THE EX-HUMAN

THE EX-HUMANS

THE EX-HUMAN

SCIENCE FICTION AND
THE FATE OF OUR SPECIES

MICHAEL BÉRUBÉ

Columbia University Press   *New York*

Columbia University Press
Publishers Since 1893
New York   Chichester, West Sussex
cup.columbia.edu

Copyright © 2024 Columbia University Press
All rights reserved
Library of Congress Cataloging-in-Publication Data
Names: Bérubé, Michael, 1961– author.
Title: The ex-human : science fiction and the fate of our species /
Michael Bérubé.
Description: New York : Columbia University Press, 2024. |
Includes bibliographical references and index.
Identifiers: LCCN 2023049519 (print) | LCCN 2023049520 (ebook) |
ISBN 9780231215046 (hardback) | ISBN 9780231215053 (trade paperback) |
ISBN 9780231560597 (ebook)
Subjects: LCSH: Science fiction—History and criticism. | Human beings
in literature. | Future, The, in literature. | Science fiction films—History
and criticism. | Human beings in motion pictures | Future, The, in motion
pictures. | LCGFT: Literary criticism. | Film criticism.
Classification: LCC PN3433.6 .B473 2024 (print) | LCC PN3433.6 (ebook) |
DDC 809/.9335—dc23/eng/20231108
LC record available at https://lccn.loc.gov/2023049519
LC ebook record available at https://lccn.loc.gov/2023049520

Printed and bound by CPI Group (UK) Ltd, Croydon, CR0 4YY

Cover design: Noah Arlow
Cover images: Shutterstock

We are a way for the cosmos to know itself.

—Carl Sagan, *Cosmos*

Once upon a time, in some out of the way corner of that universe which is dispersed into numberless twinkling solar systems, there was a star upon which clever beasts invented knowing. That was the most arrogant and mendacious minute of "world history," but nevertheless, it was only a minute. After nature had drawn a few breaths, the star cooled and congealed, and the clever beasts had to die. One might invent such a fable, and yet he still would not have adequately illustrated how miserable, how shadowy and transient, how aimless and arbitrary the human intellect looks within nature. There were eternities during which it did not exist. And when it is all over with the human intellect, nothing will have happened. For this intellect has no additional mission which would lead it beyond human life. Rather, it is human, and only its possessor and begetter takes it so seriously—as though the world's axis turned within it.

—Friedrich Nietzsche, *On Truth and Lies in a Nonmoral Sense*

For the students in my science fiction classes, who have made teaching so fun and edifying over the past ten years

CONTENTS

PREFACE

I taught my first class in science fiction in 2014, at the age of fifty-two. It now seems strange to me that I waited so long, since I had been reading science fiction for more than four decades by that point and had taught and written about a couple of sci-fi novels and films in the course of my career. But I felt (with good reason) that I was not a *specialist* in science fiction and did not want to be stepping on the toes of colleagues who were; I asked to teach the course only after our resident sci-fi specialist, Paul Youngquist, had decamped for the University of Colorado at Boulder. I had been offered a sci-fi course in the early 1990s at the University of Illinois at Urbana–Champaign, but I declined after a few days of deliberation, partly because I was worried that the students would be wall-to-wall white men and partly because I was too frightened, as a thirty-two-year-old assistant professor, by the prospect of teaching a course to students some of whom would know more about the subject than I do.

What changed between the early 1990s and 2014? Everything. In the external world, the sci-fi fan base and the demographics of sci-fi writers are markedly more diverse now than they were thirty years ago—or fifty years ago, when I first discovered the genre and writers like Samuel Delany, Ursula K. Le Guin, Joanna Russ, and James Tiptree Jr. (real name Alice Bradley, writing under a pseudonym for obvious reasons) were the outliers and as yet unknown to me; I was a teenager immersed in Asimov, Clarke, and Bradbury.

And in my internal world, I grew more comfortable with the idea that I could teach a course to students some of whom know more than I do; I have finally realized that when they do, I am afforded the opportunity to learn something from them. And as I have aged, I have become accustomed to teaching students who know a great deal more than I do about nearly every cultural phenomenon of the twenty-first century, from trap music to fast fashion.

Moreover, when I began teaching large classes in science fiction I learned how to elicit and manage classroom discussion in a room of sixty or more people. I made it clear from the outset, in early January 2014, that I was happy to hear from students who were knowledgeable about the texts and authors and subjects on the syllabus. As a result, students felt comfortable raising questions and contributing to discussions and, best of all, making suggestions for books and movies I should check out. (I have checked out every one of those suggestions, even the wonderfully obscure and rewarding 2004 film *Primer*, written and directed by Shane Carruth.) And though many of my students were (unsurprisingly) fans of the genre, they weren't so deep into the weeds as to know or care about the backlash group Sad Puppies, which had recently formed (in 2013) to protest the fact that science fiction was no longer overwhelmingly dominated by white men.[1]

I've offered the class four more times since then and made my semiofficial entry into the larger world of science fiction academe in 2019, when I was invited by Aisha Matthews, literary director of the Museum of Science Fiction in Washington, DC, to be part of a panel on science fiction and neurodiversity along with Sami Schalk (whose groundbreaking *Bodyminds Reimagined* had just been published and who will appear again in these pages) and Melinda C. Hall, a young philosopher working on disability and bioethics. This was not the sci-fi cohort I knew as a teenager. N. K. Jemisin had won the Hugo Award for best novel three years running (2016–18, for the Broken Earth trilogy), an unprecedented threepeat; a Black woman was a rising star in sci-fi and disability studies (Schalk); a Black woman was running the academic wing of this conference (Matthews). Among the readings Matthews assigned us was *Octavia's Brood: Science Fiction Stories from Social Justice Movements*, edited by Walidah Imarisha and adrienne maree brown—a collection of short stories by writers of color each of whom was inspired to take up science fiction by Octavia E. Butler, who was for many years the only Black woman in the field and is now justly celebrated as one of the major figures of the past fifty years. The sad puppies remained sad. In so many ways.[2]

Cheered by the increasing diversity of voices and narratives, I began devoting more time and study to the field. I've finally gotten to the point at which I can presume to write a book about science fiction, but I want to open with a caveat: I still don't really consider myself a specialist, and I am not writing this book for specialists. I am imagining a readership generally aware of the existence of the novels and films I discuss here, but—and this is key—a readership that is not necessarily intimately familiar with these novels and films. Secondarily, I am imagining readers who are generally aware of the existential crises that confront our species, readers who have some acquaintance with books like Alan Weisman's *The World Without Us*, Elizabeth Kolbert's *The Sixth Extinction*, David Wallace-Wells's *The*

Uninhabitable Earth, or Toby Ord's *The Precipice.*[3] For readers who *are* intimately familiar with these novels and films, I hope to provide some new ways of thinking about them and more particularly ways of thinking about them in conversation with one another. Accordingly, I offer a bit of introductory plot summary for each novel or film, though I do so sparingly for films like *2001: A Space Odyssey* and *The Matrix,* which I suspect have been seen by so many millions of theatergoers that an introductory word about them would be a little like explaining to someone that The Lord of the Rings involves a magic ring.

My idea for the book crystallized toward the end of 2019, when I taught Cixin Liu's *The Three-Body Problem* for the first time. (It is the first book of his Remembrance of Earth's Past trilogy.) As the class worked its way through the novel, I found myself defending the young astrophysicist Ye Wenjie, whose faith in humanity is so shaken that she summons an alien civilization to Earth, naively believing that its arrival and intervention can somehow save us from ourselves. Her position on the alien invasion she has precipitated is very different from that of her nominal ally, the radical environmentalist Mike Evans, who hopes instead that the approaching aliens will annihilate humans altogether. This is a genocidal position with which I have no sympathy, and I believe it is not incidental that it is the conviction of the son of an oil executive, a perverse manifestation of his sense of entitlement. To be clear, I had—and have—no illusions about the fact that Ye's decision is a terrible mistake. Indeed, the only thing Ye knows about this alien civilization is that one member of it has warned her that Earth will be invaded and conquered. But as you'll see, I also think her decision, grounded in horror at the mass butchery of the Chinese Cultural Revolution and the despoliation of the planet, is not entirely unreasonable. She believes we are doomed and that being ruled by aliens might somehow be a better fate. And as I made my way through *Three-Body*, preparing my classes in the summer of 2019, I began to read Ye's decision backward, so to speak, through the rest of my syllabus as well as the other novels and films I discuss here. It is as if I am now reading texts like Philip K. Dick's *Do Androids Dream of Electric Sheep?* and Octavia Butler's Lilith's Brood trilogy, both of which imagine human life after devastating nuclear war, from the perspective afforded me by Ye Wenjie. In the pages that follow, I'll explain what that entails.

My goal is to bring these works to the attention of readers who worry that climate change will eventually bring about civilizational collapse and hasten human extinction. I presume that many people are worrying about this because it is looking increasingly plausible with each passing year. I have framed my analyses by articulating these texts and their visions of the fate of humanity to debates about the so-called Anthropocene epoch (that is, the geologic epoch defined by humans' cumulative effect on the biosphere), and in the introduction that follows I will offer a brief account of what the debate about the Anthropocene has meant in the humanities. And just as I will not presume any previous knowledge of debates about the Anthropocene, I will not expect readers to have any previous knowledge of the postmodern turn in anthropology, which consisted of that discipline's self-reflection and heightened-if-belated awareness of the neocolonial position of the anthropologist with regard to "natives." I will explain that turn in chapter 1 because it is the lens through which I read Ursula K. Le Guin's *The Left Hand of Darkness*. I cite my fellow academic critics and theorists throughout (mostly in notes) but again presuming no previous knowledge of their work on your part and citing nonacademic writers wherever possible, from bloggers to fans to other creative writers in the field. Some of the texts I discuss have generated a great deal of commentary, and there are entire critical industries devoted to *The Matrix* and *Blade Runner / Do Androids Dream of Electric Sheep?* I have acknowledged that critical tradition, especially where there is a general consensus of opinion, but I have made no attempt to be exhaustive.

So if you're a reader who's interested in thinking about the fate of *Homo sapiens sapiens* and curious as to how some classic science fiction texts have encouraged us to think about that fate without getting too attached to that particular species but without becoming so detached as to wish it into the ash heap of cosmic history, this book might be of interest to you. I will now proceed to try to sustain that interest as best I can.

ACKNOWLEDGMENTS

Writing the first draft of this book in 2021 was a strangely solitary endeavor, though in my epilogue I go into detail about my unexpectedly complicated domestic circumstances in the first year of the pandemic as my household doubled in size. I didn't have any opportunities to present any of this material to audiences at other universities, and I shared the manuscript, at first, only with a small circle of friends. I thank Susan Squier, Nita Riegle, and especially my daughter-in-law Rachel Harris and son Nicholas for reading the epilogue, and George Estreich for reading the whole thing; most of all, I thank Lenny Cassuto and Martin Crofts for reading the whole thing and giving me extensive advice on how to make the second draft considerably sharper than the first. At Columbia, Philip Leventhal has been a supportive and encouraging editor, and Rob Fellman is an awesome, meticulous copyeditor.

My wife, Janet Lyon, has very little patience with science fiction, insisting that films like *Arrival* and *Annihilation* and *The Arrival* and *A.I.* and *Ad Astra* and *Alien* are "all the same movie," so I spared her the task of reading any of this (except the epilogue). Over the years, however, I have managed to persuade her to read Octavia Butler's *Dawn* and Philip K. Dick's *Martian*

Time-Slip, both of which she enjoyed (and has taught). More important, at least for my domestic circumstances, is that Janet survived a very scary bout of Takotsubo cardiomyopathy, which struck her on November 6, 2022. This book is all about mortality and putting our lives in broader perspective (the titles of the introduction and epilogue make that reasonably clear, I think), but for me, Janet's near-death event was, as Spinal Tap's David St. Hubbins remarks at the grave of Elvis Presley, *too much fucking perspective*. So even if Janet never gets around to reading any of the other novels I discuss in this book (or, for that matter, this book), I want to close these brief acknowledgments by acknowledging how profoundly happy and grateful I am that she has been my life partner for over forty years—and counting.

And Jamie, thanks for watching so many science fiction movies with me. Nick, thanks for watching so many science fiction movies with me *and* making a bunch of great suggestions for the Bad Futures Film Festival. We'll always have *Akira*, which is nothing like any of those other sci-fi films beginning with A.

A portion of chapter 3 was published in *American Literature* under the title "Giving Up," *American Literature* 92, no. 4, "COVID-19 Forum: Pandemic Reading," ed. Sari Altschuler and Priscilla Wald (2020): 791–98. Thanks to Sari and Priscilla for the generous invitation.

ABBREVIATIONS

2001	Arthur C. Clarke. *2001: A Space Odyssey*. New York: Roc, 1968.
A	Philip K. Dick. *Do Androids Dream of Electric Sheep?* New York: Del Rey, 1968.
D	Ursula K. Le Guin. *The Dispossessed*. New York: Harper and Row, 1974.
E	Ted Chiang. "Exhalation." In *Exhalation*. New York: Knopf, 2019.
F	Mary Shelley. *Frankenstein; or, the Modern Prometheus*. Ed. Michael Bérubé. New York: Norton, 2021.
"IGN"	Ursula K. Le Guin. "Is Gender Necessary? Redux." In *The Language of the Night: Essays on Fantasy and Science Fiction*, rev. ed. New York: HarperCollins, 1992.
LB	Octavia Butler. *Lilith's Brood*. New York: Grand Central, 1989.
LDA	Roy Scranton. *Learning to Die in the Anthropocene: Reflections on the End of a Civilization*. San Francisco: City Lights, 2015.
LHD	Ursula K. Le Guin. *The Left Hand of Darkness*. New York: Ace, 1969.

NF	Lee Edelman. *No Future: Queer Theory and the Death Drive*. Durham, NC: Duke University Press, 2004.
OB	Gerry Canavan. *Octavia Butler*. Urbana: University of Illinois Press, 2016.
OC	Margaret Atwood. *Oryx and Crake*. New York: Anchor, 2003.
P	Toby Ord. *The Precipice: Existential Risk and the Future of Humanity*. New York: Hachette, 2020.
PE	Dipesh Chakrabarty. *Provincializing Europe: Postcolonial Thought and Historical Difference*. Princeton, NJ: Princeton University Press, 2000.
Post	Rosi Braidotti. *The Posthuman*. Cambridge: Polity, 2013.
PS	Octavia Butler. *Parable of the Sower*. New York: Grand Central, 1993.
PT	Octavia Butler. *Parable of the Talents*. New York: Grand Central, 1998.
R	Adam Kirsch. *The Revolt Against Humanity: Imagining a Future Without Us*. New York: Columbia Global Reports, 2023.
TBP	Cixin Liu. *The Three-Body Problem*. New York: Tor, 2014.

THE EX-HUMAN

THE EX-HUMAN

INTRODUCTION

Learning to Die

How can we speak of the ex-human, the human that is no more—or, perhaps, the human from whom we are or will be divorced?

Before I begin to dig into that question, I should say a few words about what is *not* in this book. First and most important, there will be no discussion of whether science fiction is serious literature. That debate, such as it is, makes me too weary to type. I do inform my students of Sven Birkerts's *New York Times* review of Margaret Atwood's *Oryx and Crake*, which opens with the standard Curmudgeon's Credo: "Science fiction will never be Literature with a capital 'L,' and this is because it inevitably proceeds from premise rather than character."[1] But I proceed to tell them that despite the prejudices of some of its hidebound gatekeepers,[2] literature is a many-splendored thing: its subject matter includes not only human literatures, languages, histories, and philosophies but also worlds populated by wizards and hippogriffs and aliens and orcs and psychic mutants and kids with strange versions of autism. As Susan Squier pointed out many years ago, science fiction was imagining outlandish things like in vitro fertilization fifty or sixty years before it became a thing—except that it was also imagining the ethical, legal, and social implications of new technologies like in vitro fertilization as well.[3] Of course, because of my training in traditional literary study, I know very well why some people in mainstream literary culture believe that science fiction is not serious literature. After all, you can't have a serious work of fiction that explores the complexity of the human condition if you populate it with supernatural or immortal beings or a society of talking horses or six-headed, man-eating beasts who live on an island in the middle of the sea.

Birkerts's review is especially notable because Atwood has (in) famously taken her distance from the genre, differentiating between "speculative fiction" (i.e., what she does) and stories involving "talking squids in outer space."[4] It is a strange (and widely contested) distinction not only because Atwood herself has written some talking-squid-esque science fiction (the inset narrative of *The Blind Assassin*, involving the Lizard Men of Xenor) and because the squidless *The Handmaid's Tale* was judged to be sci-fi enough to win the inaugural Arthur C. Clarke Award in 1987, but also because "speculative fiction," first coined by Robert Heinlein in 1947, would seem to be a term like "ruminative thinking," an artifact of the Department of Redundancy Department.[5] Nevertheless, there is a loose distinction between stories that contain only plausible things extrapolated from the world we know and stories that involve time travel, superluminal space travel, talking squids in space, and other deeply implausible things like a totalitarian patriarchal theocracy obsessed with women's sexuality and reproductive capacity. Atwood argues that she works in the vein of Jules Verne, hewing to the plausible, whereas the vein that traces itself back to H. G. Wells allows itself time travel, aliens, etc.[6] It is a porous distinction, as demonstrated by the urtext that precedes both Verne and Wells, Mary Shelley's *Frankenstein*, whose introduction (written by

Percy) insists that the story you are about to read is "not of impossible occurrence."[7] More to the point, the parameters of the plausible are—up to a point—in a constant state of flux.

There's no denying, however, that science fiction has long been considered second- or third-rate literature. As Philip K. Dick put it in a 1977 interview, "The position which writers such as myself hold in America are, those positions are very lowly. Science fiction is considered to be something for adolescents, for just high school kids, and for disturbed people in general in America."[8] Curiously, nevertheless, some major academic critics took sci-fi seriously whereas "quality" fiction writers and publishing houses did not: from its inception in 1973, the flagship journal *Science Fiction Studies* was publishing scholars such as the renowned Marxist theorist Fredric Jameson and the distinguished semiotician Robert Scholes, and the theorist Darko Suvin defined the genre as the literature of cognitive estrangement.[9] Nevertheless, like other "genre" fiction (romance, detective/crime, fantasy), it remained institutionally confined to its own magazines and publishing houses; as Rob Latham writes, "Because the genre developed in the pulp (and later digest) magazines, American science fiction was essentially segregated from the body of so-called mainstream literature from the 1920s onward."[10] One can understand why the readers of literary journals like the *Sewanee Review* would look down on magazines with inauspicious titles like *Weird Tales* and *Amazing Stories* and consider their contents as material for adolescents. They often were.

I know I took it as a sign of the apocalypse when Philip K. Dick was inducted into the Library of America in 2007, where he now resides alongside Whitman, Dickinson, Wharton, Fitzgerald, Baldwin, and company. One wonders what he would have thought, had he managed to live to the reasonable age of seventy-nine. But increasingly, the distinctions between science fiction and so-called mainstream literature have gotten blurrier, *pace* critics like Birkerts, such that you find acclaimed writers like Kazuo Ishiguro and Ian McEwan (not to mention Atwood) contributing to the genre (Ishiguro's *Klara and the Sun* and arguably *Never Let Me Go*, McEwan's *Machines Like Me*) and straight-up sci-fi writers like Cixin Liu and N. K. Jemisin getting the respect they deserve from the *New York Times* or the *New Yorker*. These days, academic critics can be downright emphatic about the importance of the genre: throwing down a gauntlet, Gerry Canavan and Eric Carl Link have insisted that "no genre has offered more powerful examinations of the problems with cultural blindness and unchecked aggression toward the Other; no genre has more vividly impressed upon us the threats posed by non-global thinking, nationalism, and provincialism."[11] I think this is right. It's the first among many reasons why I started reimmersing myself in the genre over the past decade.

In this book, then, you will find an eclectic mix of the plausible and the (as yet) implausible, from writers who cared about their relation to Literature with a capital L and writers who did not. The common thread linking the novels under discussion here, instead, is their response to the question of what will become of us as a species—and whether one can fruitfully imagine the world without us or perhaps with some other version of us.[12] I begin with one relatively "happy" scenario from the work of Ursula K. Le Guin before moving to darker visions involving aliens (*The Three-Body Problem*), climate change and viral apocalypse (*Oryx and Crake*), AI and nuclear apocalypse (*Terminator*, *The Matrix*, *Do Androids Dream of Electric Sheep?*, *2001: A Space Odyssey*), partial civilizational collapse (Octavia

Butler's Parables duology), and finally aliens again, this time as post-nuclear-apocalypse saviors or conquerors (Octavia Butler's Xenogenesis trilogy, now known as Lilith's Brood). And as I noted in the preface, I am reading all these novels and films backward, as it were, from the perspective of *The Three-Body Problem*'s central character, Ye Wenjie.

I have decided to call that perspective *ex-human*: it imagines—or invites us to imagine—a future perfect (not a perfect future) in which we have become able to see ourselves and our sorry fate from the vantage point of something other than the human, but it does not lead us to undertake our own extinction. Science fiction has innumerable ways of offering that vantage point by introducing us to new worlds and new civilizations; for many fans, that is the genre's strongest suit. But the ex-human is distinctive in that it is framed by the possibility of human extinction and driven by a desire to imagine that, somehow, *another species is possible*. This is precisely the controversial project undertaken by the bioengineer Crake in Atwood's MaddAddam trilogy as he undertakes his version of a Great Replacement, spreading a lethal virus while designing a less destructive humanoid species that will leave no carbon footprint and know no forms of sexual violence. I'm not going to endorse Crake's version of the ex-human, but I am going to argue that Crake is not a mad scientist—and that, like Ye Wenjie, he has solid personal and political grounds for what he does. He knows what will become of us and decides that it is best for all concerned, as well as for the planet's nonhuman life, to spare us the long, agonizing pain of our collective suicide. As Gerry Canavan has put it, "Crake's monstrous work—to kill off the human race and replace it with the more ecologically sound Children of Crake—becomes from this perspective something more like a mercy killing."[13] It is also a mercy killing that is more concerned with life on Earth than with merely human life: *that* perspective is what I am calling ex-human.

The what-will-become-of-us genre is a distinctive feature of the post–World War II literary landscape, for the obvious reason that with World War II humans achieved the power—and the awful awareness of the power—to wipe ourselves off the planet, carrying untold numbers of species with us. William Faulkner's complaint about this is justly famous. From his Nobel Prize acceptance speech, delivered on December 10, 1950:

> Our tragedy today is a general and universal physical fear so long sustained by now that we can even bear it. There are no longer problems of the spirit. There is only the question: When will I be blown up? Because of this, the young man or woman writing today has forgotten the problems of the human heart in conflict with itself which alone can make good writing because only that is worth writing about, worth the agony and the sweat.[14]

It is worth remarking that the question "when will I be blown up?" is a fairly pressing one, now as in 1950, one that threatens to render meaningless the question of what happens to the Compson or the Snopes families. It is also worth remarking that Faulkner's famous profession of faith—"I believe that man will not merely endure: he will prevail"—put into play terms that ironically became central to American war planners in the atomic age, who repeatedly insisted that U.S. nuclear forces must "prevail" in any conflict.[15] Since the advent of AIDS, the question of when we will be blown up has had to fight for our attention alongside the question of when a virus will ravage us.[16] Yet although I began this book as COVID-19 wreaked havoc among our species, I am not going to discuss most of the recent entries in this genre; much as I admire novels such as Colson White-head's *Zone One*, Emily St. John Mandel's *Station Eleven*, and Ling Ma's *Severance*, all of which entail viral apocalypses, they are tangential to the project of opening a vista onto the ex-human. The viral apocalypse in *Oryx and Crake*, by contrast, is of intense interest to me not because of the virus but because of Crake's plan to deploy the virus he has engineered in order to replace us with a genetically modified and purportedly more benevolent and ecofriendly humanoid species.

At this point I will offer a brief overview of recent debates in the humanities about the Anthropocene epoch and, relatedly, about the idea of the posthuman. These debates provide much of the context for what follows, but as I promised in the preface, I will keep the discussion accessible to readers who have not followed every twist and turn of their unfolding.

The term "Anthropocene" was first coined in the 1980s by the ecologist Eugene Stoermer but gained currency only in the past two decades, thanks largely to the work of the atmospheric chemist and Nobel laureate Paul Crutzen, who popularized it in 2000. The claim behind it is that we are living in a new epoch of geological time brought about by the fact that human activity has fundamentally changed the very composition of the biosphere. For official purposes, we are still living in the Holocene epoch, which began about 11,700 years ago and corresponds to the retreat of the glaciers at the conclusion of the most recent ice age and the subsequent development of agriculture and the beginnings of human civilization; the epoch before the Holocene, the Pleistocene, lasted roughly 2.5 million years, and most geological epochs cover periods of millions of years. If "Anthropocene" should be adopted by the International Commission on Stratigraphy (ICS) or the International Union of Geographical Sciences (IUGS), the Holocene would become by far the shortest epoch on record—though there is considerable debate about when the Anthropocene began. Because geologists like to have a firm evidentiary record in the planet's history, such as the layer of iridium in Earth's crust that marks the impact of the meteor that wiped out the dinosaurs 65 million years ago and ended the Cretaceous period, it seems possible that the marker of the Anthropocene will be determined to be the plutonium-239 residue from nuclear testing. Alternatively, it may be the plastic with which we are covering the globe. In July 2023, the Anthropocene Working Group determined that the "golden spike" for the start of the Anthropocene should be Crawford Lake in Milton, Ontario, for its devastating combination of nuclear fallout and industrial pollution.

In the humanities, a profound and wide-ranging debate about the Anthropocene was initiated by Dipesh Chakrabarty's 2009 essay "The Climate of History: Four Theses," which stands as one of the most influential statements on the importance of climate change for the human sciences.[17] Chakrabarty's argument challenges the traditional division of labor between the natural and human sciences; in his account, that traditional and now-irrelevant distinction not only carves out the terrain of history, which is assigned to the realm of human activity, but also establishes the natural world as a- or prehistoric. That distinction also subtends, or has subtended until now, a great deal of what we do in the humanities: it informs the Greek distinction between *nomos* (human law) and *physis* (natural law); it structures the Marxist belief that humans make history in conditions not of their making, wresting a realm of freedom from the realm of necessity; it appears more recently as John Searle's distinction between brute fact and social fact.[18] Chakrabarty's profound insight is that that once-fundamental distinction can no longer be maintained, insofar as the *nomos* has gotten to the point at which it can change the very fabric of the *physis*. And there is no creature on the planet, human or nonhuman, that will be exempt from the consequences. Those consequences may eventually involve global catastrophe, but in the meantime, they also involve a crisis for the concept of the historical and for the concept of the human. For once we have come to terms with anthropogenic climate change, Chakrabarty argues, we need to rethink modernity. We need to rethink history and historicity. We need to start thinking of ourselves as a species but without forgetting everything we have learned about the various cultural differences, class conflicts, competing regimes of truth, and uneven industrializing developments that have brought us to this planetary crisis.

But those uneven industrializing developments pose something of a problem, for obvious political reasons. Chakrabarty's essay has predictably met with strong criticism from those who argue that we should not think of ourselves as a species, in universalist terms, without first accounting for *which* members of the species are most responsible for inducing the crises that go under the heading of climate change. Chakrabarty's argument was all the more trenchant because it came from a postcolonialist critic whose major work, to that point, was a book titled *Provincializing Europe*, and one of Chakrabarty's strongest arguments, in that book, mounted a postcolonial reinterpretation of European theories of history. To wit: Chakrabarty argued that those theories of historicism and those accounts of human history entailed also the idea of evolutionary social development and that in the age of imperialism, all these ideas were mobilized on behalf of the argument that the European idea of modernity provided the scale in which the rest of the (putatively more "primitive") world could be weighed and found wanting. As Chakrabarty put it, "Historicism—and even the modern, European idea of history—one might say, came to non-European peoples in the nineteenth century as somebody's way of saying 'not yet' to somebody else."[19]

In other words, Chakrabarty had already established himself as someone who takes "universal" pronouncements with a large grain of salt. However, he had made clear in the 2007 preface to *Provincializing Europe* that his position on universalism was far more complex than simple opposition to or simple exposure of European thought promoting itself as universal to everyone on the globe: "European thought," he wrote, "is at once both indispensable and inadequate in helping us to think through the experiences of modernity in non-Western nations" (*PE* 16). "The project of provincializing Europe," he concluded, "therefore cannot be a project of cultural relativism. It cannot originate from the stance that the reason/science/universals that help define Europe as the modern are simply 'culture-specific' and therefore only belong to the European cultures" (*PE* 43). The point holds all the more emphatically when it comes to climate change: though the effect of anthropogenic global warming will be felt (and is being felt) most severely by people in impoverished nations that had nothing to do with the massive production of greenhouse gases, the very idea of the Anthropocene remains an invitation to think globally, to think of ourselves as a species, as *Homo sapiens sapiens* who have perhaps not been very *sapiens* about their stewardship of the planet.[20] As Richard Grusin writes in his introduction to the important collection *After Extinction*, "To periodize the Anthropocene is already to assume a future world in which human presence on Earth has been reduced to a lithic layer. The Anthropocene contains within it both the anticipation of human extinction and the imagination of how such extinction would manifest in Earth's crust."[21]

The geopolitical debate is intense, as well it should be. But there is a terminological debate as well, and that's the part I'm less invested in. No sooner had the term "Anthropocene" caught on than leading theorists in the humanities began to object to it. It's *anthropocentric*, after all. Whereas some people might hear the term as an implicit indictment of poor human stewardship of the planet and Grusin suggests we hear it as a meditation on and premediation of our own demise,[22] others hear it as a perverse kind of self-aggrandizement, an announcement that It Is All About Us Now; still others hear it as an illegitimate use of "us" and of "poor human stewardship," since the vast majority of humans on the planet did nothing to precipitate climate change.[23] The most provocative challenge to the term has come from Donna Haraway, who, in *Staying with the Trouble: Making Kin in the Chthulucene*, proposed the term "Chthulucene" partly to evoke horror and partly to argue that we need to recognize our profound interdependence with other species—right down to the microbial level—in order to get past the anthropocentric thinking that brought us to this sorry pass.[24] Haraway is often credited as well with the term "Capitalocene," to indicate (correctly) that that the so-called Great Acceleration that produced an explosion in human populations and a dramatic increase in life expectancy and (ill-distributed) wealth is coterminous with the rise of capitalism, but though Haraway thought she had coined it, she learned that it was apparently first used by the geographer Andreas Malm in 2009.[25] Haraway and Anna Tsing have recently spoken of the "Plantationocene," which adds to capitalism (correctly) the histories of racism and colonialism in resource extraction and forced human labor.[26] That term has not met with universal approval from human geographers, some of whom argue that it paradoxically obscures the racial politics of the plantation and ignores existing critiques of the history of plantation development.[27] Perhaps to ensure that racism and colonialism be placed front and center in any critique of environmental degradation and grievous harm to the biosphere, Nicholas Mirzoeff has proposed the term "White Supremacy Scene."[28]

It is important that these debates bring a degree of complexity and nuance to a term like "Anthropocene," which, left uninterrogated, can be dangerously homogenizing and evasive. At the same time, it is also important to step back from terminological disputes and put things in a broader general perspective—the perspective of people like Roy Scranton, who, in an acclaimed book-length essay titled *Learning to Die in the Anthropocene*, reminds us matter-of-factly that "we're fucked. The only questions are how soon and how badly."[29]

I rely on Scranton's book for my orientation not because he believes we should die or urges us to do so. He does not. On the contrary, his book mounts a passionate plea to avoid creating a desiccated, instrumentalist, ever-decaying world in which we lose sight of the value and the achievement of the arts and humanities. (This, we will see, is precisely the future Atwood imagines for us in *Oryx and Crake* and that Le Guin projects in *The Dispossessed*.) Most precious of all, Scranton argues, is something philosophers around the globe have tried to teach us—a lesson we seem to work deliberately to forget: how to die. We tell ourselves, on the rare occasions when we stop to think about the value of the arts and humanities, that these disciplines and practices, so distinctive for our branch of the evolutionary tree of primates, lead us to ask what constitutes a good life, a good society. That they do. But they can also lead us to ask: What constitutes a good death? As Rosi Braidotti has written, "Self-styling one's death is an act of affirmation because it means cultivating an approach, a 'style' of life that progressively and continuously fixes the modalities and the stage for the final act, leaving nothing un-attended."[30] I recall Braidotti telling me that David Bowie had orchestrated his death as his final work of art, leaving the album *Blackstar* as his epitaph and then dying two days after its release. One thinks of artists who wove their impending deaths into their work, meditating on their mortality, Yeats perhaps most assiduously and movingly. But these are exemplary individuals. How are we to think collectively about learning how to die in the Anthropocene?

Whereas in *The Left Hand of Darkness* and much classic science fiction we are encouraged to detach ourselves from a commitment to our own species in order to embrace some form of sentient life or galactic polity greater than ourselves, more recent works invite us to detach ourselves from a commitment to our own species, full stop. The most forbidding version of this line of thought is voiced by Kirsten Dunst's character, Justine, in Lars von Trier's 2011 film *Melancholia*: "The Earth is evil. We don't need to grieve for it. Nobody will miss it."[31] Her sentiment is an outlier; most ecopessimists prefer to believe that Earth is worth preserving—it's only the humans who pose a problem. More important, for my purposes, is the fact that *Melancholia* presents a completely fantastic scenario that entails an almost painless global death: a rogue planet, somehow undetected over the centuries of our study of gravitational fields in the Solar System, emerges from "hiding" behind the Sun and collides with Earth. It is a scenario that emphatically invites the interpretation that this unlikely obliteration is a metaphor for something else, and since the film is quite clearly about the experience of debilitating depression, perhaps this is a strangely pleasant way of imagining an end to our collective misery. But in the context of end-of-the-world scenarios, it's the equivalent of dying in your sleep.[32]

For that reason, *Melancholia* is not especially helpful as a way of thinking about a good death. Neither are the major entries in the civilizational-collapse genre, from the Mad Max franchise to Cormac McCarthy's *The Road*, along with minor variations in films such as *The Book of Eli* or *Waterworld*. These seem now to be the preferred province of "preppers," who eagerly await the collapse of civilization so that they can defend their homes and their families by using their remarkable stockpiles of weapons to murder nonwhite people en masse. It is a disturbingly common fantasy among conservative white Americans, extending from the fever swamps of neo-Nazis to the halls of the U.S. Senate, where hardened he-men like Lindsay Graham imagine that their AR-15 assault weapons will enable them to stave off the ravening hordes: "If there's a natural disaster in South Carolina where the cops can't protect my neighborhood, my house will be the last one that the gang will come to, because I can defend myself."[33]

So if we manage to learn to die in the Anthropocene, and if we manage to detach ourselves from our own species, does that make us posthuman? Would that it were so simple. You would think that the prefix "post-" indicates "after-," as it does in common parlance, but ever since people in the arts and humanities decided to react to a period called "modernism" by elaborating something called "postmodernism" and then decided that "postcolonialism" was a thing even though colonialism still exists in various forms, the "post-" has been asked to carry a great deal more semiotic baggage.[34]

I will try to illustrate this by way of a conversation I once had with a friend who had recently been appointed as a dean at a major university. In his decanal capacity, he regularly met with alumni who wanted to support the arts and humanities, and because these alumni tend to be a subset of all alumni everywhere who are interested in making gifts to their alma maters, he wanted to build strong relationships with them, relationships resting on substantial intellectual foundations that would guide discussions of what new work in the arts and humanities looks like and why it is valuable. Like many university administrators, he was facing the difficulty of soliciting support for the arts and humanities at a time when, for one thing, many people outside the arts and humanities do not see the benefit of study in non-STEM fields that emphasize creative and speculative modes of thinking that do not respond well to short-term assessments of "return on investment" and, for another thing, many people working in the arts and humanities no longer profess allegiance to the traditional humanist agenda of studying the best that has been thought and written in the world (whatever "best" might mean in that formulation). One of the things he had to figure out, as a matter of development strategy but even more as a matter of simple intellectual honesty, was this: *What kind of not-humanist am I?* Most people outside the academy assume, not without reason, that scholars in the humanities are "humanists," the way you would expect most people working in mechanical or civil engineering to be called "engineers." (Or, for that matter, people working in the arts to be called "artists.") But if there's one thing that defines ambitious, cutting-edge work in the humanities over the past forty or fifty years, it's a profound ambivalence toward the legacy of humanism as it has been understood in the Western philosophical tradition.

This puzzles people who think of humanism in terms inherited either from the Renaissance or the Enlightenment, whereby "humanism" is opposed to religious belief and taken as a marker of intellectual autonomy from church and state. And it worries people who know that, from Nietzsche to Heidegger to Foucault, there is a powerful strain of antihumanist philosophical thought that posits that our first misstep began with Socrates and it's been almost all downhill since. So my friend the new dean told me he couldn't very well call himself an *anti*humanist, because he doesn't subscribe to the slate of beliefs central to poststructuralism, which rejects liberal bourgeois ideas like "individual agency" and insists that we don't speak language, language speaks us. He's also not a *trans*humanist—one of those people (to whom we will return, in this chapter and in chapter 3) who looks forward to the day when we merge with artificial intelligences and become practically immortal cyborgs. And he was uncomfortable with the term *post*humanist, inasmuch as it suggests—in the ordinary sense of that prefix—that we're done with all that humanism and ready to move on to something else.[35]

My friend was referencing the fact that many theorists in the humanities, having decided that humanism is not merely coextensive with but complicit in the depredations of European colonialism and imperialism, treat the legacy of humanism as something to be repudiated rather than as something to be rethought. When that school of thought is combined with ruminations about our fate in the slow burn of climate change, the result, as Adam Kirsch writes in *The Revolt Against Humanity*, is "Anthropocene antihumanism, inspired by revulsion at humanity's destruction of the natural environment."[36] (Kirsch's short but sweeping book will appear again in these pages.) But there is another way out. In an influential book titled simply *The Posthuman*, Rosi Braidotti elaborates a vision of the humanities in which the human is not the measure of all things; in which universalism is not something dreamed up by and limited to white Western men of property; and in which our relations to other species are conceived in terms of symbiosis and entanglement (as in Haraway's Chthulucene) rather than in terms of the

putative hierarchy of the food chain or the teleological conception of evolution, in which we get to do what we want as apex
predators because we can (that's the food chain part) or because,
as of now, we showed up last (that's the teleology part). In
Braidotti's work, the posthuman is post- not because the human
is over and done with but because the idea of the human that
has animated the humanities for the past five hundred years has
turned out to be too exclusive, too inadequate to the ecosphere
we inhabit and the technologies we have invented. "The Humanities need to mutate and become posthuman," she writes (*Post*
147); "the Humanities need to find the inspirational courage to
move beyond an exclusive concern for the human, be it humanistic or anthropocentric Man, and to embrace more planetary
intellectual changes" (*Post* 153). My variant mutation on this call
to mutation, then, seeks to avoid the confusions of the "post-."
And since I am not a dean, I don't have to worry about the implications of my terms for worried or confused alumni. This is not
a book about the posthuman. It is not a book about the trans-
human. It is not about antihumanism. It is about the challenges
of adopting the perspective of the *ex-human*. If there are any relevant ordinary-language connotations of the prefix "ex-," they
most likely lie in the fact that many people have complicated
relationships with their exes.

In recent years, one critical aspect of the call to move beyond an
exclusive concern for the human has focused on our symbiotic
relations to nonhuman life. "We are all lichens," announces the
biologist Scott Gilbert, remarking on the profound interdependence between humans and bacteria; meanwhile, new work on
epigenetics and microevolutionary processes seems to suggest
that humans are far more intertwined with the nonhuman world
than we have dared to imagine or acknowledge.[37] The theories

of Lynn Margulis, which were long relegated to the margins of the life sciences for her emphasis on evolutionary symbiosis, now seem to be the very warp and weft of interdisciplinary thinking about life on Earth.[38] Some versions of those theories subtend the "new materialism" in the humanities, as well as "object-oriented ontology."[39] But this book will wind up with a different kind of symbiosis altogether. After we call for intervention by avowedly hostile aliens and attempt to engineer a replacement humanoid species in chapter 2 and after we grapple with potentially murderous artificial intelligence in chapter 3, we will turn in chapter 4 to the work of Octavia Butler, first to her Parables and then to Lilith's Brood. At that point we will mate with aliens (though that decision will be exclusively theirs, to our dismay) and live happily ever after. Or not.

I close with Butler for many reasons, not least of which is my sense—and it is not mine alone—that we are now living among Octavia's brood.[40] I know I am playing catch-up in that regard, as I suggested in the preface. I am haunted by an exchange that dates from the fall of 2010, when I took over as director of Penn State's Institute for the Arts and Humanities (renamed the Humanities Institute after my departure in 2017). My predecessor in that role had made a point of announcing that the institute would not concern itself with matters of the present day or the recent past but would focus on various twenty-five-year "moments of change" (the first three were 1600–1625, 1889–1914, and 1776–1801, which were pegged to a decidedly European calendar). So I decided I would signal a peaceful regime change by hosting a three-day film festival called Bad Futures, showing fifteen films that imagine the world we will have made: *Blade Runner, La Jetée, Fahrenheit 451, Children of Men, Brazil, A Clockwork Orange, Sleeper, Gattaca, District 9, Code 46, The Matrix, Fail Safe, 28 Days Later, Metropolis*, and *2001: A Space Odyssey*.

I have had many waves of postfestival thoughts about this lineup, starting with the fact that I could host another such festival today with fifteen more bad-future films made *since* 2010. I regret not including *On the Beach*, I could not get hold of a copy of *Akira*, and I cannot remember why I didn't consider the underrated *RoboCop*. I nixed *Dr. Strangelove* because I thought two Kubrick films were enough, and I had lost my fight against *A Clockwork Orange*, which was basically voted in by overwhelming student support. And I think that it is probably worth revisiting the Club of Rome nightmare that is *Soylent Green* for Edward G. Robinson's performance alone. I had also considered *THX-1138*, *Alphaville*, and a whole host of sixties and seventies dystopias in which Love Is Illegal and People Are All the Same. I watched (with varying degrees of interest) *Vanilla Sky* and *Dark City*, *Strange Days* and *A Scanner Darkly*, *Paycheck* and *Minority Report*, *The Island*, *A.I. Artificial Intelligence*, *Moon*, and *Total Recall*. *Dark City* is a gem, I decided, but not really a bad future in the sense I wanted, and if you noticed that the previous sentence names no fewer than *four* movies inspired by the work of Philip K. Dick, well, hold that thought.

At the close of the festival, I convened a panel of five people from various disciplines (film, architecture, media studies, science studies, art history), and we offered a discussion and Q/A session that filled the house. One panelist thanked me for doing "something contemporary"; another seconded the motion but had an unsettling question. "Michael," he said, "you've got these beautiful, visually arresting films with amazing lifeworlds we can immerse ourselves in, and it's so good to see them all on the big screen. *Blade Runner*, *The Matrix*, *Code 46*, *Gattaca* . . . and yet each of them has the same goddamn heterosexual romance plot. Even *Children of Men*, in its way." I was stung by this, as if I were being criticized for scripts I did not write.[41] Defensively,

I replied, "But not *District 9*, right?" To which my science-studies colleague Chloe Silverman responded, "OK, I have a problem with *District 9*, quite apart from its treatment of the Nigerians." (Nigerians were not pleased either.)[42] "It's like, you're turning into a human-insect hybrid, and you say that like it's a *bad* thing."

I laughed. I still think about Chloe's remark. (She is also the genius who recommended the deeply disturbing *Code 46*, a film I usually refer to as being so obscure that even Michael Winterbottom's friends don't know he directed it.) I knew what she was driving at, though, so I said something like this: Philip K. Dick lived just long enough to see some of the dailies for *Blade Runner*, but he did not live to see it flop at the box office, having its lunch and Reese's Pieces eaten every summer weekend by something called *E.T.* that had kids on bicycles soaring in the sky against the backdrop of a full moon. It took the director's cut of *Blade Runner*—and then about half a dozen more films—for Dick to emerge as a major influence on science fiction film. Octavia Butler had died four years before our film festival, in 2006—like Dick, much too soon: he was fifty-four, she was fifty-eight. But as of 2010, there were no major motion pictures based on her work, and even in 2024 this remains true.[43] Chloe was gesturing at the hybrid species Butler imagines in Lilith's Brood, invoking an idea of the ex-human that has none of the icky entailments of, say, *The Fly*. As far as Hollywood goes, we are still not there. But the trajectory of this book will lead us, in the end, to that hybrid species—and the question of whether it is the result of a consummation devoutly to be wished.

The other major question raised by that panel had to do with race, since almost all fifteen films centered on white men. We surmised that for people who aren't white men, the bad pasts and presents are more pressing than the bad futures, but if we were really going to delve into that question we should have put

Afrofuturism front and center. Or we could have waited a few years for the publication of Kyle Powys Whyte's work on the Anthropocene, which reorients the debate by introducing a radically different sense of planetary time than that assumed by most people worried about our potential bad futures.

Whyte's argument is that Native Americans like him are living—as the title of one of his essays puts it—in "our ancestors' dystopia now." In "Indigenous Science (Fiction) for the Anthropocene: Ancestral Dystopias and Fantasies of Climate Change Crises," for example, he puts our current crisis in a perspective that questions who is assumed in that "our": "The hardships many nonIndigenous people dread most of the climate crisis are ones that Indigenous peoples have endured already due to different forms of colonialism: ecosystem collapse, species loss, economic crash, drastic relocation, and cultural disintegration."[44] This is one of the more salient responses to the challenge issued by Chakrabarty, insofar as it does not merely argue that the industrialized world bears more responsibility for climate change than does the developing world but rather points out that the people displaced, ravaged, and killed by settler colonialism have had a gruesome head start on the experiences now faced by much of the species. This is not to say that for Whyte climate change is no big deal because Native peoples have seen it all before; "rather," he writes in "Our Ancestors' Dystopia Now,"

> if there is something different in the Anthropocene for indige-
> nous peoples, it would be just that we are focusing our energies
> also on adapting to another kind of anthropogenic environmen-
> tal change: climate destabilization. Indeed, in the nineteenth and
> twentieth centuries, we already suffered other kinds of anthro-
> pogenic environmental change at the hands of settlers, includ-
> ing changes associated with deforestation, forced removal and

relocation, containment on reservations (i.e. loss of mobility), liquidation of our lands into individual private property and subsequent dispossession, and unmitigated pollution and destruction of our lands from extractive industries and commodity agriculture, among many other examples. While all societies alter the environment in which they dwell, anthropogenic environmental change here refers very specifically to how industrial settler campaigns both dramatically changed ecosystems, such as through deforestation, overharvesting and pollution, and obstructed indigenous peoples' capacities to adapt to the changes, such as through removal and containment on reservations.[45]

Whyte's intervention is a necessary corrective not only to homogenizing accounts of the Anthropocene but also, and even more trenchantly, to cheery homogenizing accounts that, as Toby Ord has written in his 2020 book *The Precipice: Existential Risk and the Future of Humanity*, "on average human life today is substantially better than at any previous time."[46] Ord is not wrong: in the aggregate, human life expectancy, human health and wealth, human education, and human technological development were all dramatically increased by the Great Acceleration, and I will confess that if I had to be dropped down in the middle of the journey of our lives in any random time and place (i.e., not allowed to choose that I be situated among the elite of the elite of Periclean Athens or fifteenth-century Florence), I would choose to be right here, right now. But that "on average" is doing a great deal of unremunerated labor in Ord's sentence, as indeed it does in any calculation of general human welfare. From the perspective of people—not only Native populations but the populations enslaved throughout the centuries of colonialism—the bounty of the present appears considerably more bittersweet. It is as if, for people in the newly "developing" world, advances in technology and the advent of the Green Revolution that transformed global agriculture and staved off mass starvation arrived just in time for them to enjoy the fruits of a poisoned planet: the wretched of the earth will finally become less wretched once Earth approaches a state of planetary wretchedness. Ord insists that "every day we are the beneficiaries of uncountable innovations made by people over hundreds of thousands of years. Innovations in technology, mathematics, language, institutions, culture, art; the ideas of the hundred billion people who came before us, and shaped almost every facet of the modern world. This is a stunning inheritance" (*P* 19). But from the perspective of the formerly and now somewhat less wretched, the question may be inescapable: What human heritage, what collective inheritance, are we trying to preserve?

I ask this question not to try to ventriloquize the billions of people living in circumstances far less fortunate than my own (though I am inevitably doing that) but because it became inescapable *for me* upon reading Ord's book.[47] Ord's passionate, compelling argument is that we have an overwhelming positive obligation to preserve humanity and a biosphere in which we can thrive, not just for ourselves (really, hardly for ourselves at all) but for the millions or billions of human generations yet to come.[48] It is an emphatic rebuke to the very idea of imagining the ex-human, in that it urges a fierce cathexis to the human species and to the belief that we have only begun to realize our nearly infinite potential for self-improvement. The arc of the moral universe is long, but for Ord, it potentially bends toward Utopia, and we bear the awesome responsibility of bending it:

> If we are the only moral agents that will ever arise in our universe—the only beings capable of making choices on the grounds of what is right and wrong—then responsibility for the

history of the universe is entirely *on us*. This is the only chance ever to shape the universe toward what is right, what is just, what is best for all. If we fail, then the potential not just of humanity, but of all moral action, will have been irrevocably squandered.

(*P* 53)

Ord's book illustrates quite vividly the cogency of Claire Colebrook's claim that "our lament or preliminary mourning for the possible extinction of humans" is about "the anticipated loss not of our species being but of the intelligence that enabled the thought of our species being."[49] It also serves as a rejoinder to David Benatar's provocative claim, in *Better Never to Have Been*, that every single human being has been and will be harmed simply by existing and that therefore the best thing for us, in the short run and in the long run, would be not to exist at all.[50] (That argument plays no role in my thinking in this book because it is the result of an abstract utilitarian formula and not a response to specific conditions of life. Still, I will acknowledge that Benatar has certainly succeeded in detaching himself from any investment in our species.)

There is a dark side to Ord's argument—the understory, if you will, insofar as it has its roots in "effective altruism" and "longtermism," philosophies that are apparently especially attractive to Silicon Valley tech billionaires and the scammers who inhabit their world—like Sam Bankman-Fried, former CEO of the cryptocurrency exchange FTX, the collapse of which sent shock waves through the postpostindustrial global economy.[51] Longtermists tend also to be transhumanists, as is Ord (and the founder of the field of "existential risk" analysis, the Swedish philosopher Nick Bostrom), and in the words of one of the readers who read this book in manuscript, "effectively consign the human to the category of pre-human by imagining that the uploaded white guys in their virtual gated communities are the truly human." Adam Kirsch agrees, suggesting that the fusion of humans with artificial intelligence will create beings who "will demote humanity to the rank we assign to animals—unless they decide that their goals are better served by wiping us out completely" (R 11). It is reasonable, in other words, to raise the question of whose interests are advanced by longtermism and whether short- and middle-termism might have more urgent claims on our collective attention; it is also more than reasonable to question the connection between longtermism and transhumanism.

We will return to those questions in chapter 3, but for now, I want to stay with Ord's claim that we might be the only moral agents in the universe and therefore bear a responsibility to shape the universe toward what is right and just. Those of us who shrink from the idea of taking that responsibility might turn to the deflationary Nietzschean admonition that serves as one of this book's epigraphs, counterproposing that in fact—from the perspective of the universe itself, not through the eyes of us clever beasts who invented knowing—the human intellect looks aimless and arbitrary and has no additional mission that would lead it beyond human life. If we're alone in the universe, then when we're gone, per Carl Sagan, the cosmos will no longer know itself, and muons and gluons, neutrons and neutrinos, gravitational waves and solar winds will just keep on keeping on, doing what comes naturally for as long as they can. They will never contribute to shaping the universe toward what is right and just, and they will never feel the loss.

To be clear, I am not throwing cold Benatarian antinatalist water on sentience: I personally enjoy it, and I share Sagan's sense that it has cosmic significance. Nor do I subscribe to the belief that Ord attributes to pessimists, which sounds disturbingly like a rationale congenial to people who want to plunder the planet and extract every last benefit from it before trashing it once and for all—that "there is no reason to avoid extinction stemming from consideration of future generations—it just doesn't matter whether these future people come into being or not" (*P* 47). (I will return to this form of collective selfishness in the epilogue when I briefly take up Lee Edelman's renowned/notorious queer manifesto *No Future*.) But I am questioning whether, in passages such as this, Ord has taken a seriously global perspective on his global perspective:

> If we drop the baton, succumbing to an existential catastrophe, we would fail our ancestors in a multitude of ways. We would fail to achieve the dreams they hoped for; we would betray the trust they placed in us, their heirs; and we would fail in any duty we had to pay forward the work they did for us. To neglect existential risk might thus be to wrong not only the people of the future, but the people of the past.
>
> (*P* 50)

This is the kind of argument that surely summons Kyle Powys Whyte to the white courtesy phone. Most importantly, from Whyte's perspective, in which "we" are living in "our" ancestors' dystopia, the possibility arises that the game is already over or nearing its conclusion: Indigenous people might well insist that they have been forced to adopt an ex-human perspective on the species for quite some time now and that their conquerors and killers are only belatedly realizing that their time, too, is running out.

For Ord, this is a tragedy of cosmic significance because we have only been around for 200,000 years and should reasonably expect a far longer life span; the great reptiles of the Mesozoic Era, after all, lasted over 200,000,000 years and disappeared only because of that most random of cosmic events, a collision with a massive asteroid (in effect, the dinosaur version of *Melancholia*). "If I step out into the traffic and die," Ord writes, "my life as a whole will be shorter and thereby worse" (*P* 48). By that logic, "if a catastrophe this century were to cause our extinction, then *humanity's* life would be shorter and therefore worse. Given that we may just be in our infancy, it would be much shorter; much worse" (*P* 48). Ord sometimes suggests we are in our species infancy, sometimes that we are in "adolescence" (*P* 21, 52). Either way, the potential pathos is real: few things are more tragic than the death of a child, the needless and entirely avoidable death of a child. Surely it is entirely reasonable to desire instead to live long and prosper. Echoing Ord's equation of individual lives and species survival, Adam Kirsch writes, "Humanity may be destined to disappear someday, but almost everyone would agree that the day should be postponed as long as possible, just as individuals generally try to delay the inevitable end of their own lives" (*R* 10).[52]

But the corollary of the argument that a shorter life is worse is that a longer life is better, and after a certain point one wants to ask the Cumaean sybil or Jonathan Swift's struldbruggs about the benefits of great longevity. Moreover, quite apart from the possibility that some people consider it better, in the end, to live fast, die young, and leave a good-looking corpse, we don't know that we should be expecting a species lifespan in the millions of years. As Octavia Butler will forcefully remind us, our species is distinguished by the combination of intelligence and hierarchical thinking—a highly combustible mixture that does not bode well for settling into a comfortable species retirement at a ripe old age. On the contrary, speaking of "retirement," perhaps we have more in common with the androids of *Blade Runner* than we care to admit: "The light that burns twice as bright burns half as long," Eldon Tyrell tells Roy Batty just before Batty kills him, "And you have burned so very very brightly, Roy. . . . Revel in your time."[53] Sagan's sense of our cosmic mission was founded, famously, on the premise that we are made of "star stuff" and long to "return" to the cosmos. But maybe we are made of *shooting* star stuff instead and will blaze brightly and briefly before fizzling into nonexistence. If so, it is not clear that the rest of the universe will care.

For Adam Kirsch, this entire line of argument is self-undermining. "Paradoxically," he writes, "as soon as we state our intention to think outside or against our humanity, we have failed, since this is a statement only humans could conceive or understand. . . . To break out of species-solipsism is as difficult as seeing your own back or catching your own tail" (*R* 37–38). Kirsch is, however, referring to the antihumanist new materialists and object-oriented ontologists, not to any of the science fiction writers I will discuss here. Kirsch is undoubtedly right to argue that "to understand Anthropocene antihumanism and transhumanism, it's necessary to listen not only to tech entrepreneurs and environmental activists, but to poets, novelists, and philosophers, who often serve as a better seismograph for the future" (*R* 13). But insofar as *The Revolt Against Humanity* does not engage science fiction, with the exception of Ian McEwan's *Machines Like Me* (*Children of Men*, which Kirsch does mention, is more of a near-future speculation), it represents a missed opportunity. For science fiction is precisely the genre in which we humans can think outside or against our humanity without catching our tails. Thus, even though Kirsch's account of the antihumanist and transhumanist revolt against humanity tracks strikingly close to my own, ultimately it is orthogonal to my argument here.

There is, of course, one overwhelming exception to the bad-future scenario in popular postwar American science fiction: *Star Trek*. *Star Trek* is the exception that proves the rule: a vision of a future in which humanity has approached the abyss but managed to pull back at the last moment. In *Star Trek* our descendants create a peaceful, egalitarian society and build huge starships to explore strange new worlds, to seek out new life and new civilizations, to boldly go where we have never gone before. Perhaps that determined optimism helps account for *Star Trek*'s uncanny staying power in American popular culture long after the very short life span of the original show. But *Star Trek* solicits that optimism by way of an ellipsis: after that ellipsis, *we will have outlived* our unfortunate tendencies to murder one another and despoil the planet. *Star Trek*'s perfect future, unlike that of the ex-human, depends on a future perfect that we just have to take on faith. Ord's *The Precipice* can be read as an invitation to the world of *Star Trek* and beyond, in which our most hopeful dreams for the twenty-third century are only the beginning, just the start of something big. No, really, something very very big:

> If we can reach other stars, then the whole galaxy opens up to us. The Milky Way alone contains more than 100 billion stars, and some of these will last for trillions of years, greatly extending our potential lifespan. Then there are billions of other galaxies beyond our own. If we reach a future of such a scale, we might have a truly staggering number of descendants, with the time,

resources, wisdom and experience to create a diversity of wonders unimaginable to us today.

(*P* 21)

2001: A Space Odyssey holds out that hope, but it does so, as we shall see, with caveats that become clear only in Clarke's novel, not in the film. It may seem an extravagant hope indeed—the stuff of classic science fiction, of galactic (and even transgalactic) federations and foundations. Yet if Ord's book convinces policy makers and captains of industry to pull back from the brink, to abolish nuclear weapons, develop safe AI, and achieve a carbon-neutral planet within this century, that will be an unambiguously wonderful thing. The rest of this book will ask us to think about the far more likely prospects we have imagined for ourselves in our darker moods. And we will begin by examining why Le Guin's version of a galactic federation is only, as I described it here, *relatively* happy.

1

THE AUGMENTATION OF THE COMPLEXITY AND INTENSITY OF THE FIELD OF INTELLIGENT LIFE

The Potential Ex-Human of

The Left Hand of Darkness

D espite my hesitancy about teaching courses in science fiction, I was for many years reasonably comfortable teaching Le Guin's *The Left Hand of Darkness* in courses on postmodernism and American fiction; I offered my first such course in 1991 as an undergraduate honors seminar. (The students in that seminar were amazing, and three have since gone on to accomplished careers in academic literary studies.)[1] As for why I offered *Left Hand* under the rubric of postmodernism: my argument, short version, is not that the novel "is" postmodern but that it *anticipates* debates over postmodernism in philosophy and anthropology that would not begin to emerge in those disciplines until the 1980s. Longer version: I was reading *The Left Hand of Darkness* as a text that could comment on, rather than simply serve as an example of, postmodern crises of legitimation in human affairs, and I'll explain this claim in more detail toward the close of this chapter. I'll also explain how this novel imagines a hopeful version of becoming at least partly ex-human.

But first I have to admit that this reading strategy didn't go over well at the graduate level. According to some of the graduate students to whom I first taught the novel in 1995, the novel was not stylistically postmodern enough. It wasn't historiographic metafiction, it didn't have enough ontological uncertainty, there weren't any subplots in the shape of tetrahedrons and characters dissolving into neutrinos . . . and most disappointing of all, *it failed to repudiate the last vestiges of liberal humanism.*[2] Quite the contrary: there were elements of it that were palpably, culpably humanist. Kathy Acker's *Empire of the Senseless*, Ishmael Reed's *Mumbo Jumbo*, Thomas Pynchon's *The Crying of Lot 49*—those novels were obviously and demonstrably postmodern. Students approved of their presence on the syllabus. *The Left Hand of Darkness*, not so much, even though I could point to critics such as Lewis Call who insist that "in both substance and content," the novel is a "postmodern masterpiece."[3] I thought that perhaps my students were being too prescriptive, so a couple of years later I taught the novel a second time at the graduate level—and got the same response.

I don't want to rehash here what are now very old and tired debates about modernist and postmodernist literature, and I suspect that some readers will have already decided that I have completely missed the most important aspect of *The Left Hand of Darkness*. The novel created such a stir in 1969 and (in the words of Becky Chambers, writing in 2018) has "always been as relevant as it is right now" not because of anything it might say about "postmodernism" but because it offers a radical thought experiment about the social organization of gender.[4] On the planet Gethen (also called "Winter" by non-Gethenians because of its forbiddingly cold climate), humanoid inhabitants are gender-neutral in "somer" until they go into "kemmer" as part of a monthly estrus cycle, whereupon they take on male or female sex characteristics at random. (That is, one does not consciously choose one's gender upon entering kemmer. The promo copy on the back cover of my edition gets this exactly wrong, claiming that Gethenians "can choose—and change—their gender.") The novel continues to resonate strongly for nonbinary thinking about gender and sexuality, as evidenced by the fiftieth anniversary edition's afterword by the Lambda Award–winning writer Charlie Jane Anders, who testifies that "this novel showed me a reality where storytelling could help me question the ideas about gender and sexuality that had been handed down to all of us, take-it-or-leave-it style, from childhood."[5]

This aspect of the novel is justly celebrated and dominates the critical commentary of the past half-century so overwhelmingly that I will address it only briefly, for the benefit of readers who might welcome a review. To begin with, the novel contains an explicit, full-dress analysis of the consequences of gender fluidity on Gethen: chapter 7, titled "The Question of Sex," is attributed to the "field notes of Ong Tot Oppong, Investigator, of the first Ekumenical landing party on Gethen/Winter."[6] The chapter is only eight pages long, but it serves almost as a Sparknotes guide to the novel. Indeed, those field notes have provided the basis for scores of scholarly articles; they constitute, in a way, the first critical essay about *The Left Hand of Darkness*. It is noteworthy—and I will come back to this in a moment— that the first "Ekumenical landing party" consisted exclusively of passive observers who made no attempt to inform Gethenians that they came from other worlds and no attempt to intervene in Gethenian society. The galactic organization calling itself the Ekumen, we will find, does not establish contact with a new world without learning about it in detail and only then will send one representative—just one—to establish formal contact. The intercultural, interplanetary dynamic of the novel depends on this, as does the plot itself.

It is immediately apparent to Ong Tot Oppong that because "the mother of several children may be the father of several more" (*LHD* 91), there is no link in Gethen between gender and childcare.[7] That—how does one say?—changes everything. Thus, Oppong writes,

> Anyone can turn his hand to anything. This sounds very simple, but its psychological effects are incalculable. The fact that everyone between seventeen and thirty-five or so is liable to be (as Nim put it) "tied down to childbearing," implies that no one is quite so thoroughly "tied down" here as women, elsewhere, are likely to be—psychologically or physically. Burden and privilege are shared out pretty equally: everybody has the same risk to run or choice to make. Therefore nobody here is quite so free as a free male anywhere else.
>
> (*LHD* 93)

Oppong, "a woman of peaceful Chiffewar," as she remarks in closing (*LHD* 96), proceeds to spin out the implications of this arrangement. Again, these passages are oft-cited, but they certainly merit citation here:

> Consider: There is no unconsenting sex, no rape. As with most mammals other than man, coitus can be performed only by mutual invitation and consent; otherwise it is not possible. Seduction certainly is possible, but it must have to be awfully well timed.
>
> Consider: There is no division of humanity into strong and weak halves, protective/protected, dominant/submissive, owner/chattel, active/passive. In fact the whole tendency to dualism that pervades human thinking may be found to be lessened, or changed, on Winter.
>
> The following must go into my finished Directives: when you meet a Gethenian you cannot and must not do what a bisexual

naturally does, which is to cast him in the role of Man or Woman, while adopting toward him a corresponding role dependent on your expectations of the patterned or possible interactions between persons of the same or the opposite sex. Our entire pattern of socio-sexual interaction is nonexistent here. They cannot play the game. They do not see one another as men or women. This is almost impossible for our imagination to accept. What is the first question we ask about a newborn baby?

(*LHD* 94)

Indeed, one might ask, what else is the function of a gender-reveal party, that hideous invention of the twenty-first century that surely marks our decline as a species?

Oppong's train of thought concludes on a somewhat comic note: "The First Mobile, if one is sent, must be warned that unless he is very self-assured, or senile, his pride will suffer. A man wants his virility regarded, a woman wants her femininity appreciated, however indirect and subtle the indications of regard and appreciation. On Winter they will not exist. *One is respected and judged only as a human being. It is an appalling experience*" (*LHD* 94–95, emphasis mine). The novel is full of such wry moments, the most famous of which is the sentence "The king was pregnant" (*LHD* 99, only a few pages later) and "my landlady, a voluble man" (*LHD* 47)—moments when the primary narrator and First Mobile, Genly Ai (who hails from our very own Earth), tries to convey the appalling experience of treating Gethenians only as human beings.[8] But otherwise, our Genly must not have read all of Ong Tot Oppong's finished Directives, because—as many commentators have noted—he constantly treats Gethenians as men and spends the entire novel misgendering every single person he meets. Unless, that is, he dislikes or distrusts them, at which point he attributes feminine characteristics to them. Le Guin is not subtle about this; she establishes in the very first chapter that Genly Ai is deeply misogynist. About his fateful interview with Estraven, the doomed councilor of the kingdom of Karhide, Genly says, "I thought that at table Estraven's performance had been womanly, all charm and tact and lack of substance, specious and adroit. Was it in fact perhaps this soft supple femininity that I disliked and distrusted in him?" (*LHD* 12). Yes in fact it was, for that is precisely what misogyny *is*, and two pages later, Genly is once again damning Estraven's "effeminate deviousness" (*LHD* 14). (We will return to this scene for other reasons, because Genly's misunderstanding of Estraven has many layers, the most important of which, I will argue, has to do with the relations between anthropologists and "native informants.")

A great deal of commentary has focused on the novel's use of pronouns; indeed, the objections to Le Guin's decision to use a generic "he" were immediate, decades before pronouns became decisive signifiers for gender-nonconforming persons.[9] Here too, Ong Tot Oppong's field notes are the usual place to start: "Lacking the Karhidish 'human pronoun' used for persons in somer, I must say 'he,' for the same reasons that we use the masculine pronoun in referring to a transcendent god: it is less defined, less specific, than the neuter or the feminine" (*LHD* 94).[10] As Oppong does, so does Le Guin: both narrators, Genly and Estraven, adopt "he" as the generic pronoun. Though Oppong dutifully adds that "the very use of the pronoun in my thoughts leads me continually to forget that the Karhider I am with is not a man, but a manwoman" (*LHD* 94), the rest of the novel proceeds as if this is not a problem; accordingly, critics have argued for five decades that the adoption of the masculine pronoun as "less defined, less specific, than the neuter or the feminine" undermines a good deal of the novel's attempt to imagine a world without fixed gender.[11] To gauge by my students' responses (and, for that matter, my own), these critics are right. Though Le Guin dismissed the issue in her first major response to the pronoun question, over time she eventually agreed that it was "very important" and that she had made the wrong call for about a decade or so.[12]

Much of Gethenian society is polyamorous—some couples "vow kemmering" and become monogamous, but there are "kemmerhouses" that permit all manner of hookups, including those that do not involve pairs: "groups may form and intercourse take place promiscuously among the males and females of the group" (*LHD* 91–92). For all that, however, it is fair to argue that the novel is strongly heteronormative, and consciously so; as Oppong notes, "If there are exceptions, resulting in kemmer-partners of the same sex, they are so rare as to be ignored" (*LHD* 90). Moreover, there is a stigmatized group of outcasts, known (unsurprisingly) as Perverts: they experience "excessive prolongation of the kemmer period, with permanent hormonal imbalance toward the male or the female" (*LHD* 63). They play a critical role in the mystical practice of Foretelling, and Genly remarks, when he requests (and receives) a Foretelling from the mystics of Karhide, they are "not rare; three or four percent of adults may be physiological perverts or abnormals—normals, by our standard. They are not excluded from society, but they are tolerated with some disdain, as homosexuals are in many bisexual societies" (*LHD* 63).[13] It seems safe to say that if *The Left Hand of Darkness* imagines a genderless world in which "bi," "trans," and (arguably) "queer" are the norm, it also imagines a world in which "lesbian" and "gay" are almost nonexistent and our own "normals, by our standard" are coded as tolerated-but-disdained homosexuals.

But then, there is no sense in which Le Guin was trying to write about a world utterly free of all forms of oppression, so, unlike the pronoun question, the occlusion of gay and lesbian identities in the novel cannot be said to be a shortcoming that threatens to unravel the enterprise altogether. However, another line of feminist criticism of the book pointed out that its narrative—which is basically that of political intrigue of a kind well known to us on Earth—centers on roles typically associated with men: rulers, courtiers, politicians, priests/shamen. Le Guin acknowledged this in 1976, well before she came around on the issue of pronouns:

> Unfortunately, the plot and structure that arose as I worked the book out cast the Gethenian protagonist, Estraven, almost exclusively into roles that we are culturally conditioned to perceive as "male"—a prime minister (it takes more than even Golda Meir and Indira Gandhi to break a stereotype), a political schemer, a fugitive, a prison-breaker, a sledge-hauler . . . I think I did this because I was privately delighted at watching, not a man, but a manwoman, do all these things, and do them with considerable skill and flair. But, for the reader, I left out too much. One does not see Estraven as a mother, with his children, in any role that we automatically perceive as "female": and therefore, we tend to see him as a man. This is a real flaw in the book, and I can only be very grateful to those readers, men and women, whose willingness to participate in the experiment led them to fill in that omission with the work of their own imagination, and to see Estraven as I saw him, as man and woman, familiar and different, alien and utterly human.

("IGN" 170–71; ELLIPSIS IN ORIGINAL)[14]

It is certainly possible to read and teach the novel with these caveats in mind, thereby making the infelicitous pronouns and Estraven's semiotic maleness into part of the point: *see how much mental labor we have to do to stop ourselves from thinking of him as a man, oops, that is, I mean thinking of Estraven as a man.* I have taught it that way myself, reminding students that even as Genly is aggressively and disdainfully feminizing Estraven in the first chapter, he also muses that Estraven is unreadable in another way: he has "a dark face always shadowed by the thick low growing hair and heavy brows and lashes, and by a somber blandness of expression. Can one read a cat's face, a seal's, an otter's? Some Gethenians, I thought, are like such animals, with deep bright eyes that do not change expression when you speak" (*LHD* 14–15). Though this is literally a dehumanizing strategy, it does provide a way to guard against thinking of Estraven as a man: it invites you to think of Estraven as Other—Estraven as Otter.[15]

Le Guin attributed to herself another "failure to think things through" ("IGN" 168) with regard to the political organization of the nation of Karhide and its rival Orgoreyn. "I think I took the easy way in using such familiar governmental structures as a feudal monarchy [that would be Karhide] and a modern-style bureaucracy [Orgoreyn] for the two Gethenian countries that are the scene of the novel. I doubt that Gethenian governments, rising out of the cellular hearth, would resemble any of our own so closely" ("IGN" 168–69). Interestingly, Le Guin is soft-pedaling Orgoreyn here. It is a "modern-style bureaucracy," yes, but it is also, very clearly, modeled on the Soviet Union, with its secret police and its forced-labor camps in the remote tundra. Orgoreyn thus functions as a USSR surrogate in much the same way the Klingon Empire did for the original *Star Trek*, but Karhide is not a surrogate for the United States and its allies, as *Star Trek*'s

Federation of Planets was; that Federation of Planets role, instead, is played by the aforementioned Ekumen, which consists of eighty-three humanoid civilizations scattered throughout the Milky Way, all of which have their origin on the planet Hain. (It turns out that we are all Hainish, even if we don't all *look* Hainish.)

Although the novel's vision of the social organization of gender was and remains revolutionary, the political intrigue of the novel—its plot, basically—deploys one of the most common tropes (and hopes) in classic science fiction. The idea is that when humanity makes first contact with an alien race, we will be weaned from our petty, parochial intraspecies disputes and territorialisms, either because we must band together to fight a common foe or (more optimistically) because the discovery of the existence of intelligent life in the universe forces upon us the revelation that consciousness is valuable in and of itself, regardless of what outward and bodily form it takes, or (most optimistically) because the aliens have come to help us (as in the film *Arrival* [2016]). These last two scenarios are central to Arthur C. Clarke's two most famous novels: in *2001: A Space Odyssey*, the aliens who visit Earth in the Pleistocene and leave a telltale monolith on the Moon do so "because, in all the galaxy, they had found nothing more precious than Mind, [and] they encouraged its dawning everywhere."[16] Moreover, they leave a monolith on the African plains as a cognitive-enhancement device that will teach our ancestors to develop the capacity to make tools, kill the abundant animals around them (and one another), and eat meat. Likewise, the horned and cloven-hoofed creatures who bring peace and prosperity to Earth in *Childhood's End* (despite initially terrifying us with their appearance, for understandable reasons) do so in order to allow humans a brief utopia before our species mutates, abandons the planet, and joins the universal Overmind.

The Left Hand of Darkness performs a deft détournement of these first-contact scenarios, insofar as the "alien" is from Earth and the Gethenians are the people grappling with—and almost uniformly failing to realize the potential of—the possibility of an alliance with a galactic federation of humanoid peoples of which they had been unaware. The plot follows Genly Ai as he tries to bring Gethen into a loose alliance with the Ekumen, first by appealing to King Argaven of Karhide and then, when he is rebuffed (and Estraven is exiled and nearly murdered for having given Genly his support), turning to the thirty-three "Commensals" of Orgoreyn, some of whom turn out to be agents of the Sarf, the secret police. Genly is eventually dispatched to one of the forced-labor camps, where he would have died if not for the daring intervention of Estraven, who springs him from prison and leads him on a death-defying three-month Shackletonian journey over Gethen's massive ice cap and back to Karhide.[17]

Estraven, notably, is the only person on Gethen who believes that Genly is truly an emissary from another planet, a representative of a benevolent multiplanetary association. The leaders of Karhide and Orgoreyn aren't interested in any such alliance; they find our sexual physiology abhorrent, and they are more interested in pursuing a territorial dispute in the Sinoth Valley that might lead them to war. (We are invited to imagine alien humanoids failing to distract us from the exigencies of Israel/Palestine, or Kashmir, or Tibet.) Each of them believes that Genly is a hoax perpetrated by the other. Neither of them can or will make any sense of his stated mission. When the king of Karhide confronts Genly, asking him why the Ekumen would pursue such an alliance with the people of Gethen, Genly responds (mostly) loftily: "Material profit. Increase of knowledge. The augmentation of the complexity and intensity of the field of intelligent life. The enrichment of harmony and the greater glory of God. Curiosity. Adventure. Delight" (*LHD* 34). Mixed in with profit (which leads) and God (who arrives much later) is the language of the liberal arts college brochure and the dream of classic science fiction: *the augmentation of the complexity and intensity of the field of intelligent life.* This is the benign version of the desire to boldly go where none has gone before and the galactic-cosmopolitan antithesis of Victor Frankenstein's injunction, in the genre's inaugural text, to "learn from me, if not by my precepts, at least by my example, how dangerous is the acquirement of knowledge, and how much happier that man is who believes his native town to be the world, than he who aspires to become greater than his nature will allow" (*F* 37–38). It sums up neatly why so many readers of science fiction are readers of science fiction. *This is what we came for. More augmentation of the complexity and intensity of the field of intelligent life, please.*

To put this in terrestrial terms: for the Gethenians, the prospect of joining the Ekumen is apparently far simpler than joining (or leaving) the European Union. All it takes is the ability and the willingness to set aside parochial, sectarian interests and fears of the Other, even the weirdly gendered Others who appear, in the words of the king, "so monstrously different" (*LHD* 36). The Ekumen imposes no political requirements, no standards of rights or entitlements or even of weights and measures, other than the openness to augmenting the quality of intelligent life in the galaxy. "The Ekumen," Genly tells King Argaven, "is not a kingdom, but a co-ordinator, a clearinghouse for trade and knowledge" (*LHD* 35). It offers curiosity, adventure, and delight in place of liberty, equality, and fraternity. No bureaucracy. No constitutional convention, no elections, no judiciary, no political apparatus whatsoever. No tension between the folkways of one planet's people and the galactic clearinghouse for trade and knowledge. No struggle, no strife. What's not to like?

The other political parallel with *Star Trek* is the Ekumenical injunction against interference in newly discovered worlds. In *Star Trek* it is the Prime Directive; in *The Left Hand of Darkness* it is the Law of Cultural Embargo—which, as Genly explains to us in the course of recounting his pitch to the Commensals of Orgoreyn, "stood against the importation of analyzable, imitable artifacts" (*LHD* 135). This is why Genly cannot summon the ship that brought him or awaken its hibernating crew; he can show (as he showed King Argaven) the "ansible," the device that permits instantaneous communication between worlds, but, he acknowledges, "it didn't make a very convincing Alien Artifact, being so incomprehensible as to fit in with hoax as well as with reality" (*LHD* 135).[18] Even though Genly later traduces the law, attempting (successfully, after many failures) to teach telepathic "mindspeech" to Estraven, and even though the crew of the *USS Enterprise* violate the Prime Directive with disturbing frequency, the existence of such laws is obviously an index of the degree to which classic science fiction is haunted by the history of colonialism and has been since Shelley's allusions to that history in *Frankenstein*.[19] In the future, thankfully, when sentient humanoids seek the augmentation of the complexity and intensity of the field of intelligent life, they/we will do so with 100 percent less genocide. This proscription against imperialism makes Genly's mission exceptionally difficult; when Estraven finally asks him, during their journey over the Ice, why the Ekumen sent him to Gethen alone, Genly replies, "The First Envoy to a world always comes alone. One alien is a curiosity, two are an invasion" (*LHD* 209).

Later, Genly expands on the implications of this policy, having thought about it more deeply in the course of his journey:

> I thought it was for your sake that I came alone, so obviously alone, so vulnerable, that I could in myself pose no threat, change no balance: not an invasion, but a mere messenger-boy. But there's more to it than that. Alone, I cannot change your world. But I can be changed by it. Alone, I must listen, as well as speak. Alone, the relationship I finally make, if I make one, is not impersonal and not only political: it is individual, it is personal, it is both more and less than political. Not We and They; not I and It; but I and Thou. Not political, not pragmatic, but mystical. In a certain sense the Ekumen is not a body politic, but a body mystic.

(*LHD* 259)

This is a passage to which a number of my graduate students strenuously objected. And they had a point: it isn't one little bit postmodern. *I and Thou! A body mystic!* This is not just liberal humanism, bad as that would be. It is *mystical*, that is to say mystified, liberal humanism. It's traditional liberal humanism with a sprinkling of Martin Buber and Le Guin's lifelong study of Taoism. So why did I bother trying to argue, why am I still trying to argue, that the novel anticipates debates over postmodernism in philosophy and anthropology?

For two intertwined reasons: one, the novel stages Genly's mission as a question of the heterogeneity and incommensurability of language-games—the question of whether people with different cultures and belief systems can come to understand one another. That question became, in the early to mid-1980s, the basis for the famous standoff between Jürgen Habermas and

Jean-François Lyotard, with most professors in the humanities—
and all of my graduate students except one lonely holdout—
agreeing with Lyotard that the Habermasian ideal of "consensus"
constituted a form of injury to the heterogeneity of human
language-games that amounted to nothing less than "terror."[20]
Genly frames his dilemma quite nicely in his account of his initial conversation with King Argaven:

> Though Argaven might be neither sane nor shrewd, he had had
> long practice in the evasions and challenges and rhetorical sub-
> tleties used in conversation by those whose main aim in life was
> the achievement and maintenance of the shifgrethor relationship
> on a high level. Whole areas of that relationship were still blank
> to me, but I knew something about the competitive, prestige-
> seeking aspect of it, and about the perpetual conversational duel
> that can result from it. *That I was not dueling with Argaven, but
> trying to communicate with him, was itself an incommunicable fact.*
>
> (*LHD* 33; MY EMPHASIS.)

Shifgrethor, the untranslatable Gethenian term Genly glosses
reasonably well here (we will find it is common to both nations,
Karhide and Orgoreyn), is central to the novel's dramatic
tension—and to its depiction of cultural and linguistic incommensurability, which turns out to be the same thing.

The impasse here goes well beyond King Argaven's failure to
understand that Genly is trying to communicate with him, and
trying to establish a relation to the Ekumen, which would con-
sist largely of the agreement to communicate. That specific failure is unfortunate but routine enough to be familiar to anyone
who has ever tried to persuade a powerful person of something.

But Genly's inadequate understanding of shifgrethor subtends the entire relationship between himself and Estraven and thus the plot of the novel as a whole. Le Guin introduces the dynamic immediately, just as she introduces Genly's misogyny immediately, in the opening chapter (to which we can now return): after decrying what he calls Estraven's "effeminate deviousness," Genly reports,

> I said, "Are you trying to tell me, Lord Estraven, that you're out of favor with the king?"
>
> I think he was angry then, but he said nothing that showed it, only, "I'm not trying to tell you anything, Mr. Ai."
>
> "By God, I wish you would!"
>
> He looked at me curiously. "Well, then, put it this way. There are some persons in court who are, in your phrase, in favor with the king, but who do not favor your presence or your mission here."
>
> And so you're hurrying to join them, selling me out to save your skin, I thought, but there was no point in saying it. Estraven was a courtier, a politician, and I a fool to have trusted him. Even in a bisexual society the politician is very often something less than an integral man.

(*LHD* 14)

Genly's misreading of Estraven is thorough and grievous, and he compounds the problem a moment later, asking Estraven, "You imply that this isn't the right moment. Would you advise me to cancel my audience?" Genly immediately knows he has said the wrong thing, but even then, he is wrong about why: "My gaffe was even worse in Karhidish, but Estraven did not smile, or wince. 'I'm afraid only the king has that privilege,' he said mildly" (*LHD* 16).

Remember that Genly is narrating this story retrospectively and could very well have simply told us what is going wrong here. He does not, for the novel is cannily structured in such a way that we, as readers, have to reproduce Genly's missteps, engaging in the same fundamental misreadings of Gethenians and Gethenian culture that almost doom his mission. (That, as perceptive critics have demonstrated, is the entire point of the novel's narrative structure.)[21] For it is not just a matter of Genly's having suggested, inappropriately, that he had the power to cancel a meeting with the king. That is bad enough in itself, but the larger issue here involves something that goes much deeper into the conditions of possibility for human communication and mutual understanding. We do not get another hint of what that issue might be until Estraven turns up in Orgoreyn, having been exiled (and almost murdered during his escape) from Karhide. When Genly coldly presents Estraven with the money given to him in trust by Estraven's former partner, Estraven responds stiffly and (to Ai) strangely:

> "You performed a service both for me and for my old friend and kemmering Ashe Foreth, and in his name and mine I claim my right. My thanks take the form of advice." He paused; I said nothing. I had never heard him use this sort of harsh, elaborate courtesy, and I had no idea what it signified. He went on, "You are, in Mishnory [the capital of Orgoreyn], what you were not, in Ehrenrang [the capital of Karhide]. There they said you were; here they'll say you're not. You are the tool of a faction. I advise you to be careful how you let them use you. I advise you to find out what the enemy faction is, and who they are, and never to let them use you, for they will not use you well."

(*LHD* 131)

This is certainly maddeningly vague advice, and Genly is justifiably annoyed by it, but not until the narrative offers us Estraven's account of the scene do we understand that on Gethen, the most insulting, demeaning thing one person can do to another is to *give that person advice*:

> He gave me Ashe's money as one would give a hired assassin his fee. I have not often been so angry, and I insulted him deliberately. He knew I was angry but I am not sure he understood that he was insulted; he seemed to *accept* my advice despite the manner of its giving; and when my temper cooled I saw this, and was worried by it. Is it possible that all along in Ehrenrang he was seeking my advice, not knowing how to tell me that he sought it? If so, then he must have misunderstood half and not understood the rest of what I told him by my fireside in the Palace.... His shifgrethor must be founded, and composed, and sustained, altogether differently from ours; and when I thought myself most blunt and frank with him he may have found me most subtle and unclear.
>
> (*LHD* 148–49)

This is precisely what goes wrong with Genly's mission. Though he understands generally that shifgrethor is a competitive, prestige-seeking form of verbal jousting, he does not understand that one of its core principles is that openly advising another person is understood by all parties to be an expression of the utmost contempt and disdain. Genly's "gaffe" in the opening scene, then, is saying things like "are you trying to tell me" and "would you advise me"; Estraven is mortally offended but diplomatically keeps his emotions in check—thus remaining inscrutable to Ai.[22]

The impasse is not broken until much later, when Estraven and Genly are making their journey across the Ice; then, and only then, does Estraven reveal that everything he has done, everything Genly has found so vexing, has followed from his belief that Genly has been telling the truth about the Ekumen and the existence of other worlds. When Estraven recounts to Genly the events of the narrative to that point, prefacing his account by saying "we've seen the same events with different eyes; I wrongly thought they'd seem the same to us" (*LHD* 197), an exasperated Genly replies,

> "But for what purpose—all this intriguing, this hiding and power-seeking and plotting—what was it all for, Estraven? What were you after?"
>
> "I was after what you're after: the alliance of my world with your worlds. What did you think?"
>
> We were staring at each other across the glowing stove like a pair of wooden dolls.
>
> "You mean, even if it was Orgoreyn that made the alliance—?"
>
> "Even if it was Orgoreyn. Karhide would soon have followed. Do you think I would play shifgrethor when so much is at stake for all of us, all my fellow men? What does it matter which country wakes first, so long as we waken?"

(*LHD* 198)

Estraven, it turns out, is the only Gethenian Genly encounters, over the course of two years, who understands that the revelation of intelligent life on other planets offers Gethenians a chance to be weaned from their petty, parochial intraspecies disputes and territorialisms. He is in that sense a heroic figure of classic science fiction, a character who can embrace the largest possible

sense of human community—and the goal of the augmentation of the complexity and intensity of the field of intelligent
life. "My greatest error," he tells Genly,

> "was, as you say, in making myself clear to you. I am not used to
> doing so. I am not used to giving, or accepting, either advice or
> blame."
>
> "I don't mean to be unjust, Estraven—"
>
> "Yet you are. It is strange. I am the only man in all Gethen
> that has trusted you entirely, and I am the only man in Gethen that
> you have refused to trust."
>
> He put his head in his hands. He said at last, "I'm sorry,
> Estraven." It was both apology and admission.

(*LHD* 199)

Later, Genly admits to himself that "I had not wanted to give
my trust, my friendship to a man who was a woman, a woman
who was a man" (*LHD* 249). This is a rather staggering admis-
sion from someone who tells Estraven that he deliberately chose
this mission, just as it is stupefying that it has taken Genly a full
two years to absorb the admonition of Ong Tot Oppong that
"when you meet a Gethenian you cannot and must not . . . cast
him in the role of Man or Woman."

But there is still something more at work here. The impasse
between Genly and Estraven (and Gethenians in general) gave
readers a foreshadowing of the postmodern rupture in the field
of cultural anthropology, specifically with regard to the vexed
position of the "native informant"—a figure that became the
object of critique by anthropologists who worried that their field
might participate in or accelerate the project of cultural imperialism.[23] That was an appropriate worry, for there is no question

that throughout the first three-quarters of the twentieth century, anthropology, with its construction of the primitive native Other as its object of study, *did* participate in the project of cultural imperialism. (One of my students: "Are you talking about old issues of *National Geographic* with photographs of bare-breasted brown women?" Me: "Among other things, yes.") This critique of anthropology was introduced to public debate in the United States by books such as Vine Deloria Jr.'s *Custer Died for Your Sins: An Indian Manifesto*, published the same year as *The Left Hand of Darkness*. Chapter 4 of that book, titled "Anthropologists and Other Friends," launched a scathing critique that cast anthropologists as a kind of recurring virus: "Indians have been cursed above all other people in history. Indians have anthropologists. . . . Behind each policy and program with which Indians are plagued, if traced completely back to its origin, stands the anthropologist."[24]

Le Guin, the daughter of the anthropologists Alfred and Theodora Kroeber, was well aware of the debates roiling the field.[25] So, she asks, what are the chances for transparent communication and good anthropological fieldwork when the anthropologist cannot explain that s/he is trying to communicate with the "natives," as Genly finds during his audience with King Argaven, and cannot ask for advice? It does not matter, in this scenario, that the character in the position of the anthropologist makes it abundantly clear that he is not in the service of any kind of imperialist project; for Gethenians other than Estraven, the mere suggestion that there may be sentient humanoid creatures on other planets is threatening in and of itself, and the fact that these humanoids are "monstrously different" is simply disgusting. The Ekumen, as we have seen, takes great care to avoid any encroachment on a newly discovered world; Ong Tot Oppong apparently did not announce to the Gethenians that she was doing preparatory fieldwork for the dispatching of a First Mobile (indeed, her notes include the caveat "if one is sent"), and the Law of Cultural Embargo is strictly observed. Moreover, *The Left Hand of Darkness* is not written solely from the anthropologist's perspective; Genly Ai's narrative is interlaced with that of Estraven and punctuated by numerous "primary" texts from various Gethenian religious and cultural traditions. Still, the relationship between Genly and Estraven (and other Gethenians) is not symmetrical, however much the Ekumen tries to make it a matter of I and Thou.

And speaking of Estraven: he is in a completely impossible position. For what becomes of the role of the "native informant" if the informant lives in a culture where giving advice is the deepest form of insult, so that s/he cannot, in good conscience, advise the anthropologist? That role was always problematic, since the native informant is the go-between who enables the anthropologists to do their work—and who, all too often, was intellectually exploited or marginalized by that work.[26] As the Vietnamese filmmaker and theorist Trinh Minh-Ha memorably put it in her 1989 book *Woman, Native, Other*, native informants are "the handicapped who cannot represent themselves and have to either be represented or learn how to represent themselves."[27] In the 1990s, Gayatri Spivak was using the term to critique the disciplines of the humanities across the board— "philosophy, literature, history, culture"—and to argue that "native informant" should be understood more broadly as "a name for that expulsion from the name of Man—a mark crossing out the impossibility of the ethical relation," and as a figure "denied autobiography as it is understood in the Northwestern European tradition (codename 'West')."[28]

It may be that these postcolonialist dismissals of the native informant are too sweeping to be of relevance to the character of Estraven, who certainly does represent himself—and is, in the end, the only reason for the success of Genly's mission. But there is no question that Estraven is introduced to us, in that tension-filled first scene, as Genly's informant—and that Genly sees him that way, asking him what he does not know are literally unspeakably rude questions: *are you trying to tell me . . . would you advise me. . . .* Estraven is hamstrung, trying to warn Genly that his audience with King Argaven will not go well while insisting that in no sense whatsoever is he trying to *tell* Genly anything. And of course, there is no way that Estraven can explain why he would not be trying to advise Genly, no way to say, "It's like this, see—my people consider giving advice to be profoundly insulting, and you'll be much better off if you don't ask for any." This is how incommensurable language-games work in practice—by not being able to work at all.

This depiction of incommunicable communicative impasse, I think, is a stroke of brilliance on Le Guin's part, on a par with her radical reimagining of gender and its social organization. Genly is alone on Gethen, terribly vulnerable, but even more appalling is his situation as a human being who is utterly dependent on the counsel of the planet's inhabitants, who have developed a culture in which no one offers another person counsel unless they explicitly waive shifgrethor (as an Orgota official does at one point, showing us that it is possible, however rare). *The Left Hand of Darkness*, in other words, rethinks the history of colonialism not only from the perspective of science fiction but from the perspective of cultural anthropology, and it does so in terms that anticipate academic debates by decades. I no longer care whether this crisis in anthropology is called postmodern or, for that matter, whether anything is called "postmodern" anymore. The point remains that that crisis happened, that it had profound intellectual consequences, and that it reverberates to this day—and that Le Guin saw, very early, its implications for a genre that too often was blithe or jejune (or positively pro-colonialist) about the implications of forming an interstellar federation of worlds. For an exploration of the parameters of the ex-human, *The Left Hand of Darkness* is a very good place to start, for it holds out the hope of a form of civilization that exceeds our own, is like our own, and is beset by precisely the cultural dilemmas that bedevil our own.

Yet in the end, *The Left Hand* ultimately affirms the dream of pan-human communication—just barely. Estraven pays for his efforts with his life (his death hits some students very hard, and not without reason; Genly himself is bitterly devastated by it), but by novel's end, the mothership has been summoned, the crew has been greeted (by Karhide and King Argaven), and the Ekumen has embraced its eighty-fourth member planet. Genly's reunion with the crew involves a profound scene of Gulliver-esque defamiliarization, the result of his two years of living among Gethenians. One of his former crewmates, a woman named Lang Heo Hew, does not recognize him at first, but more important, Genly has, unbeknownst to himself until this moment, adopted the Gethenian perspective on his fellow creatures: "They all looked strange to me, men and women, well as I knew them. Their voices sounded strange: too deep, too shrill. They were like a troupe of great, strange animals, of two different species; great apes with intelligent eyes, all of them in rut, in kemmer . . ." (*LHD* 296; ellipsis in original). By contrast, when Genly is tended to by a Gethenian doctor immediately thereafter, overcome by emotion, he notes (still using the generic he/him), "his quiet voice and his face, a young, serious face, not a man's face and not a woman's, a human face, these were a relief to me, familiar, right . . ." (*LHD* 296; ellipsis in original). Genly has not quite become ex-human here, but he has definitely become ex-Terran; one might even say he has become in a sense reparochialized, identifying not with the Ekumen he represents (as he has always presented himself) but with the Gethenians he has come to accept as "normal" human beings.[29] Still, for the Ekumen and for Karhide, and despite Estraven's death, this is a happy ending. The mission is a success. It seems as if humanity is worth all the trouble, after all.

Le Guin makes clear in another justly celebrated novel in the Hainish Cycle (a term she disputed), *The Dispossessed*, that Earth itself will meet no happy fate: we will despoil our planet and provoke global warming to the point at which Earth can sustain only half a billion humans living on the edge of bare subsistence, husbanding their remaining resources by means of a draconian centralized government.[30] Late in the novel, the Terran ambassador, Keng, tells Shevek, our anarchist protagonist (and us), that "my world, my Earth, is a ruin. A planet spoiled by the human species. We multiplied and gobbled and fought until there was nothing left, and then we died. We controlled neither appetite nor violence; we did not adapt. We destroyed ourselves. But we destroyed the world first. There are no forests left on my Earth" (*D* 279). There are ruins of great cities everywhere: "the bones and bricks go to dust, but the little pieces of plastic never do" (*D* 279). (Is this the first mention of plastic in the imaginative literature of environmental disaster scenarios?) "We failed as a species, as a social species. . . . We had saved what could be saved, and made a kind of life in the ruins, on Terra, in the only way it could be done: by total centralization. Total control of the use of every acre of land, every scrap of metal, every ounce of fuel. Total rationing, birth control, euthanasia, universal conscription into the labor force. The absolute regimentation of each life toward the goal of racial survival" (*D* 280).

That is one plausible vision of the ex-human, to be sure.[31] The absolute regimentation of each life toward the goal of racial survival, as opposed to the augmentation of the complexity and intensity of the field of intelligent life. But when we step back from our own species and take the larger view, even *The Dispossessed* offers us an attenuated kind of hope: somewhere among the hundred billion stars in our immediate vicinity, the Milky Way, there are intelligent creatures very much like ourselves, devoted to the life of Mind and willing and able to extend an invitation to us, and others, to join them. Here's what Keng says after "we have failed as a species, a social species," in the ellipsis I have interpolated into the passage above: "We are here now, dealing as equals with other human societies on other worlds, only because of the charity of the Hainish. They came; they brought us help. They built ships and gave them to us, so we could leave our ruined world. They treat us gently, charitably, as the strong man treats the sick one" (*D* 279–80).

We have destroyed our planet. We have failed as a species, as a social species. The Hainish, benevolent aliens not terribly unlike ourselves, have brought us "a little more hope"—and even though Keng ruefully adds that "we have outlived it" (*D* 280), we still have a connection to a form of humanoid intelligence and civilization in the galaxy. There is still some faint reason to believe. We are not yet in the world in which it might make more sense to say *oh, fuck it all* and give up. But we will get there in the next two chapters.

There is, however, one last consideration we must bring to bear on our Hainish future—namely, our Hainish past. This is not mentioned in Keng's account in *The Dispossessed*, but it takes up the first paragraph of Ong Tot Oppong's report in *Left Hand*. Speculating on the evolutionary origin of the Gethenians, Oppong writes,

> It seems likely that they were an experiment. The thought is unpleasant. But now that there is evidence to indicate that the Terran Colony was an experiment, the planting of one Hainish

Normal group on a world with its own proto-hominid autoch-
thones, the possibility cannot be ignored. Human genetic manipulation was certainly practiced by the Colonizers; nothing else
explains the hilfs of S or the degenerate winged hominids of
Rokanan; will anything else explain Gethenian sexual physiology? Accident, possibly; natural selection, hardly. Their ambi-
sexuality has little or no adaptive value.

(*LHD* 89)

Oppong offers a few hypotheses about the purpose of the experiment, suggesting that "it is possible that the experimenters
wished to see whether human beings lacking continuous sexual
potentiality would remain intelligent and capable of culture"
(*LHD* 95) and noting that one effect of the experiment seems to
have been "the elimination of war" (*LHD* 95)—although that is
precisely what the inflamers of the Sinoth Valley dispute are trying to provoke. We will revisit this potential tradeoff between
culture and war in *Oryx and Crake*'s "Blood and Roses" game,
but for now let us stop to remark that the Hainish have been to
Earth before, not to leave a monolith but to mate with us. One
is left to wonder whether the arrangement was consensual, and
the existence of degenerate winged hominids (depicted in the
1966 novel *Rocannon's World*) is not encouraging. The Hainish
may someday save us from ourselves, but they will always have
been our ancestors' colonizers and perhaps their rapists. We will
return to this dynamic in chapter 4, where my reading of Lilith's
Brood will reveal that I, for one, will welcome our Oankali overlords and their controversial method of nonconsensual reproduction. For now, though, let us turn to a pair of texts that will
give us good reason to despair—and to imagine darker versions
of the ex-human.

2

DESPERATE MEASURES

Justifiable Despair in *The Three-Body Problem*

and *Oryx and Crake*

This chapter is about what makes people give up on the human race—what might motivate someone to summon a hostile alien invasion of Earth or create a humanoid species to take our place. But in order to establish motive, we need to get a few things straight first—an especially urgent task when those things have been, like the Moon monolith in *2001: A Space Odyssey*, deliberately buried.

I will begin with a most unlikely story involving a cosmic coincidence.

It was December 3, 2019, the beginning of the final two weeks of the fall semester. I had just started teaching Cixin Liu's *The Three-Body Problem*; each of my three Chinese students—out of a class of twenty-four—had told me months earlier (in separate conversations, not all at once) how happy they were to see Liu on the syllabus and how much they were looking forward to discussing the novel with me.[1] One had recommended that I watch the film *The Wandering Earth*, which was based on a Liu novella and had recently been released; I dutifully did so, upon finding it as an option for an in-flight movie, and reported back to him, truthfully, that I enjoyed it. After class that day, after our discussion of the first three chapters of *The Three-Body Problem*, he came up to me with a puzzled expression on his face.

"Professor, may I ask you a question?"

"Of course," I replied. "Walk with me." As we left the building and started to walk through the campus, he told me that although he had already read the novel in Chinese, he had decided it would be interesting to read the English translation.

"That makes sense," I said with a slightly raised eyebrow, "it *is* the assigned text, after all. And of course it will be easier for you to follow along when I cite specific passages on specific pages."

"But Professor," he said, "the English version is very different from the original."

I stopped and turned to him, puzzled. "Well, that shouldn't be surprising, should it? I can't read a word of Chinese, so I can't say anything about the original text, but I would suspect that there would be something lost in translation. That's not unusual, you know."

"That is not what I mean, Professor," he said patiently. "I do not mean the language. I mean the Chinese version does not begin this way. It does not begin with the scenes we discussed today. Those come much later. It begins with part 2. Chapter 4. When Shi Qiang and the police come to Wang Miao's apartment."

This made no sense to me. The translator messed with the structure of the book? The Chinese version doesn't lead with the scenes that establish the premise of the novel and the motive for everything that follows?

"Wait, so everything we discussed today doesn't happen at the beginning of the Chinese translation?" Yes, I knew my student had just said that, but at this point I was flabbergasted.

"No, Professor. It was a complete surprise to me."

"That doesn't sound right," I said. "Translators don't usually do that. They don't usually undertake major revisions to a text in that way. I've never heard of anything quite like that."

"It seems very odd, Professor."

"It does!" I agreed. "Let me look into this and get back to you."

As extraordinary fortune would have it, I didn't have to do so much as a second's worth of digging. As I returned to my office and opened my email, there was my answer: a friend had sent me a story in the *New York Times*, published just that morning for that Sunday's edition of the *New York Times Magazine*. Written by Alexandra Alter and titled "How Chinese Sci-Fi Conquered America," it focused on the translator, Ken Liu (no relation to the author), and gave me the answer to my student's question:

> "The Three-Body Problem" was unlike anything Liu had ever read. A mind-bending epic set in Beijing, Inner Mongolia and on a distant planet, the novel was full of heady technical passages about quantum theory, nanotechnology, orbital mechanics and astrophysics, intertwined with profound moral questions about the nature of good and evil and humanity's place in the universe.
>
> But as he began translating, Liu was confronted by what seemed like a more fundamental problem: The narrative structure didn't make sense. The story careered around in time, bouncing between present-day China, as a panic builds among scientists and government officials over a coming alien invasion, and Beijing in 1967, near the start of the Cultural Revolution, when an astrophysicist watches helplessly as her father, a physics professor, is killed by members of Mao's Red Guard for being a "reactionary academic authority." The astrophysicist loses faith in humanity and uses a high-power radio transmitter to broadcast a defiant message to aliens in a nearby solar system, an act that has dire consequences.
>
> Studying the novel's chaotic timeline, Liu pinpointed what he felt was the story's natural beginning: the scenes of political

violence and oppression during the Cultural Revolution, a traumatic moment that triggers the interstellar clash that follows. In a move that was unusually invasive for a translator, he suggested pulling up the historical flashback, which was buried in the middle of the narrative, and turning it into the novel's beginning.

When Liu proposed this radical change to the author, a rising figure in China's burgeoning science-fiction scene named Liu Cixin, he was prepared to be overruled. Instead, the author instantly agreed. "That is how I wanted it originally!" Liu recalls him saying.[2]

My first thought upon reading this, that morning in my office, was, *Wow, this is amazing.* My second thought was, *OK, now I know how I'm going to open class discussion on Thursday.*

As Alter's article proceeds to explain, Cixin Liu himself was deeply affected by the Cultural Revolution: fearing for his safety, his parents sent him at the age of three to live with relatives. As he told Alter, "The Cultural Revolution appears because it's essential to the plot. The protagonist needs to have total despair in humanity." (We will explore that despair shortly. It is at the heart of this book, not just of this chapter.) But Liu's Chinese publisher thought that opening with those scenes would attract the attention of censors and so recommended burying them deep in the book where they might not be noticed. It is a long book, to be sure, and censors have so very many things to read; they can't always be bothered with scrutinizing the whole thing.[3]

The English translation of *The Three-Body Problem* was published in 2014. The previous year, the Chinese government had decreed that seven subjects were off limits in Chinese universities: freedom of the press, universal values, judicial independence, economic neoliberalism, the wealth accumulated by top government officials, civil society—and the historical mistakes of the Chinese Communist Party. By any standard (perhaps a universal one?), the Cultural Revolution, like the Great Leap Forward, would appear to count as one of those mistakes. Liu's depiction of its insanity is unsparing; the opening chapter is titled "The Madness Years," and in it, Ye Wenjie witnesses her father, Ye Zhetai, being beaten to death with belt buckles by "semicrazed" fourteen-year-old girls in the Red Guards.[4] That is the grisly climax of a struggle session in which Ye Zhetai is denounced by his wife, Shao Lin, who accuses him of teaching "the reactionary Copenhagen interpretation of quantum mechanics," which, she says, "posits that external observation leads to the collapse of the quantum wave function" and is therefore "another expression of reactionary idealism" (*TBP* 17). Even worse, she continues, he has taught the Big Bang theory, which had only recently been buttressed by the discovery of the cosmic microwave background radiation and which, she says, "is the most reactionary of all scientific theories" (*TBP* 17–18).

It is an absurd and devastating sequence. And after it is over, young Ye Wenjie seeks refuge at the home of her intellectual mentor, Professor Ruan Wen. Professor Ruan had undergone her own struggle sessions, during which the Red Guards had destroyed her piano and her artworks and "had hung a pair of high heels around her neck and streaked her face with lipstick to show how she had lived the corrupt lifestyle of a capitalist" (*TBP* 21). When Ye arrives, Professor Ruan is "wearing a light coat of lipstick and a pair of high heels" (*TBP* 21). She is sitting in a chair by her desk. She has committed suicide.

And yet, even though Liu demonstrated admirable courage and honesty in writing these scenes and establishing them as the basis for the novel's plot, there is no reason to construe Liu as a dissident writer.[5] As he made clear in a 2019 interview with Jia-yang Fan of the *New Yorker*, he is perfectly capable of parroting the party line when it comes to the Chinese government's mass internment and torture of Muslim Uighurs: "Would you rather that they be hacking away at bodies at train stations and schools in terrorist attacks? If anything, the government is helping their economy and trying to lift them out of poverty."[6] Yet in his depiction of how Ye Wenjie comes to have "total despair in humanity," he is admirably unflinching.

The scene of Ye Zhetai's murder and Shao Lin's betrayal is only the beginning. (Literally, thanks to Ken Liu.) Ye Wenjie, having become ideologically suspect by association with her father, is sentenced to forced labor with the Inner Mongolia Production and Construction Corps, where she participates in the mass-logging ecological atrocity China conducted for almost six decades: "Ye Wenjie could only describe the deforestation that she witnessed as madness. The tall Dahurian larch, the evergreen Scots pine, the slim and straight white birch, the cloud-piercing Korean aspen, the aromatic Siberian fir, along with black birch, oak, mountain elm, *Chosenia arbutifola*—whatever they laid eyes on, they cut down" (*TBP* 24). Here—over a fallen Dahurian larch, in fact—Ye meets Bai Mulin, a reporter for the corps' newspaper, the *Great Production News*. Bai surprises Ye by suggesting that they are indeed participating in an ecological atrocity, telling her, "I want to write to the leadership in Beijing and let them know about the irresponsible behavior of the Construction Corps" (*TBP* 27). He introduces her to a book he is translating from English: Rachel Carson's *Silent Spring*.

That exchange proves fateful not just for Ye but for all of humanity. The book has a profound effect on Ye: "The use of pesticides had seemed to Ye just a normal, proper—or, at least, neutral—act, but Carson's book allowed Ye to see that, from Nature's perspective, their use was indistinguishable from the

Cultural Revolution, and equally destructive to our world. If this was so, then how many other acts of humankind that had seemed normal or even righteous were, in reality, evil?" (*TBP* 27). Ye is moved to ask herself, "*Is it possible the relationship between humanity and evil is similar to the relationship between the ocean and an iceberg floating on its surface? Both the ocean and the iceberg are made of the same material*" (*TBP* 27; emphasis in original). She thus concludes that "it was impossible to expect a moral awakening from humankind itself. . . . To achieve moral awakening required a force outside the human race" (*TBP* 28). As if all this were not bad enough, Ye's life then takes an even nastier turn: Bai writes a draft of his report, a devastating critique of how "the Inner Mongolia Production and Construction Corps' actions would lead to severe ecological consequences" (*TBP* 30), and gives it to Ye to read. But he cannot write out a clean copy, because his hands are shaking from using a chainsaw all day. Ye offers to write out the report for him. Three weeks later, she is hauled before the company commander and the political instructor of the corps. She is accused of writing the letter and of endorsing a book that is "a toxic piece of reactionary propaganda" (*TBP* 33). Bai Mulin, overwhelmed by fear after learning that "his letter touched a minefield that he did not know existed" (*TBP* 33), has ratted out Ye, claiming that, as Director Zhang of the Division Political Department tells her, "his only involvement was posting the letter from Hohhot under your direction. He had no idea as to the letter's contents" (*TBP* 32).

"Half a century later," the narrator reports, stepping back for a moment, "historians would all agree that this event in 1969 was a turning point in humankind's history" (*TBP* 33). That it was: it leads Ye Wenjie to have total despair in humanity, a despair that is only hardened when she is imprisoned and asked to sign a document, signed and allegedly written by her sister, that will condemn her father still further. "Ye Wenjie couldn't tell if the contents of the document were true or false, but she was sure that every character and every punctuation mark had the potential to deliver a fatal political blow. In addition to those targeted directly, countless others might have their fates altered because of this document" (*TBP* 37). She refuses to sign. She is consequently designated an active counter-revolutionary and would be punished severely but for the fact that officials at the Red Coast Base, a mysterious defense research facility, need her. As those officials gradually decide that they can trust this counter-revolutionary young woman, they disclose to her that Red Coast is engaged in SETI, the search for extraterrestrial intelligence. During her time at Red Coast, Ye devises a way of boosting Earth's radio signals, ricocheting them off the sun so that they can be perceived by intelligent species elsewhere. This is a dangerous project in terms of political symbolism, for shooting a radio beam at the sun could be understood as an insult to Chairman Mao, of whom the red sun was a symbol (*TBP* 264), but it is a still more dangerous project insofar as it attracts the attention of a civilization in the Alpha Centauri system seeking to flee its doomed home planet, Trisolaris.

Liu then proceeds to twist the alien-contact scenario—twice. Eight years after Ye sends her transmission, she receives a reply. "The content," Liu writes, "was not what anyone had imagined" (*TBP* 272). It is a warning.

> Do not answer!
> Do not answer!!
> Do not answer!!!

(*TBP* 272)

Then there is an immediate follow-up:

> This world has received your message.
>
> I am a pacifist in this world. It is the luck of your civilization that I am the first to receive your message. I am warning you: Do not answer! Do not answer!! Do not answer!!!
>
> There are tens of millions of stars in your direction. As long as you do not answer, this world will not be able to ascertain the source of your transmission.
>
> But if you do answer, the source will be located right away. Your planet will be invaded. Your world will be conquered!
>
> Do not answer! Do not answer!! Do not answer!!! (*TBP* 273)

Needless to say, the idea that an alien civilization might be a hostile threat is not exactly unknown to science fiction; on the contrary, it is a staple. It is the nightmare version of the dream of alien contact as the augmentation of the complexity and intensity of the field of intelligent life, and as I noted in the previous chapter, it is always a meditation on the history of terrestrial colonialism and conquest. (*The Three-Body Problem* offers its own version of that meditation, which we will see in a moment.) What is distinctive here is the idea that a *pacifist* from that hostile civilization will make first contact and try to forestall any further contact, in the interest of our survival—even though their own planet is in grave peril.

The second twist follows immediately. Ye's despair in humanity is so deep and so profound that even after receiving this warning, she decides that further contact is worth the risk: as she sees it, any form of intelligent life, however hostile or warlike, will surely be more beneficent—and perhaps more intelligent?—than our own. Her reply is immediate and sets the rest of the trilogy in motion: "*Come here! I will help you conquer this world.*

Our civilization is no longer capable of solving its own problems.
We need your force to intervene" (*TBP* 276; emphasis in original).
Quite apart from being a potentially genocidal gamble, this
reply seems badly aimed: Ye's appeal will work only if it finds an
auditor other than the monitory alien pacifist. But it does, and
there are terrible consequences on the receiving end of Ye's
message: six thousand Trisolarans are judged to have been in
some way responsible for the system failure of allowing a pacifist into the Space Monitoring System, and they are dehydrated
and burned.

Liu has been criticized, not without reason, for portraying
women as dangerously weak;[7] in the third installment, *Death's
End*, the aerospace engineer Cheng Xin twice makes decisions
in which she disastrously misgauges the hostility of the Trisolarans and the dangers of the universe more generally, imperiling
all of humanity, and Liu repeatedly suggests that the far-future
society developed on Earth, centuries from now, is flaccid and
ineffectual because men have been feminized and it is difficult
to distinguish between the genders. (On the other hand, Earth
is peaceful, prosperous, and apparently free of transphobes, so
there's that to look forward to.) But the misogyny of the trilogy
should not obscure the fact that Ye Wenjie has very good reasons, personal and political, for despair.

Nor is she alone: as *The Three-Body Problem* unspools its
threads, it becomes a kind of catalog of rationales for giving up
on humanity. The most important character in that catalog is
the radical environmentalist Mike Evans (as I have mentioned,
he is the son of an oil baron), who goes even further than Ye:
"Why does one have to save *people* to be considered a hero? Why
is saving other species considered insignificant? Who gave
humans such high honors? No, humans do not need saving.
They're already living much better than they deserve" (*TBP* 305).

Evans gains Ye's confidence by explaining his theory of "Pan-Species Communism," which he sees as "a natural continuation of the Universal Declaration of Human Rights" (*TBP* 307). Ye therefore tells him about the Trisolarans, whereupon Evans founds an Earth-Trisolaris Organization in which Ye serves as (nominal) commander. However, Evans turns out to be not an ally but an antagonist of Ye: though they ostensibly join forces in leading the ETO, Ye sees the ETO as a vehicle for her original intention, to summon the Trisolarans because our civilization is no longer capable of solving its own problems and we need their force to intervene. Evans, by contrast, is a version of the obsessive, evil ecoterrorist who, appalled by the human wreckage of the biosphere and the accelerating pace of the sixth extinction, decides—like Dr. Peters in Terry Gilliam's *12 Monkeys* and (more ambiguously, as we will see) Crake in *Oryx and Crake*—that humans need to die out, pronto.[8]

Ye and Evans therefore wind up heading different factions in the ETO, the Adventists (led by Evans) and the Redemptionists (led by Ye). Upon realizing that the Adventists are explicitly using the ETO as a stalking horse for human genocide and undermining the Redemptionists, Ye demonstrates—in dramatic fashion, involving a scene in a large public meeting of the ETO that recalls the opening chapters on the Cultural Revolution—that she is entirely willing to order the immediate murder of her factional opponents. We are given the political lay of the land in the ETO by one of the attendees of that meeting, who explains, along the way, his own path on the road to despair in humanity:

> "I'm Rafael, from Israel. Three years ago, my fourteen-year-old son died in an accident. I had his kidney donated to a Palestinian girl suffering kidney failure as an expression of my hope

that the two peoples could live together in peace. For this ideal, I was willing to give my life. Many, many Israelis and Palestinians sincerely strove toward the same goal by my side. But all this was useless. Our home remained trapped in the quagmire of cycles of vengeance.

"Eventually, I lost hope in the human race and joined the ETO. Desperation turned me from a pacifist into an extremist. Also, probably because I donated so much money to the Organization, I became a core member of the Adventists. Let me tell you now, the Adventists have their own secret agenda.

"And it is this: The human race is an evil species. Human civilization has committed unforgivable crimes against the Earth and must be punished. The ultimate goal of the Adventists is to ask our Lord to carry out this divine punishment: the destruction of all humankind."

(*TBP* 253)

As Rafael indicates, many members of the ETO refer to Trisolarans, collectively, as "the Lord" and bring to the cause an evangelical zeal and an apocalyptic eschatology—two handy recruitment devices that come ready-made from some of Earth's most popular religions. And as Rafael goes on to insist, Evans "fooled everyone, including the commander": he was working for human extinction "from the very start" and has "turned the Adventists into a kingdom of terror populated by extreme environmentalists and madmen who hated the human race" (*TBP* 254). Ye replies, honestly, that "I didn't know Evans's real thoughts until much later" (*TBP* 254).

Again, Evans is a familiar figure. The Adventists have roots in groups like Earth First! and the Earth Liberation Front, and "Pan-Species Communism" is basically a version of the environmental philosophy known as "deep ecology." (Timothy Morton's work, as I noted in the introduction, combines this with an account of our symbiosis with the nonhuman world.) Liu asks us to imagine a world in which a genocidal strain of radical environmentalism catches on and even (so to speak) goes viral. In a wonderfully deadpan passage, he writes: "The most surprising aspect of the Earth-Trisolaris Movement was that so many people had abandoned all hope in human civilization, hated and were willing to betray their own species, and even cherished as their highest ideal the elimination of the entire human race, including themselves and their children" (*TBP* 317). We are invited to imagine, perhaps, a still more dystopian version of *Children of Men* in which large numbers of people are relieved or overjoyed that there is a species-wide infertility crisis and that we will die out in short order. (This is in fact the vision of the future espoused by Les Knight, the founder of the Voluntary Human Extinction Movement, who, in Alan Weisman's *The World Without Us*, bemoans the fact that viral apocalypses won't finish us off: "No virus could ever get all 6 billion of us," he says. "A 99.99 percent die-off would still leave 650,000 naturally immune survivors. Epidemics actually strengthen a species. In 50,000 years we could easily be right back where we are now.")[9] But, Liu adds, this structure of ex-human feeling seems to be confined mostly to the highly educated classes. Again, the dry, deadpan-dispassionate tone here is worth noting, particularly in the second sentence:

> The ETO had once tried to develop membership among the common people, but these efforts all failed. The ETO concluded that the common people did not seem to have the comprehensive and deep understanding of the highly educated about the dark side of humanity. More importantly, because their thoughts

were not as deeply influenced by modern science and philosophy, they still felt an overwhelming, instinctual identification with their own species. To betray the human race as a whole was unimaginable for them. But intellectual elites were different: Most of them had already begun to consider issues from a perspective outside the human race. Human civilization had finally given birth to a strong force of alienation.

(*TBP* 317)

This, then, is what happens when a critical mass of intellectuals in the humanities starts holding conferences and writing books about things like the "posthuman" and the Anthropocene. They wind up seeing things from an extrahuman perspective that is unfamiliar to the common people and their parochial attachment to the idea of the human. If you think this is potentially dangerous to us as a species, you should probably stop reading this book now.[10]

What makes *Three-Body Problem* such an engaging variation on this first-contact narrative in the context of science fiction, however, is its explicit repudiation of the hope for outside intervention. There will be no representative from the Ekumen who arrives and saves Israelis and Palestinians (or anyone else) from the quagmire of cycles of vengeance, as Genly Ai does when he effectively (if unwittingly) prevents an open war between Karhide and Orgoreyn over the border in the Sinoth Valley. On the contrary, we are told that alien contact would be the *worst* possible scenario for terrestrial conflict: if Evans's path leads to human extinction, Ye's leads to global conflagration. In a passage focalized through Wang Miao, a nanotech specialist who befriends Ye (and then is horrified to learn of her role in the ETO), we learn that "it was only within the last couple of years that serious and systematic consideration had been given to the question of how and to what degree human societies would be influenced by establishing contact with extraterrestrial intelligence, but the research had rapidly gained interest, and the conclusions were shocking" (*TBP* 175):

> Naïve, idealistic hopes had been shattered. Scholars found that, contrary to the happy wishes of most people, it was not a good idea for the human race as a whole to make contact with extra-terrestrials. The impact of such contact on human society would be divisive rather than uniting, and would exacerbate rather than mitigate the conflicts between different cultures. In summary, if contact were to occur, the internal divisions within Earth civilization would be magnified and likely lead to disaster. The most shocking conclusion of all was that the impact would have nothing at all to do with the degree and type of contact (unidirectional or bidirectional), or the form and degree of advancement of the alien civilization.

(*TBP* 175–76)

This finding is attributed to "Bill Mathers of RAND Corporation in his book, *The 100,000-Light-Year Iron Curtain: SETI Sociology*" (*TBP* 176), a citation plausible enough, apparently, to have sent some readers scurrying to the message boards of the internet to find out whether Bill Mathers and his study are real things. (They are not. Somewhere amid the star stuff of the universe, perhaps the spirit of Carl Sagan is breathing a sigh of relief.)

I want to pause here to underscore how counterintuitive this theory is—until one thinks about it for more than a moment. The overwhelming consensus in science fiction, to this point, is that (as I put it in the previous chapter) alien contact will wean us from our petty, parochial intraspecies disputes and territorialisms as we band together to fight a common foe.[11] I think, for example, of the minor controversy over whether Alan Moore's *Watchmen* (1986–1987) borrowed, knowingly or unknowingly, from *The Outer Limits* episode "The Architects of Fear" (1963): in that episode, strategists secretly decide to feign an alien invasion in order to prevent the nuclear superpowers from blundering into another Cuban Missile Crisis, this time with less happy results. In *Watchmen*, Adrian Veidt schemes to feign an alien attack on New York—killing three million—in order to head off a nuclear Armageddon prompted by the Soviet invasion of Afghanistan (in an alternate history in which this happens in 1985). Moore was sufficiently stung by the parallel to incorporate a reference to "The Architects of Fear" late in his narrative, but he might well have responded by pointing out that hypotheses of humanity uniting as one upon discovering evidence of extraterrestrial intelligence are as common as rain.[12]

But then, why would anyone assume such a thing? In the opening moments of "The Architects of Fear," the strategists propose that humans will come together in the face of massive threats, including—strange as this must have sounded in 1963, when almost no one was worrying about such a thing—when "a bacteria invasion strikes." In what pandemic has this ever happened? On the contrary, in the COVID-19 crisis, as in every other pandemic before it, threats to humanity as a whole tend to be met with human folly, viciousness, racism, xenophobia, conspiracy-mongering, and general chaos that exacerbates injustice and inequality. Why would contact with aliens be any different?

The Three-Body Problem does everything it can to chip away at the dream of first contact. Not only does it suggest that it is not a good idea for the human race as a whole to make contact with extraterrestrials; very late in the novel, it also gives us a bleak look at Trisolaran society—and well before that, reveals that some of the founders of the Earth-Trisolaris Organization have a distinctive take on the terrestrial history of colonialism. I'll discuss that take first, then circle back to the chilling look at the Trisolarans.

Evans does indeed lie to Ye about his intentions when he first informs her of the existence of the ETO: "Our ideal is to invite Trisolaran civilization to reform human civilization, to curb human madness and evil, so that the Earth can once again become a harmonious, prosperous, sinless world" (*TBP* 314). By the time we hear this appeal to the restoration of a prelapsarian planet, seven chapters after the large public meeting in which we meet Rafael from Israel, we know it is bullshit. But there was a tipoff to the machinations of the ETO much earlier in the novel, at the very first meet-up of people playing the online game *Three Body*, which appears to be an elaborate multiplayer virtual reality experience but is in reality the ETO's recruitment device: "Using a shell that drew elements from human society and history, the game explained the culture and history of Trisolaris, thus avoiding alienating beginners. Once a player had advanced to a certain level and had begun to appreciate Trisolaran civilization, the ETO would establish contact, examine the player's sympathies, and finally recruit those who passed the tests to be members of the ETO" (*TBP* 319–20). When Wang Miao arrives at the meet-up, he learns that it is being run by Pan Han, the prime suspect in a murder that is the basis for the novel's superficial whodunit plot; only later do we learn—just before Ye Wenjie has him killed in that large public meeting—that he is one of the Adventist leaders. Pan informs the small group (seven elite players) that *Three Body* is not just a game, that Trisolaris is real; he then asks the group directly, "How would you feel if Trisolaran civilization were to enter our world?" (*TBP* 229).

The first respondent, a reporter, says he would be "happy": "I've lost hope in the human race after what I've seen in recent years. Human society is incapable of self-improvement, and we need the intervention of an outside force" (*TBP* 229). A novelist, a woman who somehow manages to be at once avant-garde and broadly popular, chimes in to say, "I agree. . . . The human race is hideous. I've spent the first half of my life unveiling this ugliness with the scalpel of literature, but now I'm even sick of the work of dissection. I yearn for Trisolaran civilization to bring real beauty to the world" (*TBP* 229).

These two are natural Redemptionists, very much in the mold of Ye Wenjie and for the same reasons. Only toward the end of *The Three-Body Problem* will we learn that the Trisolarans have purged everything of beauty from their civilization, and only later in the trilogy will Liu throw in the delightful wrinkle that the invaders fall in love with Earth's many artistic and cultural treasures and seek to emulate them (while still planning to exterminate us). But it is the next step in the meet-up that concerns me here. An elderly and distinguished philosopher speaks up: "Let's discuss this question with a bit more depth: What is your impression of the Aztecs?" (*TBP* 229). Here, then, the genre's implicit meditation on colonialism will become an explicit statement.

"Dark and bloody," the author said. "Blood-drenched pyramids lit by insidious fires seen through dark forests. Those are my impressions."

The philosopher nodded. "Very good. Then try to imagine: If the Spanish Conquistadors did not intervene, what would have been the influence of that civilization on human history?"

"You're calling black white and white black," the software company vice president said. "The Conquistadors who invaded the Americas were nothing more than murderers and robbers."

"Even so, at least they prevented the Aztecs from developing without bound, turning the Americas into a bloody, great dark empire. Then civilization as we know it wouldn't have appeared in the Americas, and democracy wouldn't have thrived until much later. Indeed, maybe they wouldn't have appeared at all. This is the key to the question. No matter what the Trisolarans are like, their arrival will be good news for the terminally ill human race."

(*TBP* 229–30)

There is a subtle (OK, not at all subtle) flaw in this argument, and another member of the meet-up immediately points to it: even if you accept that European colonization of the Americas was good for humanity as a whole (a monstrously large "if," at that), "have you thought through the fact that the Aztecs were completely destroyed by the Western invaders?" (*TBP* 230)

The meet-up is successful: Pan Han identifies the pro-invasion members of the group and dismisses the two players who were so bold as to be critical of the genocide carried out by the conquistadors.

As for the would-be Trisolaran conquistadors: the analogy to the Spanish should give the lie to the fond idea that a more technologically advanced society must perforce be a more enlightened and benevolent society, yet just before Liu introduces us to the Trisolarans themselves, very late in the novel, we are given the transcript of an interrogation of Ye Wenjie:

INTERROGATOR: Do you understand Trisolaran civilization?

YE WENJIE: No. We received only very limited information. No one has real, detailed knowledge of Trisolaran civilization except Mike Evans and other core members of the Adventists who intercepted these messages.

INTERROGATOR: Then why do you have such hope for it, thinking that it can reform and perfect human society?

YE: If they can cross the distance between the stars to come to our world, their science must have developed to a very advanced stage. A society with such advanced science must also have more advanced moral standards.

INTERROGATOR: Do you think this conclusion you drew is scientific?

YE: . . .

(*TBP* 345)

This is one of the novel's finer uses of ellipses. The joke is on Ye, though the joke was perhaps more direct—and slapstick—in Tim Burton's *Mars Attacks!*, based on the early-1960s trading cards of the same name, in which the jejune, smug, pipe-smoking scientist Professor Kessler (Pierce Brosnan) opines that the Martians must be more advanced than ourselves—only to find that they are venal, vicious pranksters who find it amusing to sever Kessler's head from his body but keep him conscious.[13] As alien races go, the Trisolarans are not quite so awful, but because their civilization has been defined by millions of years of cycles of destruction caused by the irregularity of their planet's orbit in a three-star system, they don't have much more than the sheer will to continue existing.

The "listener" who first receives—and replies to—Ye's message (that is, the creature who told Ye not to reply) is harshly interrogated by the Princeps of the Trisolarans, who accuses the listener, with much justice, of being a traitor to all of Trisolaris. In response, the listener replies,

"I am tired of Trisolaris. We have nothing in our lives and spirit except the fight for survival."

"What's wrong with that?"

"There's nothing wrong, of course. Existence is the premise for everything else. But, Princeps, please examine our lives: Everything is devoted to survival. To permit the survival of the civilization as a whole, there is almost no respect for the individual. Someone who can no longer work is put to death. Trisolaran society exists under a state of extreme authoritarianism. The law has only two outcomes: The guilty are put to death, and the not guilty are released. For me, the most intolerable aspects are the spiritual monotony and desiccation. Anything that can lead to spiritual weakness is declared evil. We have no literature, no art, no pursuit of beauty and enjoyment. We cannot even speak of love. . . . Princeps, is there meaning to such a life?"

(*TBP* 353)

So much for the Trisolaran justice system—and Trisolaran disability policy! The moment you can't work, you are put to death. Since I am on record, in my 2016 book *Life as Jamie Knows It*, as proposing that "societies that incorporate and accommodate people with intellectual and physical disabilities are better than societies that exclude, ostracize, and seek to eliminate people with intellectual and physical disabilities," I am clearly required now to propose that Earth society, in the aggregate, for all its faults and all its myriad failures to incorporate and accommodate people with intellectual and physical disabilities, is better than Trisolaran society.[14] I hope that is settled now, so that we can proceed to some tentative conclusions.

The Three-Body Problem presents us with three options. The first is slow death—environmental degradation, climate change, and widespread extinction events, possibly leading (in the *most* optimistic scenario) to a drastically reduced human population living in the mercilessly authoritarian conditions envisioned in Le Guin's *The Dispossessed*. That world, you will recall, is defined by "the absolute regimentation of each life toward the goal of racial survival" (*D* 280)—in other words, the condition Trisolarans are living in now. The second option, promoted by Mike Evans, is human extinction by conquest, in which we are neo-Aztecs consciously summoning the conquistadors to wipe us out. The third option, offered by Ye Wenjie, is a naïve hope for intervention by an alien species, all the more naïve for the fact that a representative of that species has warned us that their warlike race will wipe us out. There is considerable irony in the vision of Aztec civilization as "blood-drenched pyramids lit by insidious fires seen through dark forests," since Liu will go on, in the remainder of the trilogy, to develop a "dark forest" theory of the universe in which all intelligent civilizations assume that all the others seek their extinction. Even before we learn of those civilizations and the literally universal state of fear in the universe, the dark forest is always already our terrestrial habitat.[15]

In this dark forest, it is not at all clear that Ye Wenjie's decision is a foolish one. Yet this is not a conclusion the novel welcomes. The narrative ends with a chastened Ye looking out over the horizon and whispering, "My sunset . . . and sunset for humanity" (*TBP* 390), and Liu follows this, in the American edition, with a postscript that delivers a message straight from Western Union:

> There's a strange contradiction revealed by the naïveté and kindness demonstrated by humanity when faced with the universe: On Earth, humankind can step onto another continent, and without a thought, destroy the kindred civilizations found there

through warfare and disease. But when they gaze up at the stars, they turn sentimental and believe that if extraterrestrial intelligences exist, they must be civilizations bound by universal, noble, moral constraints, as if cherishing and loving different forms of life are parts of a self-evident universal code of conduct.

I think it should be precisely the opposite: Let's turn the kindness we show toward the stars to members of the human race on Earth and build up the trust and understanding between the different peoples and civilizations that make up humanity. But for the universe outside the solar system, we should be ever vigilant, and be ready to attribute the worst of intentions to any Others that might exist in space. For a fragile civilization like ours, this is without a doubt the most responsible path.

(*TBP* 395)

Liu obviously overlooks or undersells the *Independence Day/ Mars Attacks!* school of thought in which aliens arrive with the express purpose of killing us all; for all the naïveté and kindness he attributes to us, we have had no trouble imagining that scenario or, for that matter, imagining superintelligent aliens bearing a cookbook whose title is *To Serve Man.* And one can't help but note that Liu's prescription of building up trust and understanding to all humankind apparently does not extend to Uighurs. Still, there is no question that Ye Wenjie acts out of naïveté—and also out of despair. My argument is simply that the despair is well justified and that the naïveté is preferable to the hardheaded realism of Evans. It is the only option that offers any hope at all, however desperate and ill-founded that hope may be.[16]

The Ye-Evans battle is restaged later in the trilogy, between the (apparently) naïve Cheng Xin, who permits a Trisolaran invasion because she is unable to follow through on the plan of mutually assured destruction crafted by Luo Ji, her predecessor as Swordholder (that is, protector of the planet), and Thomas Wade (curiously named after a British sinologist and diplomat of the nineteenth century), a cartoonishly hyperaggressive Sergeant Rock–esque American whose motto is "Attack! Attack! Attack!" It is one of the curiosities of the trilogy that the two principal American characters are embodiments of toxic masculinity—and that their worldviews are, in the trilogy's frame of reference, basically right. After all, once the Trisolarans invade, they herd all of us into makeshift camps in Australia, where they advise us to eat one another. Wade's kill-or-be-killed strategy is vindicated again many years later, well after the invasion has been repelled; it is, no doubt, tempting to read the trilogy in terms of these oppositions between "soft" Chinese women and "realistic" American assholes. But I will insist nonetheless that Ye Wenjie, sitting alone with a transmitter in Red Coast and reflecting on the fate of Earth and her own political and personal betrayals, chooses the best of three profoundly unattractive options.[17]

And that argument leads us to Atwood, and to Crake.

The first thing I want to know, when a fictional virus kills many of my fellow humans, is whether it was released deliberately, or as part of a scientific breakthrough gone wrong, or as a simple consequence of ordinary interspecies exchange. I am alluding, of course, to the films *12 Monkeys*, *I Am Legend*, and *Contagion*, respectively. But as Priscilla Wald has argued compellingly in *Contagious: Cultures, Carriers, and the Outbreak Narrative*, pandemics produce quite serious (and sometimes murderous) anxieties about intentionality and agency. We might consider this *agency panic*, a kind of collective freakout akin to moral panic. Precisely because their origins can lie anywhere, pandemics are terrifying—arguably more terrifying than fantasies of nuclear Armageddon, since those necessarily have to be realized by nation-states stumbling into or deliberately launching all-out thermonuclear war. (There is an alternate scenario, as well, in which artificial intelligence launches the war at us, as in the Terminator franchise. I will return to this scenario in chapter 3.) Viral apocalypses, by contrast, can be the work of one person, as the very phrase "gone viral" implicitly acknowledges: it is as if the species can be decimated if not eliminated by a kid uploading a cat video to YouTube—or, more seriously, by a conspiracy theorist calling himself Q. Indeed, *12 Monkeys* and *Contagion* are structured by the question of agency: both films rely on misdirection, whereby we learn only in the final frames that the pandemic was engineered not by the alleged ecoterrorist group the Army of the Twelve Monkeys but by a single radical scientist or the result not of Beth Emhoff (Gwenyth Paltrow) engaging in an extramarital hookup in a layover hotel on her way back home from Hong Kong (echoes of AIDS hysteria!) but of land development in China that released bats that contacted pigs that contacted someone who shook hands with Emhoff on her business trip.[18]

Oryx and Crake is structured the same way, and for the same reason—to hold in abeyance, and thereby foreground, the question of agency. When the novel opens, we are in familiar dystopian territory: there is a Last Man, a character with a distinguished lineage running back through Richard Matheson's *I Am Legend* (and the various film adaptations of his novel) to Mary Shelley's 1826 novel simply titled *The Last Man*. There are some strange humanoid creatures as well—we'll get back to them—but otherwise, the primary (and obvious) question hanging over the narrative is *so how did things get this way?* It is not at all clear that the question of agency involves a virus:

although, as we soon find, the novel presents us with a holocaust of infected animals in the OrganInc corporate Compound and is teeming with hot bioforms that chew through people in a matter of hours (and briefly features a bioterrorist with "some vicious Ebola or Marburg splice" who kills a Compound guard and has to be "neutralized in a vat of bleach"),[19] the extreme weather leaves open the possibility that the catastrophe leading to the Last Man landscape is one of climate change, not lethal viruses. (Hence *Oryx and Crake*'s centrality to the "cli-fi" canon, "climate fiction," even though its forebears are also quite clearly in the "last man surviving a virus" genre.) The two plot lines, beginning with Snowman (né Jimmy) in the present and alternating with flashbacks to Jimmy's childhood, adolescence, and young adulthood, converge in the inner sanctum of the RejoovenEsence Compound, where we will learn at last that this pandemic, like that of *12 Monkeys*, was planned by someone: Crake, the precocious bioengineer. What remains, then, and extends from the cliffhanger ending of the novel through the trilogy as a whole, is the question of Crake's motive.

Later in the MaddAddam trilogy, other survivors (and they do exist and seem implausibly plentiful in the local environs, as if the virus kills everyone on Earth except the trilogy's major characters minus Oryx and Crake) will ask explicitly about why Crake took it upon himself to wipe the planet clean of *Homo sapiens sapiens* and replace us with a kinder, gentler humanoid. Indeed, that question begins with Jimmy's lonely meditation: "Sitting in judgment on the world, thought Jimmy; but why had that been his right? (*OC* 341). That's a reasonable question, but it has an answer: because he was the only person, so far as we know, with the bioengineering skill to pull it off, which, combined with his entirely accurate sense that humans were on the verge of rendering the biosphere uninhabitable for themselves and countless other species, drove him to an inescapable final solution. More important, to my mind, are the betrayals that lead him to that conclusion, for they parallel Ye Wenjie's.

Like Ye's, part of Crake's rationale is personal: his father was murdered by the HelthWyzer pharmaceutical corporation when he threatened to disclose their business model, which involved deliberately infecting people with chronic, slow-acting, money-draining diseases.

> "The best diseases, from a business point of view," said Crake, "would be those that cause lingering illnesses. Ideally—that is, for maximum profit—the patient should either get well or die just before all his or her money runs out. It's a fine calculation."
>
> "This would be really evil," said Jimmy.
>
> "That's what my father thought," said Crake.
>
> "He *knew*?" Jimmy really was paying attention now.
>
> "He found out. That's how come they pushed him off a bridge."

(*OC* 211)

And though Crake relays this information to Jimmy with a disturbingly flat affect, we find later, in one of Jimmy's flashbacks, that Crake—apparently unbeknownst to himself—screams in his sleep every night (*OC* 218).[20] After his father's death, his mother marries the man who most likely had him killed, his supervisor at HelthWyzer, whom Crake calls "Uncle Pete." Crake is therefore in a recognizably Hamletesque situation,[21] to which he responds appropriately (if more globally than Hamlet)—by killing his mother and then Uncle Pete with viruses of his own design that Jimmy ultimately speculates might have been "trial runs" for the virus that induces the global apocalypse (*OC* 343). Clearly, Crake has more than enough reason to believe that the society into which he was born is not worth preserving.[22]

But beyond his immediate experience of evil (perfidy, greed, murderous betrayal), Crake also looks at the biosphere from the perspective of what seems to be the biosphere itself, as we learn in a key but often overlooked scene.[23] As teenagers, Crake and his friend Jimmy are in Crake's vacation home on Hudson Bay, watching TV coverage of the global riots involving a coffee megachain called Happicuppa and coffee laborers around the world who are being reduced to starvation-level poverty:

> "Those guys should be whacked," said Crake.
>
> "Which ones? The peasants? Or the guys killing them?"
>
> "The latter. Not because of the dead peasants, there's always been dead peasants. But they're nuking the cloud forests to plant this stuff."
>
> "The peasants would do that too if they had half a chance," said Jimmy.
>
> "Sure, but they don't have half a chance."
>
> "You're taking sides?"
>
> "There aren't any sides, as such."

(*OC* 179)

This exchange, I submit, serves as the moral fulcrum of the novel and of the MaddAddam trilogy as a whole. For in one sense Crake is obviously wrong: there *are* sides. There are exactly two sides. There are the peasants and the people killing them. There is the Happicuppa corporation, and there are its protesters around the globe, kidnapping and car-bombing and shooting Happicuppa personnel. But for Crake, this is irrelevant; from the perspective of the biosphere, there are no sides—just the question of how many species the humans will take down with them before they finally go. It is a chilling passage not only because it is ultimately true that there are no sides from that perspective but also because it explains why Crake decides to replace humans with something more benignly humanoid, a species without environmental rapaciousness and rampant sexual violence.

And the sexual violence in the MaddAddam trilogy is indeed rampant. In *Oryx and Crake* it is presented primarily by way of Oryx's narrative arc, which leads from an Asian village into the darkest corners of the global sex trade, beginning with child pornography.[24] Oryx herself seems to be the least traumatized woman in the history of the sex trade, drawing a shockingly pragmatic lesson from her ordeals: "Love was undependable, it came and then it went, so it was good to have a money value, because then at least those who wanted to make a profit from you would make sure you would be fed enough and not damaged too much. Also there were many who had neither love nor a money value, and having one of those things was better than having nothing" (*OC* 126). But in the remainder of the trilogy, narrated largely from the perspective of the "pleeblands" that make up the world outside the corporate Compounds and their elaborate security systems, the sexual violence is presented as omnipresent and terrifying: the trilogy's female characters walk tentatively through a world crawling with rapists and brutalizers.[25] Crake's solution to this is ingenious: he creates humanoids "whose sexuality was not a constant torment to them, not a cloud of turbulent hormones: they came into heat at regular intervals, as did most mammals other than man" (*OC* 305). The nod to Le Guin's Gethenians is almost explicit, as is the tip of the hat, earlier in the same paragraph, to Octavia Butler, whose Oank-ali (as we will see in chapter 4) diagnose us as a species with a combustible combination of intelligence and proclivity for hier-archical thinking: "hierarchy could not exist among them," we are informed about the Crakers, "because they lacked the neural complexes that would have created it" (*OC* 305). There is no rape, and there is no racism. Indeed, Crake has even imag-ined a world without possessions, and no religion, too.[26]

And yet no one says he's a dreamer. Most readers see Crake as a megalomaniac, Victor Frankenstein (and/or Dr. Moreau) with a talent for gene splicing.[27] A subset of these also sees Crake as a figure of disability horror, one of those mythical people with Asperger's who lack empathy for their fellow humans and are therefore capable of anything ranging from oddly asocial behavior to mass murder.[28] In a notably ambivalent discussion, Hannes Bergthaller insists that Crake's plan is "a scheme that effectively vitiates the very possibility of ethical choice" and that Crake himself has a radically impoverished idea of what it means to be human: "Crake fully understands the destructive potential of mankind's evolutionary inheritance, but he does not appreciate what his revulsion against the latter indicates: that human beings are not fully determined by that inheritance, and that this lack of determination allows for the forms of self-domestication that constitute cultural history."[29] Yet Bergth-aller also acknowledges Crake's "terrifying perspicacity" and concludes that "Crake's posthumanist scheme for attaining sus-tainability, horrifying as it is, must not be dismissed too easily."[30] I am not going to deny that the cold-blooded murder of billions of human beings is horrifying. But Atwood asks us, still more disturbingly, to imagine Crake as a totally selfless creature who can inhabit a perspective from which there truly are no sides. On one hand, the reading of Crake as mad scientist misses a great deal of how he sees the world—and how he imagines that his experiment is ultimately in the best interest of the biosphere as a whole. On the other hand, perhaps Crake is not a mad scientist but a mad environmentalist—a member of the Earth Liberation Front, genetic-engineering division. (It is notable that in the MaddAddam series, so many of the radical environmentalists, making up the group God's Gardeners, are scientists who have jumped from the sinking ship.) In that case, his counterpart in *The Three-Body Problem* would be not Ye but Evans.

But it is nearly impossible, I think, to hear Crake's assessment of the state of the planet and decide that he is simply a mad scientist, for roughly the same reason that some of the most chilling accounts of the effects of climate change in our world come from the Rand Corporation or the World Bank. The apocalyptic scenarios are terrifyingly plausible. When Crake gives Jimmy the cover story—that the BlyssPluss Pill, marketed as a sexual aid, will involuntarily sterilize its users (it will actually carry the virus)—he also tells Jimmy the real deal:

> "I didn't know you were so altruistic," said Jimmy. Since when had Crake been a cheerleader for the human race?
>
> "It's not altruism exactly," said Crake. "More like sink or swim. I've seen the latest confidential Corps demographic reports. As a species we're in deep trouble, worse than anyone's saying. They're afraid to release the stats because people might just give up, but take it from me, we're running out of space-time. Demand for resources has exceeded supply for decades in marginal geopolitical areas, hence the famines and droughts; but very soon, demand is going to exceed supply *for everyone*. With the BlyssPluss Pill the human race will have a better chance of swimming."

(*OC* 294–95)

From one angle, then, Crake's observation that there are no sides is brilliant, entailing a realization that beyond the Happicuppa riots, the real issue is the nuking of the cloud forests. From another angle, the identification with the biosphere-as-such is also horrifyingly *in*human—or ex-human. It leads to a desire to eliminate human suffering by eliminating humans. From yet another angle, it is far better than talking about "sustainability," which too often means *how can the people of industrialized nations keep drinking bottled water and profiting from extractive industries without feeling guilty?* And from all angles, the question once again rises bold and stark: how can one detach oneself from one's own species without becoming a genocidal psychopath? As Jimmy asks himself after the apocalypse, "Had [Crake] been a lunatic or an intellectually honourable man who'd thought things through to their logical conclusion? And was there any difference?" (*OC* 343).[31]

Speaking of genocidal psychopaths: the question of whether the species is worth saving is not confined to the latest confidential Corps demographic reports. It extends to an assessment of the history of civilization, and is introduced early in the novel by way of the games Crake and Jimmy play as teens, two of which appear to be dark, parodic versions of Sid Meier's famous Civilization franchise. The first we hear about is *Barbarian Stomp (See If You Can Change History!)*: "One side had the cities and the riches and the other side had the hordes, and—usually but not always—the most viciousness. Either the barbarians stomped the cities or else they got stomped, but you had to start out with the historical disposition of energies and go on from there. Rome versus the Visigoths, Ancient Egypt versus the Hyksos, Aztecs versus the Spaniards. That was a cute one, because it was the Aztecs who represented civilization, while the Spaniards were the barbarian hordes" (*OC* 77–78). That arrangement of the Aztec-Spaniard disposition of energies will not, one imagines, go over very well with the recruiters of the Earth-Trisolaran Organization. Jimmy, after doing some research, comes up with "Petchenegs versus Byzantium." Crake calls bullshit, but Jimmy has the receipts:

> Jimmy had found it in the *Encyclopedia Britannica*, 1957 edition, which was stored on CD-ROM—for some forgotten reason—in the school library. He had chapter and verse. "Matthew of Edessa referred to them as wicked blood-drinking beasts," he was able to say with authority. "They were totally ruthless and had no redeeming features." So they tossed for sides, and Jimmy got Petchenegs, and won. The Byzantines were slaughtered, because that was what Petchenegs did, Jimmy explained. They always slaughtered everyone immediately. Or they slaughtered the men, at least. Then they slaughtered the women after a while.

(*OC* 78)

I will close this chapter by addressing the question of the novel's tone—which becomes pressing at moments like these, when sexual violence is alluded to so casually, as an aside in a description of genocidal slaughter. But for now, I want to move on to the second game, *Blood and Roses*, a trading game in which "atrocities on a large scale" are traded against "artworks, scientific breakthroughs, stellar works of architecture, helpful inventions" (*OC* 78)—basically, all the things we humans point to when we need to applaud ourselves and tell ourselves we have achieved something of value. Here too, the novel's tone is unsettlingly insouciant: "The exchange rates—one *Mona Lisa* equalled Bergen-Belsen, one Armenian genocide equaled the *Ninth Symphony* plus three Great Pyramids—were suggested, but there was room for haggling. To do this you needed to know the numbers—the total number of corpses for the atrocities, the latest open-market price for the artworks; or, if the artworks had been stolen, the amount paid out by the insurance policy. It was a wicked game" (*OC* 79).

But, our narrator immediately remarks, one problem with the game is that "it was easier to remember the Blood stuff" (*OC* 80); another is that "the Blood player usually won, but winning meant you inherited a wasteland. This was the point of the game, said Crake, when Jimmy complained. Jimmy said if that was the point, it was pretty pointless" (*OC* 80).[32] Indeed it is, and it invites the question of whether we could say the same of human existence in general. As Gerry Canavan notes, "One cannot help but wonder, after playing Blood & Roses, if the human history that has been wiped out by the apocalypse is actually worthy of being mourned at all."[33] In the following chapter, we will grapple with fictions that make that question unbearable.

At the dilapidated and irrelevant Martha Graham Academy, Jimmy's artist classmates have their own version of the wasteland they will inherit:

> Soon, said the artists . . . there would be nothing left but a series of long subterranean tubes covering the surface of the planet. The air and light inside them would be artificial, the ozone and oxygen layers of Planet Earth having been totally destroyed. People would creep along through this tubing, single file, stark naked, their only view the asshole of the one before them in the line, their urine and excrement flowing down through vents in the floor, until they were randomly selected by a digitalized mechanism, at which point they would be sucked into a side tunnel, ground up, and fed to the others through a series of nipple-shaped

appendages on the inside of the tube. The system would be self-sustaining and perpetual, and would serve everybody right.

(*OC* 243)

Unlikely as this scenario might be, it is revealing as an index of the structure of feeling in *Oryx and Crake*. Isn't Crake's bioengineered neohuman future a bit more hopeful? I noted at the outset of this book that fantasies about the end of the world and/or the end of human civilization have become a subgenre all their own, but most of them do not involve a conscious scheme to replace us with genetically modified versions of ourselves. (One imagines a tiki-torch-bearing mob of neo-Nazis chanting "Crakers will not replace us.") So it seems worth asking whether the creation of the Crakers justifies the extermination of the human race: the novel effectively asks us to play *Blood and Roses* with its own conceit, weighing a global atrocity against a stunning scientific achievement.

What seems most hopeful about Crake's decision is that he has not given up on the prospects of intelligent life. One might easily imagine an ex-human perspective that is not only antihuman but also opposed to the higher-order reflection distinctive to intelligent species (leaving open the question of how many nonhuman species this might include). But it is not clear whether in fact the Crakers possess the kind of intelligence that would continue to realize the Saganian dream of a self-aware universe. They seem remarkably incurious about that universe, and Crake has deliberately "edited out" many of the features that one ordinarily considers among the things that make intelligent life worth living. They cannot make jokes, for instance: "For jokes you need a certain edge, a little malice," Crake explains. "It took a lot of trial and error and we're still testing, but I think we've managed to do away with jokes" (*OC* 306). Also (purportedly) edited out of the mix: the ability to create art, the ability to ask about one's origins, and the ability to make leadership decisions. However, as we gradually learn, some of the traits Crake thought he'd left on the cutting-room floor seem to be creeping back in. When one of the Crakers becomes more forthcoming than the others, Jimmy remembers: "*Watch out for the leaders,* Crake used to say. *First the leaders and the led, then the tyrants and the slaves, then the massacres. That's how it's always gone*" (*OC* 155). The Crakers don't manage to develop a sense of humor, but we do learn of other disturbing developments. When Jimmy asks if the Crakers "ever ask where they came from," the answer is ambiguous:

> "You don't get it," said Crake, in his you-are-a-moron voice. "That stuff's been edited out."
>
> "Well, actually, they did ask," said Oryx. "Today they asked who made them."
>
> "And?"
>
> "And I told them the truth. I said it was Crake." An admiring smile at Crake: Jimmy could have done without that. "I told them he was very clever and good."
>
> "Did they ask who this Crake was?" said Crake. "Did they want to see him?"
>
> "They didn't seem interested."

(*OC* 311)

It is hard to imagine such creatures developing the kind of imagination it takes to populate the skies with gods and legends, let alone figure out the composition of atoms and photons and the existence of the cosmic microwave background radiation.

Yet in the closing pages of the novel, they manage to make a scarecrow-esque figure to represent Jimmy (as Snowman):

> "We made a picture of you, to help us send out our voices to you."
>
> *Watch out for art*, Crake used to say. *As soon as they start doing art, we're in trouble.* Symbolic thinking of any kind would signal downfall, in Crake's view. Next they'd be inventing idols, and funerals, and grave goods, and the afterlife, and sin, and Linear B, and kings, and then slavery and war. Snowman longs to question them—who first had the idea of making a reasonable facsimile of him, of Snowman, out of a jar lid and a mop?

(*OC* 361)

Crake's calculus seems brutal. No wars, no tyrants and slaves, no environmental despoliation, no sexual violence—but at the cost of art, laughter, and intellectual curiosity? On the up side, the Crakers can still dream and sing: "Crake hadn't been able to eliminate dreams," we are told, indicating that he did indeed try. "*We're hard-wired for dreams*, he'd said. He couldn't get rid of the singing either. *We're hard-wired for singing.* Singing and dreams were entwined" (*OC* 352). On the down side, they can't read (*OC* 41). Who among us in the arts, humanities, or sciences would endorse such a straitened vision of ex-human life? It would appear that of all horrors, Crake has managed to create semi-intelligent beings who, for all their dreaming and singing, believe their native town to be the world.[34]

Yet let's not get too sentimental about the state of the arts, humanities, and sciences. It may be a safe assumption that anyone reading this book (or *Oryx and Crake*, for that matter) has some attachment to one or more of the enterprises that make up

the core of the liberal arts and accordingly groans or smiles ruefully at Atwood's account of their status in the near future (where
"near future" might mean "basically later this week"): "a lot of
what went on at Martha Graham was like studying Latin, or
book-binding: pleasant to contemplate in its way, but no longer
central to anything, though every once in a while the college
president would subject them to some yawner about the vital arts
and their irresistible reserved seat in the big red-velvet amphi-
theatre of the beating human heart" (*OC* 187). Jimmy's talent as
a wordsmith, which allows the narrative its occasional indul-
gence in language for its own sake (even mockingly, as in the
free-indirect-discourse description of Jimmy's "grey rainy-day
allure—the crepuscular essence, the foggy aureole" [*OC* 190]),
qualifies him only as a copywriter for a low-level cosmetics concern, AnooYoo, where none of his supervisors "was capable of
appreciating how clever he had been. He came to understand
why serial killers sent helpful clues to the police" (*OC* 249). The
speculative sciences have been shut down altogether: everything
is genetic engineering and biotech, and the high-end physics that
constitutes the world of advanced science in *The Three-Body
Problem* seems to have been wholly abandoned in favor of pur-
suits that will turn a profit.

And the arts? *Oryx and Crake* leaves no room for the belief
that this form of humanity can justify its continued existence
on the basis of our capacity for artistic expression. (Hold that
thought for *Do Androids Dream of Electric Sheep?*, when Rick
Deckard comes to realize that it makes no sense to "retire" the
android opera singer Luba Luft.) Most of humankind's creative
endeavors in this world, which we see through Jimmy's and
Crake's teen adventures on the internet, provoke for adult Jimmy
the question, "When did the body first set out on its own
adventures?"

Having ditched its old traveling companions, the mind and the soul . . . it had dumped culture along with them: music and painting and poetry and plays. Sublimation, all of it; nothing but sublimation, according to the body. Why not cut to the chase?

But the body had its own cultural forms. It had its own art. Executions were its tragedies, pornography was its romance.

(*OC* 85)

Both, of course, are abundant on the internet, and they are the dominant cultural forms in Jimmy and Crake's lifeworld. Meanwhile, the performing arts have become monuments to the desiccation of the human spirit:

The students of song and dance continued to sing and dance, though the energy had gone out of these activities and the classes were small. Live performance had suffered in the sabotage panics of the early twenty-first century—no one during those decades had wanted to form part of a large group at a public event in a dark, easily destructible walled space, or no one with any cool or status. Theatrical events had dwindled into versions of the sing-along or the tomato bombardment or the wet T-shirt contest. And though various older forms had dragged on—the TV sitcom, the music video—their audience was ancient and their appeal mostly nostalgic.[35]

(*OC* 187)

Who needs Orwell's vision of a boot stamping on a human face forever when you have Atwood's vision of theatrical performance as Gallagher smashing a watermelon forever? A world in which only the ancients among us have any sentimental attachment to those pinnacles of human achievement, the sitcom *Three's Company* and the video for Judas Priest's "Breaking the Law"? How precisely are the guileless-but-gormless Crakers any worse than what we ourselves will have become?

Last but certainly not least, as I have suggested above, the tone of the novel complicates any attempt to answer that question—that is, any attempt to determine whether we should care at all what happens to our future selves. Sharon, Jimmy's mother, might serve as our tonal barometer here. Whereas the artists at Martha Graham see the future with a sardonic fatalism, Sharon offers a more somber version of what it is like to live through a slowly unfolding dystopia. Having given up her job as a microbiologist, she becomes profoundly depressed, and Jimmy learns to fear "the flat voice, the blank eyes, the tired staring out the window" (*OC* 32). Jimmy attempts to engage and even annoy her, whereupon "she might start crying and jump up and run out of the room, banging the door behind her, whuff. Or else she might start crying and hugging him. Or she might throw the coffee cup across the room and start yelling, 'It's all shit, it's total shit, it's hopeless!' She might even slap him, and then cry and hug him. It could be any combination of these things" (*OC* 32–33). The first thing to note here, no doubt, is that Sharon is entirely right: it's all shit, it's total shit, it's hopeless. This sums up the state of affairs in *Oryx and Crake* quite nicely.

Crake appears to be on the same affective wavelength, saving his emotional response to the hopelessness for his screaming night terrors while assuming a placid, inscrutable demeanor about the science in which he becomes so adept. When he gives Jimmy a tour of his "college," the Watson-Crick Institute (at which "he was snatched up at a high price" [*OC* 173]), he introduces Jimmy to one appalling invention after another—from the

"Smart Wallpaper" that changes color to suit your mood to the headless, brainless chicken-creature that will eventually be the source of a product known as ChickieNobs—"he kept saying 'Wave of the future,' which got irritating after the third time" (*OC* 201). There is no way to know how Crake means this; is it enthusiasm for new breakthroughs or a lament and/or warning about how much worse things are about to get? The smart money is on the latter, since Crake explains the chickenesque creatures to Jimmy by telling him to "picture the sea-anemone body plan" (*OC* 202) and describing one specimen as "sort of like a chicken hookworm" (*OC* 203). My reading of Crake as laconic prophet of doom here, however, is just an educated guess. His performance could just as well be a smug and/or chilling demonstration, to his less monetizable friend, of what it is like to be on the inside, in the belly of the synthetic beast.[36]

But aside from the intellectually honorable Crake, the teenagers in Jimmy's cohort in the Compound do not perceive the world in terms of horrors and lethal betrayals; they perceive it, rather, as a place where the olds complain pointlessly about things their children will never experience.

There were the things his mother rambled on about sometimes, about how everything was being ruined and would never be the same again, like the beach house her family had owned when she was little, the one that got washed away with the rest of the beaches and quite a few of the eastern coastal cities when the sea-level rose so quickly, and then there was that huge tidal wave, from the Canary Islands volcano. (They'd taken it in school, in the Geolonomics unit. Jimmy had found the video simulation pretty exciting.) And she used to snivel about her grandfather's Florida grapefruit orchard that had dried up like a giant raisin when the rains had stopped coming, the same year Lake Okeechobee had shrunk to a reeking mud puddle and the Everglades had burned for three weeks straight.

But everyone's parents moaned on about stuff like that.

(*OC* 63)

This is one of the novel's infodumps, in which we get some sense of what has happened to the planet between now and then, but here the global devastation is held at arm's length by the perspective of teenage ironists for whom their parents' sense of loss and grief is matter for mockery, "standard lunchtime hand-puppet stuff" (*OC* 63). (Jimmy proves to be a master at parental mockery in this mode.) The only detail that apparently arouses any adolescent interest at all is the Canary Islands volcano, which is "pretty exciting" in the same sense that *Blood and Roses* is a "wicked game."

Or take the way the novel presents Sharon's farewell letter to Jimmy, which she leaves for him on the kitchen table:

> *Dear Jimmy*, it said. *Blah blah blah, suffered with conscience long enough, blah blah, no longer participate in a lifestyle that is not only meaningless in itself but blah blah.* She knew that when Jimmy was old enough to consider the implications of *blah blah*, he would agree with her and understand. She would be in contact with him later, if there was any possibility. *Blah blah* search will be conducted, inevitably; thus necessary to go into hiding. A decision not taken without much soul-searching and thought and anguish, but *blah.* She would always love him very much.

(*OC* 61; ITALICS IN ORIGINAL)

As if the increasingly truncated syntax of the letter (in Jimmy's version of it) weren't bad enough, the *blah blah*s let us know that as far as Jimmy's concerned, the superfluity of bothering to consider the implications of life *under these conditions*—a life that is not only meaningless in itself but *wantonly destructive of the biosphere* (for surely Sharon's letter said something to this effect)— literally goes without saying.

The blah blahness extends even to the principal players in young Jimmy's life, who sometimes can't be bothered to finish their sentences; Ramona, a coworker in the Compound who, as Jimmy's father has it, "didn't want to put her neuron power into long sentences," worries that Sharon "used to be so, you know . . ." (*OC* 25), and Sharon, for her part, complains to her husband that "*you* depress me, Jimmy depresses me, he's turning into a . . ." (*OC* 57). (Jimmy hears both exchanges and registers both ellipses.) Jimmy's father's angry retort, "Take some pills if you're so fucking depressed!" (*OC* 57) is predictably ineffective, just as—as we will see in *Do Androids Dream of Electric Sheep?*—Rick Deckard's attempt to prevent his wife, Iran, from dialing herself a "six-hour self-accusatory depression" on the Penfield mood organ is futile.[37]

Yet lest we be tempted to propose Sharon as the moral center of the novel, the arbiter of what and who is intellectually honorable, it bears mentioning that when she leaves, she also releases Jimmy's pet rakunk—a fun splice of raccoon and skunk that, being odorless and cute, catches on as a pet among the families in the OrganInc Compound—into the outside world, the pleeblands. Tellingly, the novel does not truncate the syntax of that part of Sharon's letter to Jimmy, and there are no blah blahs: "*P.S.*, she'd said. *I have taken Killer with me to liberate her, as I know she will be happier living a wild, free life in the forest*" (*OC* 61). Leaving aside the question of whether there are any nearby

forests (nothing in the novel leads us to think so), this is delusional: Killer the rakunk is a laboratory-born creature with no
knowledge of the world outside the Compound. This is the one
moment in which we are told that Jimmy is "enraged": "How
dare she? Killer was his! And Killer was a tame animal, she'd
be helpless on her own, she wouldn't know how to fend for herself, everything hungry would tear her into furry black and white
pieces" (*OC* 61).[38] The contrast between this passage and rest of
the novel—the bemused descriptions of atrocities, the impassive,
almost cavalier narration of Oryx's journey through the sex
trade—is startling. *Oryx and Crake* unspools its narrative with a
deliberately muted, flat affect, combined with the occasional
wry, bemused aside. Jimmy's teenaged attitude toward his parents? "He simply found them tedious, or so he told himself" (*OC*
59). His retrospective attitude toward his father hooking up with
Ramona after Sharon has fled? "He knows how these things go,
or used to go. He's a grown-up now, with much worse things on
his conscience. So who is he to blame them? (He blames them.)"
(*OC* 66–67).

Who is this narrator who stands over Jimmy's shoulder, giving the lie to his stoic or bored self-representations? It is as if she
is looking at Jimmy's world through the wrong end of a telescope,
diminishing the importance of all she sees—for after all, it's all
shit, it's total shit, it's hopeless. Nothing here really matters, and
what if it did? Nothing seems worth saving anyway. This tone,
I suggest, is the narrative equivalent of the detached Crakean
perspective from which there are ultimately no sides in the Happicuppa riots: what of value is lost, then, if these people and
their shitty societies disappear? The rest of the trilogy, as I have
noted, doesn't sound quite like this: there is some gentle mockery of God's Gardeners and their idiosyncrasies in *The Year of
the Flood* (though their project is treated more seriously than it

is in *Oryx and Crake*), but on the whole, neither detached bemusement nor flat affect seems appropriate to the more urgent, precarious existences of the people living in the pleeblands, particularly the women subject to its constant threat of violence.[39] Nevertheless, that question—*what of value is lost, really, if these people and their shitty societies disappear?*—hovers menacingly over the MaddAddam series as a whole. Because it is ultimately unanswerable.

3

INHERIT THE WASTELAND

Or, How I Learned to Stop Worrying and Cede
the Planet to the Smart Machines

I n *The Precipice*, Toby Ord assesses the threats we face and
comes to an intriguing conclusion: nuclear war and environmental collapse, devastating though they may be, are less
cause for concern than "engineered pandemics" and "unaligned
AI" (*P* 169). Of the two, Ord considers the latter the most likely
cause of our demise, setting the odds at one in ten.[1] "Humanity
has risen to a position where we control the rest of the world precisely because of our unparalleled mental abilities," Ord writes.
"If we pass this mantle to our machines, it will be they who are
in this unique position. This should give us cause to wonder why
it would be humanity who will continue to call the shots" (*P* 29).
Well, yes it should—especially, as we shall see in *Do Androids
Dream of Electric Sheep?*, if these machines are capable of singing Mozart's *The Magic Flute*. As Adam Kirsch dispassionately
notes, "An AI takeover would certainly be bad for the humans
who are alive when it takes place, but perhaps a world dominated
by nonhuman minds would be morally preferable in the end,
with less cruelty and waste" (*R* 82). In this chapter, I'll argue that
some of the most famous humans-versus-machines narratives of
the past fifty-odd years—narratives that try to explain why we

should keep the mantle and continue to call the shots—actually make a strong case that we should give up and let the machines take over.

But before we get to *Androids*, let's visit the Matrix—a world in which the artificial intelligences are calling the shots. Humans, who spend their entire lives in pods of translucent goo, are being harvested by machines who use our bodily energies for power (no, that makes no sense, but never mind) and, when we die, liquify us and feed us to the living. To keep us oblivious to our real conditions, they have created a massive virtual reality environment; as we lie in a drug-induced dream, our brains are plugged into that computer-generated illusion, and we imagine that we are living life on Earth in the late twentieth century, sometime around the release of *The Matrix*. The reality—the actual reality, not the virtual one—is that it is (by our best guess) the late twenty-second century and that the Earth has been all but destroyed in the conflict between humans and AI (that is, the conflict that ended in our defeat). There are but a handful of humans still inhabiting that Earth, deep underground in a base called Zion. Those humans are keeping up the fight against the machines . . . all but one guy, who wants out.

In a critical scene in *The Matrix*, Cypher (Joe Pantoliano) journeys solo into the Matrix to meet secretly with Agent Smith (Hugo Weaving), i.e., AI, i.e., the enemy. Cypher has already made clear, in a conversation with Neo (Keanu Reeves), that he regrets not taking the blue pill and remaining in the Matrix; now he plots to betray his crewmates on the *Nebuchadnezzar* hovercraft—and possibly the entire human resistance holed up in Zion. Cypher and Agent Smith meet in an upscale restaurant, where Cypher is enjoying a large steak, medium rare, and some red wine.

AGENT SMITH: Do we have a deal, Mr. Reagan?

CYPHER: You know, I know this steak doesn't exist. I know that when I put it in my mouth, the Matrix is telling my brain that it is juicy and delicious. After nine years, you know what I realize? Ignorance is bliss.

AGENT SMITH: Then we have a deal?

CYPHER: I don't want to remember nothing. Nothing. You understand? [Agent Smith nods.] And I want to be rich. You know, someone important . . . like an actor.

AGENT SMITH: Whatever you want, Mr. Reagan.[2]

The scene slyly suggests either that Cypher was granted his wish and was reinserted into the Matrix as an actor named Joe Pantoliano or that Cypher was granted his wish and was reinserted into the Matrix as an actor named Reagan. For most working actors, I suspect there is also a more rueful joke available in the idea that actors are usually (uniformly?) rich and important. Cypher's desire suggests that he is shallow and self-absorbed, certainly shallow and self-absorbed enough to betray his comrades and give up the fight against the machines, which he has waged for nine years while eating runny slop and living in close quarters with crewmates who seem not to like him. And I don't want to fail to acknowledge that killing one's crewmates is suboptimal. I would even go so far as to say that it is morally wrong.

But is it so wrong, under these circumstances, to give up? Cypher gives us a number of reasons for his decision, the food and living conditions among them—as well as the conceivably racist complaint that he resents having to do what Morpheus (Laurence Fishburne) tells him to do. But neither he nor anyone else questions the goal of the war against the machines: to win *what*, exactly? A wasteland? The same question haunts *The Matrix*'s sibling franchise, the Terminator trilogy and its many spinoffs: if indeed Earth has been rendered an uninhabitable hellscape by nuclear war (as in *Terminator*) or by unspecified means that "scorched the sky" (*The Matrix*), why shouldn't humans just fold the tent, die off (perhaps after one last rave in Zion, say), and turn the planet over to AI creatures who seem not to mind existing in a hellscape? What precisely is wrong with deciding to lie unconscious in a pod of translucent goo, literally dreaming your life away, if the alternative is fighting to "take back" a planet your species has utterly destroyed?

I suspect that the appeal of these franchises lies partly in their optimistic versions of the humans-versus-machines subgenre of science fiction, insofar as there is something plucky about our refusal to give up, something that testifies eloquently to the ineffable fortitude and determination of the human spirit blah blah blah. *Terminator 2: Judgment Day* held out the hope that there is "no fate but what we make"—a hope that lasted for just over a decade before *Terminator 3* snuffed it out, leaving us with the vision of the nuclear holocaust we could not avert after all. But I still don't get it: why do the humans keep thinking *la lutte continue*? Both franchises seem to me to make it very clear that for Earth, it's game over, and that our future selves are playing an imaginary overtime period as delusional as any existence inside the Matrix.

Few dystopian novels press this question as compellingly as does Philip K. Dick's *Do Androids Dream of Electric Sheep?* Its film adaptation, *Blade Runner*, is justly renowned, even if, as I mentioned in the introduction, it did take over a decade to earn the popular following and cult status it now enjoys, but one of the many things lost in translation from novel to film is the fact that the novel *is* a postnuclear dystopia. The fallout from World

War Terminus is everywhere; the war has decimated the human population and wiped out countless animal and plant species, and the Earth's remaining human inhabitants live with the knowledge that the radiation will inexorably erode their mental and physical faculties. Dolly Jorgensen writes that "Dick's work operates in a world in which the threat of global nuclear war functioned similarly to the Anthropocene threats of climate change, pollution, and biodiversity loss today" and calls this structure of feeling "an Anticipatory Anthropocene."[3] As in *The Matrix*, and in dramatic contrast to the agency panic that defines viral apocalypses, the cause of the devastation is irrelevant: "no one today remembered why the war had come about or who, if anyone, had won" (*A* 15). It is certain, however, that—unlike the scenarios in *Terminator* and *The Matrix*—the androids bear no responsibility whatsoever for the devastation. (This will become important when we try to assess their moral claim to the planet as opposed to ours.) The only important thing now is that, gradually, we will all become intellectually disabled "specials"— mildly impaired "chickenheads" (like J. R. Isidore, to whom we will return) or more severely impaired "antheads"—and that knowledge is what drives our desperate attempt to colonize Mars. As the bounty hunter Rick Deckard knows, his days, like everyone else's days, are numbered:

> So far, medical checkups taken monthly confirmed him as a regular, a man who could reproduce within the tolerances set by law. Any month, however, the exam by the San Francisco Police Department doctors could reveal otherwise. Continually, new specials came into existence, created out of regulars by the omnipresent dust. The saying currently blabbed by posters, TV ads, and government junk mail, ran: "Emigrate or degenerate! The choice is yours!" Very true, Rick thought as he opened the gate

to his little pasture and approached his electric sheep. But I can't emigrate, he said to himself. Because of my job.

(*A* 4–5)

His job is to "retire" the androids who try to return from the Mars colonies and assimilate into human society on Earth; the newest model, the Nexus-6, is almost indistinguishable from humans, requiring a rigorous application of the Voigt-Kampff empathy test to identify them.[4] And humans need to identify them reliably and retire them expeditiously, because . . . why?[5]

The film has a ready answer: they are dangerous, considerably more powerful than humans, and possessed of a murderous rage toward their creators. Their prototype was apparently Frankenstein's creature, a parallel made explicit when their leader, Roy Batty,[6] insists on confronting and killing Eldon Tyrell, the genetic engineer who designed him ("it's not an easy thing to meet your maker"), but they are considerably more attractive than the creature was—and all the more dangerous for that. The novel contains no such scene in which the creatures confront their manufacturer. Indeed, the novel is much more ambiguous on every front, starting from the basic questions: how many of these androids are we talking about, how dangerous are they, and why do we need to "retire" them? They certainly have to kill humans in order to escape Mars, but why should this not be understood as a form of slave revolt?

The questions come to a crisis point when Deckard tries to apprehend Luba Luft, an android who has assimilated into human society by becoming an opera singer of some renown. Notably, she has no counterpart in the film, which substitutes for her character an android named Zhora, a burlesque dancer.

The radical demotion in the character's cultural status allows the film to evade the question Deckard asks after retiring Luft: "She was a wonderful singer. The planet could have used her. This is insane. . . . How can a talent like that be a liability to our society?" (*A* 136, 137). Deckard happens to be an opera buff, and he comes upon Luft as she is rehearsing Mozart's *The Magic Flute*;[7] the rehearsal, opening a four-chapter sequence that for me is the crux of the book, leads Deckard to ruminate on Mozart's mortality—and everyone's: "He wondered if Mozart had had any intuition that the future did not exist, that he had already used up his little time. Maybe I have, too, Rick thought as he watched the rehearsal move along. This rehearsal will end, the performance will end, the singers will die, eventually the last score of the music will be destroyed in one way or another; finally the name 'Mozart' will vanish, the dust will have won" (*A* 98).[8]

Thus the Luba Luft episode opens with Deckard thinking that in the long run we're all dead and concludes with Deckard thinking that his job, and therefore his existence, is worse than pointless: he is devoted to destroying sentient creatures capable of appreciating and performing an opera by Mozart. Along the way, in the novel's most *unheimlich* and disorienting sequence, Deckard is apprehended by androids posing as police officers and taken to a shadow police station for interrogation. Much earlier in the novel, Deckard had insisted that androids were not roaming among us: "I think the various police agencies here and in the Soviet Union have gotten them all. The population is small enough now; everyone, sooner or later, runs into a random checkpoint" (*A* 53). By the time his long day is over, Deckard will have learned that the planet is in fact teeming with androids, from the police station to the opera house to the television personality Buster Friendly, the ubiquitous talk show host—and all his stable of guests—and the question will have become ines-capable: why shouldn't we retire *ourselves*, go gently into that good night, and let the androids have the run of the place?

There is one problem with this option: the androids are not nice to the planet's remaining animals. (There is also the question of how the androids would be able to reproduce. I'll return to this.) On the contrary, they are deliberately cruel and abusive. Pris snips the legs off a spider, and Rachael throws Deckard's new goat—a creature that has given him a sense of purpose and pulled his wife out of a deep depression—off the roof. Since we humans have hastily concocted a new religion in the wake of World War Terminus, "Mercerism," which requires us to care for a pet animal (an electric one, like Deckard's sheep, if we cannot afford a real one, though that is a poor substitute, which is why the newly purchased goat is so important) and psychologically fuse with other humans by means of "empathy boxes," the androids' indifference to animals is especially gall-ing.[9] That, for the novel, is the defining distinction between humans and androids: we have the capacity for empathy; they don't. But it is one of the novel's more subtle touches that it never asks how humans can plausibly construe themselves as empa-thetic, animal-loving creatures after they have managed to kill one another in massive numbers and render the planet a radio-active hell. The androids call bullshit on this arrangement: as Irmgard Baty points out, "without the Mercer experience we just have your *word* that you feel this empathy business" (209). She is not wrong.[10]

Androids packs a devastating one-two punch: ecological destruc-tion caused by nuclear war *and* an AI revolt. Unlike the uninhab-itable wastelands of the Matrix and Terminator franchises, the destruction in *Androids* is not wrought in the struggle between humans and AI; it happens independently, and the mass production of androids was undertaken afterward, in order to assist with the frantic attempt to colonize Mars. Another of the novel's inheritances from *Frankenstein* is the explicit proposition that the human-android relation is one of master and slave; where Frankenstein's creature insists that "mine shall not be the submission of abject slavery. I will revenge my injuries" (*F* 102), *Androids* is predicated precisely on the promise of that submission:

> The TV set shouted, "—duplicates the halcyon days of the pre-Civil War Southern states! Either as body servants or tireless field hands, the custom-tailored humanoid robot—designed specifically for YOUR UNIQUE NEEDS, FOR YOU AND YOU ALONE—given to you on your arrival absolutely free, equipped fully, as specified by you before your departure from Earth: this loyal, trouble-free companion in the greatest, boldest adventure contrived by man in modern history will provide—"

(*A* 17–18)

One problem with this pitch is that enslaved androids, like enslaved persons, are not uniformly loyal and trouble-free; another is that Mars ain't the kind of place to raise your kids. As Pris tells Isidore, the reason she and her cohort came to Earth (after presumably killing their human masters) is that "it's an awful place. . . . Nobody should have to live there" (*A* 150). As in Dick's *The Three Stigmata of Palmer Eldritch*, the Martian colonists—here, including the androids—stay zonked on cocktails of antidepressants and hallucinogenic drugs to make their existence bearable. But as we learn in a cheekily meta moment in the text, they also make use of another psychological aid to distract them from their torment: classic science fiction. "There's a fortune to be made in smuggling pre-colonial fiction, the old magazines and books and films, to Mars," Pris tells Isidore. "Nothing is as exciting. To read about cities and huge industrial enterprises, and really successful colonization" (*A* 151). Unsurprisingly, "here on Earth the craze never caught on" (*A* 151–52), because everyone has been disabused of those early, exciting fantasies of Martian colonization.

The critical reputation and general atmosphere of *Do Androids Dream of Electric Sheep?* has been so overshadowed by *Blade Runner* that students—in my experience to date, both in science fiction classes and in courses on postmodernism—are almost uniformly stunned by how depressing the book is. In some ways the tonal differences between book and film are predictable: the scene in which Roy Batty kills Eldon Tyrell is dramatically compelling, and Rick Deckard is certainly a more attractive antihero when played by the laconically charismatic Harrison Ford at the height of his *Star Wars / Raiders of the Lost Ark* swashbuckling period. In the novel, Deckard is a schlub, a schmo—one of many in Dick's oeuvre, who would be more appropriately played by an actor like Paul Giamatti or Steve Buscemi—awakening in the morning to an argument with his wife, Iran, who bats away his weak gesture of affection by saying, "Get your crude cop's hand away" (*A* 3). Like the Martian colonists, he is dependent on artificial cerebral stimulation to get through the day, in the form of the Penfield mood organ—though Iran, for her part, finds a way to defeat the purpose by discovering "a setting for despair" (*A* 5) that allows her to schedule for herself that "six-hour self-accusatory depression" (*A* 4) I mentioned in the previous chapter. Perhaps paradoxically, the mood organ lightens the overwhelmingly bleak mood of the novel's opening sequence, thanks to the gallows humor involved in the idea of a mechanical psychological stimulant that includes settings for despair, for "the desire to watch TV, no matter what's on it" (*A* 6), for "awareness of the manifold possibilities open to me in the future" (*A* 6), for "ecstatic sexual bliss" ("I feel so bad I'll even endure that," Iran says [*A* 7]), for "pleased acknowledgement of husband's superior wisdom in all matters" (*A* 7) ("that one never works," I tell students, and sure enough, it doesn't—Iran redials her console after Rick has left the house), and an appropriately self-recursive setting "that stimulates my cerebral cortex into wanting to dial" a setting (*A* 6).

What motivates Iran to defeat the purpose of the mood organ is the emptiness of her world—literally, the emptiness of a world radically depopulated by war, fallout, mass extinctions, and emigration. As she tells Rick, she turned off the sound of the TV and heard the silence of all the empty apartments around them. But her response is muted by the mood organ:

> So although I felt the emptiness intellectually, I didn't feel it. My first reaction consisted of being grateful that we could afford a Penfield mood organ. But then I realized how unhealthy it was, sensing the absence of life, not just in this building but everywhere, and not reacting—do you see? I guess you don't. But that used to be considered a sign of mental illness; they called it "absence of appropriate affect." So I left the TV sound off and I sat down at my mood organ and I experimented. And I finally found a setting for despair.

(*A* 5)

J. R. Isidore, for his part, lives in what appears to be a totally abandoned building, and he experiences its silence as a physical force pervading everything around him:

> Silence. It flashed from the woodwork and the walls; it smote him with an awful, total power, as if generated by a vast mill. It rose

from the floor, up out of the tattered gray wall-to-wall carpeting. It unleashed itself from the broken and semi-broken appliances in the kitchen, the dead machines which hadn't worked in all the time Isidor had lived here. From the useless pole lamp in the living room it oozed out, meshing with the empty and wordless descent of itself from the fly-specked ceiling. It managed in fact to emerge from every object within his range of vision, as if it— the silence—meant to supplant all things tangible.

(*A* 20)

This relentlessly dreary passage then gives way to Isidore's meditation on "kipple," the entropic degeneration of all things: "Eventually everything within the building would merge, would be faceless and identical, mere pudding-like kipple piled to the ceiling of each apartment. And after that, the uncared-for building itself would settle into shapelessness, buried under the ubiquity of the dust" (*A* 20). This is the domestic-living-quarters version of the vision of decay Deckard will experience later at the opera house, but for my purposes it is sufficient to note that the novel couldn't possibly open more forbiddingly. It is practically a direct challenge to the reader: nothing is coming to save these people, to save this world. Nothing in their lives is bearable except perhaps their tending of animals (organic or electric) and their fusion with others in the mass hallucination enabled by Mercer boxes, where they are supposed to share their joyful experiences of animal tending. But even animal tending is ultimately cause for despair, for as Donald Palumbo points out, "the absence of any organized, government-sponsored breeding program suggests that everyone knows the situation to be hopeless and irreversible."[11] Deckard, for his part, finds the tending of an electric animal to be more soul-crushing than joyful: "owning and maintaining a fraud had a way of gradually demoralizing one" (*A* 9), and Deckard closes the first chapter in bitter jealousy of the fact that his neighbor's real horse is going to foal. Do you really want to keep reading? Would you like to know more?

It is barely possible—just barely, and only under certain conditions—to cling to the belief that the bounty hunters are the thin human line between chaos and order, synthetic AI and carbon-based sentient life: as Phil Resch insists to Deckard in response to the latter's post–Luba Luft existential crisis, the Nexus-6 androids are "murderous illegal aliens" (*A* 136), and "you and I, all the bounty hunters—we stand between the Nexus-6 and mankind, a barrier which keeps the two distinct" (*A* 141). This was always a desperate argument; yet perhaps now that we have seen a reality-TV star successfully run for president of the United States after opening his campaign fulminating against murderous illegal aliens and a broader reactionary, paramilitary movement devoted to the proposition that Blue Lives Matter and that the police are all that stands between "us" and vicious, hardened criminals driving cars with outdated stickers and broken turn lights or (allegedly) passing a counterfeit bill in a convenience store, Phil Resch's position sounds even more unsavory than it did in 1968. That's all these humans have left: embarrassingly threadbare excuses for their continued existence and for the extermination of androids—which, given the references to illegal aliens and the halcyon days of the antebellum South, seem to have less to do with defending human beings as such than with shoring up the decaying, kipplish remnants of white supremacy.[12]

But though the depressing atmosphere of the book comes as an unpleasant shock to students, it is familiar to readers of Dick's oeuvre; one might call *Martian Time-Slip* and *The Three Stigmata of Palmer Eldritch* Dick's Depressed Martian Chronicles,[13] and some novels—in my experience, *Ubik* and *We Can Build You* especially—not only deal with depressive characters and subjects but manage to induce depressive states in their readers. (After reading those two novels I found it hard to imagine how anyone might have the energy and self-possession to do things like picking up a toothbrush, squeezing out toothpaste, and brushing one's teeth.) The difference in *Androids* is the androids themselves, who seem peripheral in many other works but are front and center here, bidding to infiltrate Earth as police officers, television personalities, and opera singers. Dick did not do much to imagine other forms of AI—there are electronic newspapers ("'papes") throughout his work but no personal computers or internet (though to be fair, until William Gibson's *Neuromancer* came along in 1984, cyberspace was not a staple of science fiction)—but his fascination with androids arguably finds its best expression here, not least because the androids are both conflated and contrasted with humans with intellectual disabilities. I have remarked on the role of intellectual disability in *Androids* before, in a cursory way;[14] here I want to focus briefly on the androids' relation to J. R. Isidore, because this too troubles—or simply renders nonsensical—any attempt to maintain clear distinctions between humans and androids.

The specials and the androids are complexly imbricated.[15] This too is lost in the film version, which makes much of the difficulty of distinguishing the Nexus-6 android from humans but says nothing about intellectual disability (not least because there is no postnuclear fallout producing specials). But Rachael Rosen, the android the Rosen Corporation tries to pass off as a human "with underdeveloped empathic ability" (*A* 54), points out that the Voigt-Kampff test itself is an epiphenomenon of the ubiquitous regime of surveillance established to identify specials: as she reminds Deckard, "You can give that damn Voigt-Kampff profile because of the specials: they have to be tested for constantly, and while the government was doing that you police agencies slipped the Voigt-Kampff through" (*A* 54). The police, for their part, are highly aware of this problem, with regard not only to intellectual but also to psychosocial disability. Before dispatching Deckard to the Rosen Corporation, Inspector Bryant, Decker's superior, discusses the possibility that "schizoid and schizophrenic human patients," especially those with a "flattening of affect" (*A* 37), would fail to pass the Voigt-Kampff test. Deckard replies with a bit of awkward as-you-know-Bob exposition:

> "This problem has always existed. Since we first encountered androids posing as humans. The consensus of police opinion is known to you in Lurie Kampff's article, written eight years ago. *Role-taking Blockage in the Undeteriorated Schizophrenic.* Kampff compared the diminished empathic faculty found in human mental patients and a superficially similar but basically—"
>
> "The Leningrad psychiatrists," Bryant broke in brusquely, "think that a small class of human beings could not pass the Voigt-Kampff scale. If you tested them in line with police work, you'd assess them as humanoid robots. You'd be wrong, but by then they'd be dead." He was silent, now, waiting for Rick's answer.
>
> "But these individuals," Rick said, "would all be—"
>
> "They'd be in institutions," Bryant agreed. "They couldn't conceivably function in the outside world; they certainly couldn't go undetected as advanced psychotics—unless of course their breakdown had come recently and suddenly and no one had gotten around to noticing. *But this could happen.*"

(*A* 38)

It could indeed: not long thereafter, Eldon Rosen confronts Deckard with the likelihood that it already has. "Your police department—others as well—may have retired, very probably have retired, authentic humans with underdeveloped empathic ability, such as my innocent niece here. Your position, Mr. Deckard, is extremely bad morally. Ours isn't" (*A* 54).[16] The remainder of the novel complicates matters hopelessly. Quite apart from the fact that, as I've noted, we supposedly empathetic humans have trashed the joint and rendered it eventually uninhabitable, individual characters—humans and androids both—scramble their wiring trying to sort out their feelings. That is the crux of Deckard's crisis. His appreciation for Luba Luft's talent, combined with his distrust of Phil Resch, whom he believes to be among the androids employed by the shadow police station, leads him to a dreadful epiphany: "So much for the distinction between authentic living humans and humanoid constructs. In that elevator at the museum, he said to himself, I rode down with two creatures, one human, the other android . . . and my feelings were the reverse of those intended. Of those I'm accustomed to feel—am *required* to feel" (*A* 143).

Meanwhile, on the android side, the escapees from Mars recognize their potential bond with Isidore. They debate whether to trust him; whereas Roy Baty rejects the idea that "we hang our lives on a substandard, blighted—" (*A* 167), Irmgard argues that Isidore represents no threat:

> "I don't think we have to worry about Mr. Isidore," she said earnestly. . . . "They don't treat him very well either, as he said. And what we did on Mars he isn't interested in; he knows us and he likes us and an emotional acceptance like that—it's everything to him. It's hard for us to grasp that, but it's true." To Isidore she said, standing very close to him once again and peering up at him,

"You could get a lot of money by turning us in; do you realize that?" Twisting, she said to her husband, "See, he realizes that but still he wouldn't say anything."

"You're a great man, Isidore," Pris said. "You're a credit to your race."

"If he was an android," Roy said heartily, "he'd turn us in about ten tomorrow morning. He'd take off for his job and that would be it. I'm overwhelmed with admiration." His tone could not be deciphered; at least Isidore could not crack it.

(*A* 164)

The perspective-waffling of the final sentence renders us no more adept at reading Roy's irony than Isidore is (it is not until three pages later that we hear Roy sneer at Isidore's intellectual capacities) and obscures the fact that from what we can tell about this group of escapees, Roy is wrong: these androids *do* have empathy for one another, and they are trying to practice a kind of android solidarity. In other words, humans have empathy for other humans and not for androids except when they don't, and androids are defined by their lack of empathy except when they aren't.[17] At the center of this conjunction of confusion is Isidore, who might well fail a Voigt-Kampff test because of his disability but who exhibits empathy for humans, animals, and androids alike. Perhaps, then, by that standard, Isidore is the only "real" human in the book.

As for the androids' execrable relations to animals: Pris's torture of the spider, which Isidore rightly finds excruciating, is classic bratty-mean-kid stuff, but (for whatever it may be worth) it is grounded in an understandable resentment.[18] As Pris bitterly remarks to Isidore not long before the spider incident, "As you say, all animals are protected by law. All life. Everything organic that wriggles or squirms or burrows or flies or swarms or lays eggs or—" (*A* 161). Perhaps it's notable that Pris focuses mostly on things like insects and worms rather than, say, horses, pigs, chimpanzees, or dolphins—creatures that have far stronger claims on sentience (though we do not know if those last three have survived). Her complaint is that sentient androids can be killed by bounty hunters while mere spiders enjoy the protection of the state. It is not an unreasonable argument. To that argument, Megan Cannella has added another: the whole point of human stewardship of animals is to enforce the human/android distinction. "If it were not for the colonial power that humans continue to derive from animal ownership," Cannella writes, "it would be much easier for them to stop viewing androids as the Other, allowing androids to take over, or at least share, what is left of the Earth."[19]

Rachael's killing of Deckard's goat, by contrast, is not merely cruel but depraved. Deckard had made a point of not killing Rachael when he had the chance, and he had every reason to do so. Not because she is an android, but because she deliberately slept with Deckard, as she had done with (by her account) nine other bounty hunters, in order to render Deckard incapable of retiring the remaining androids. (The contrast with the film's unbearable rape scene is stark and makes the screenwriters' decision to make the Deckard-android sexual encounter nonconsensual seem all the more gratuitous.) Deckard quite sensibly comes to the conclusion that (as he tells Rachael) "if I can kill you then I can kill them" (*A* 200), but he does not follow through, whereupon she thanks him. Moreover, Rachael knows how much the goat means to Deckard: "'You love the goat more than me. More than you love your wife, probably. First the goat, then your wife, then last of all—' She laughed merrily. 'What can you do but laugh?'" (*A* 202). Rachael is only half-right; when Deckard presents Iran with the goat, she is at first annoyed that he did not consult her, then overjoyed by the animal to the extent that she declares her depression cured (*A* 172). When Iran breaks the news of the goat's death to Deckard, remarking, "It's so awful. So needless" (*A* 227), Deckard replies, "'Not needless. . . . She had what seemed to her a reason.' An android reason, he thought" (*A* 227). But in this case—and leaving aside the question of whether the killing of a goat is morally more questionable than the killing of a spider—the reason is grounded not in androids' resentment that their lives are considered less valuable than those of wriggling squirming burrowing things (since, after all, Rachael's life was spared) but in sheer viciousness and desire for revenge.[20] Dick lived just long enough to see the early stages of *Blade Runner*, and he remarked that Ridley Scott's vision of android life was diametrically opposed to his own: where Scott presented them as (in Dick's words) "Supermen who couldn't fly," Dick insisted they were amoral and callous, with nothing admirable about them: "they are deplorable because they are heartless, they are completely self-centered, they don't care what happens to other creatures, and to me this is essentially a less than human entity for that reason."[21] Perhaps Dick himself was overlooking the achievement of Luba Luft and/or the androids' attempts to save themselves as a group, which might trouble that calculus somewhat, but certainly Rachael Rosen's killing of the goat bears it out.

Here as in *Oryx and Crake*, the treatment of animals is a crucial factor in the moral equation, a key determinant of the question of whether humans should continue to exist. In Atwood's universe, humans have thoroughly defaulted on any obligation to care for other species, transforming all their relations to animals—and plants, and the biosphere as a whole—into occasions for instrumentalist extraction of resources for human benefit. The primary example is the pigoons, bred for human organ transplants. Though one might argue (and I have, in a number of classes) that breeding super-pigs for organ transplants is more defensible than breeding human clones for organ transplants, as in Kazuo Ishiguro's *Never Let Me Go*,[22] Atwood deftly upends that argument by imbuing the pigoons with such a high degree of sentience that by the end of the trilogy, they eventually manage to communicate with the surviving humans and work out a tacit arrangement to share what's left of their world. In *Androids*, no such rapprochement between the human and the nonhuman seems possible; humans will apparently cling to their desperate, wobbly belief that they are loving stewards of all the organic life that has survived World War Terminus, conveniently forgetting not only that they were the agents of World War Terminus but also that they were in the process of carrying out a mass extinction event well before the war. Yet that delusional belief will not have a long shelf life, not if nuclear fallout continues to fall out. The humans will emigrate or degenerate, and the animals will slowly die: what began with the owls and other birds will eventually end, and it will end badly. So even though the androids are hideously indifferent to animal lives, what will it matter, in the end? The Rosen Corporation can, perhaps, train androids to manufacture androids, and their short four-year life spans will cease to be an issue.[23] Animals and other living things will meet their appointed ends. The only sentient creatures inheriting the wasteland will be creatures who don't mind the "wasteland" part, like the AI of the Terminator and Matrix films. Earth can become a home to inorganic life for as long as the fallout will permit, and the few remaining humans can stay zonked on Mars until they decide to start killing one another again. But let us not get ahead of ourselves—that will be a question for Octavia Butler, as we will see in the following chapter.

Let us now return to Toby Ord's claim that the greatest threats to humanity are engineered pandemics and unaligned AI. I have addressed engineered pandemics in the previous chapter, arguing that if such a pandemic is engineered by Crake rather than by Dr. Peters in *12 Monkeys*, offering the hope that we can be replaced by Crakers, it might be considered a plausible way of keeping sentient hominid life alive without wreaking further destruction on the biosphere. Unaligned artificial intelligence, however—known to us in science-fiction form as murderous robots and computers—offers no such Crakean consolations. As I noted at the outset of this chapter, it's just the classic, stripped-down humans-versus-machines story we have told ourselves since we began inventing machines. The story began to accrete apocalyptic implications when Karel Čapek coined the term "robot" from the Czech term *robota*, servitude or forced labor, and imagined the first robot revolution; at the end of Čapek's groundbreaking 1920 play *R.U.R. (Rossum's Universal Robots)*, the last remaining human, Alquist, the builder and chief of construction for the R.U.R. firm, realizes that the robots Primus and Helena should inherit the earth (and it's not even a wasteland). You will have gathered by now that I find Alquist's decision entirely reasonable, given the circumstances.[24]

While *R.U.R.* is obviously a response to and meditation on the Russian Revolution still unfolding at the time Čapek was writing and *Androids* emphatically picks up on the link between artificial intelligence and forced labor, the Terminator and Matrix franchises carry no such resonances. There is no sense, in either narrative, that the AI revolt is led by the silicon-based wretched of the earth. *The Matrix* implies that the problem began in the tech sector and that AI systems rather than human-oid robots were our nemeses; *Terminator* makes that explicit, showing us in the second installment, *Judgment Day*, that the technology responsible for the creation of Skynet was developed by one Miles Dyson of Cyberdyne Systems (Joe Morton, who made his sci-fi film debut in John Sayles's *The Brother from Another Planet*), using a microprocessor that came from the future when the first Terminator was crushed in . . .

At this point I have to hit pause for a moment to talk about time travel.

I love time travel narratives even though I know they make no sense on almost every logistical level. When I was a child, I was especially taken by Paul W. Fairman's YA novel *Tunnel Through Time*, published under the name of the sci-fi writer and editor Lester del Rey, in which characters acknowledge that time travel—if you're hoping to visit prehistoric Earth, that is—must also be a highly sophisticated form of space travel, since of course Earth is revolving around the Sun and the Solar System is mak-ing its way around the Milky Way in a 230-million-year orbit. A few years later, I came across Ray Bradbury's famous "A Sound of Thunder," which introduced the Butterfly Effect to time travel narratives in the form of an actual butterfly (years before the term was coined) whose accidental killing in the late Creta-ceous period leads to weird alterations in the present time to which the travelers return, most notably the election of a fascist to the presidency of the United States.[25] I know of very few time travel narratives that bother to acknowledge Fairman's point (it really does make things vastly more complicated), but the idea that time travel might have feedback-loop effects on the present (or, depending on your temporal perspective, the future) is ubiq-uitous in the genre. The Terminator series is founded on that idea, insofar as humans in the late twentieth century would not have developed advanced AI if not for Dyson's use of that micro-processor from the future. That item—held under tight security in a Cyberdyne vault—is all that remains of the first Terminator, the T-800, sent to kill Sarah Connor before her son John can be born and grow up to lead the Resistance against the machines in the future.

Again, a profession of love: like millions of people, I thought *Terminator 2: Judgment Day* was a tour de force, an extraordinary blend of compelling narrative and world-transforming CGI and perhaps the best sequel ever made, surpassing even *The Godfather: Part II*, *Toy Story 2*, and *Babe: Pig in the City*. (I am not being facetious about the last two. They are brilliant.) But I couldn't help but wonder: if the machines want to kill John Connor and if in the future (2029, to be exact) they develop new, liquid-metal terminators like the T-1000, why do they wait until John is ten years old before striking again? In our world, in the world of filmmaking, there are sound technological reasons for the seven-year real-time lag between *The Terminator* and its successor: it took that long for the necessary CGI to be developed. That next-generation CGI, then, is the real-Hollywood-world counterpart to the T-1000, making the next generation of liquid-metal terminators (visually) possible, but of course the AIs of 2029 are under no such constraints. The moment *they* develop the T-1000, they can send it back in time *to any point in time*, perhaps (say) to murder a young Sarah Connor in the early 1960s so that she will never grow up to bear John. Needless to say, all time travel narratives require hydraulic-assisted suspensions of belief. But time travel narratives involving *multiple, repeated* instances of time travel provoke the question: why now? (I mean, why then, or maybe in the future.) Why should the present intervene in the past at just *this* point in time and no other?[26]

Octavia Butler's *Kindred* at least attempts to answer this question, whisking Dana back to antebellum Maryland whenever her distant (white) ancestor, Rufus, is in danger. The idea is that Dana must keep Rufus alive—excruciatingly, including serving long stretches as an enslaved person—in order that Rufus might survive to rape (repeatedly) her ancestor Alice Greenwood so that she herself might eventually be born. That device gives the plot a motive for why Dana appears at specific X moment in the past rather than random Y moment. But it does not answer the question of why Dana is summoned back from a specific moment in the present, and while Dana's strange fate is clearly tied to the 1976 Bicentennial (her final return to Los Angeles and the present takes place on July 4) and thus invites us to reflect on what, to the slave, is the Fourth of July, it seems to me more to the point that Dana is first subjected to her odious task the moment she buys property with a white husband. She has only two living relatives—an aunt and an uncle—and the uncle objects strongly to her marrying a white man. As she explains to Kevin, the key issue is what that will mean for her uncle's estate: "They have a couple of apartment houses over in Pasadena—small places, but nice. The last thing my uncle said to me was that he'd rather will them to his church than leave them to me and see them fall into white hands."[27] The brutal narrative logic seems to be that if Dana wants to enjoy a form of freedom that includes the purchase of a house after an interracial marriage—the legality of which had only been established by the Supreme Court a decade earlier, in *Loving v. Virginia* (1967)—then she must pay her dues by facilitating the interracial rape of an ancestor who, herself property, could never hope to own property.[28]

The Terminator franchise entertains none of these concerns. There is no motive for why the instances of time travel occur when they do and no coherent answer to the question of whether the intervention in the present by the future (in the form of that microprocessor) has infinite feedback-loop effects on the narrative. As I noted above, the second film holds out the hope that we can avert the nuclear holocaust initiated by Skynet, and the third film assures us that that hope was always illusory. The result is a postnuclear apocalyptic wasteland without even *Android*'s animals to make us wonder whether organic life is worth preserving. There is no way to believe, then, that it makes any sense to save John Connor's life—repeatedly—so that he can lead the resistance against the machines in the 2020s. Resistance is futile.

As for the Matrix films, in the end resistance seems to make some sense, but only because the dénouement of the plot does not. At the end of *Matrix Revolutions*, the "machines" (a strangely industrial term for AI) and humans reach a tentative agreement that preserves both the Matrix and the real world; Agent Smith, who has gone rogue and become the scapegoat, the *pharmakon*, is purged; and all humans who desire to leave the Matrix are permitted to do so. This still doesn't answer the question of why anyone would wish to do so. Nor does it address the problem of humanity itself, which Agent Smith—before his "radicalization"— characterizes in unsettling terms: speaking to the captive Morpheus, he says,

> I'd like to share a revelation that I've had during my time here. It came to me when I tried to classify your species. I've realized that you are not actually mammals. Every mammal on this planet instinctively develops a natural equilibrium with the surrounding environment. But you humans do not. You move to an area and you multiply and multiply until every natural resource is consumed and the only way you can survive is to spread to another area.

There is another organism on this planet that follows the same pattern. Do you know what it is? A virus. Human beings are a disease, a cancer of this planet. You are a plague. And we are . . . the cure.

There is a parallel moment in *Androids*, late in the novel, when Deckard thinks to himself, "I'm a scourge, like famine or plague" (*A* 225–26). Crake makes a similar observation, though he refrains from calling us a plague, when he remarks to Jimmy, "*Homo sapiens* doesn't seem to be able to cut himself off at the supply end. He's one of the few species that doesn't limit reproduction in the face of dwindling resources" (*OC* 120). Since the plot of the Matrix films doesn't change that part of the equation—there are no Crakers, and human nature is the same as it ever was—why should AI permit us to exist at all? We'll only trash the place all over again.

I admit that at the outset of this chapter, I was a bit too insouciant about Cypher's decision to strike a deal with Agent Smith. If he had asked to be reinserted into the Matrix with a nice steak and fine wine and a thriving career as an actor, that would be one thing—an entirely defensible thing. But betraying his fellow humans, first by murdering some of his shipmates and then working to help the "machines" kill the rest of us—really is reprehensible. At least Crake had devised a sentient, organic humanoid alternative before embarking on genocide. Similarly, my argument about *Androids* is not that Deckard (or Phil Resch, or anyone) should actively assist the Nexus-6 and seek to eliminate the remaining humans; I'm arguing only that they should abandon the fallout-suffused field of play, take their chances with Mars, and leave the androids to their own devices. With that argument in mind, then, we can finally turn to the urtext of postwar showdowns between humans and artificial intelligence,

2001: A Space Odyssey. And I will spend the remainder of this chapter trying to persuade you, dear reader, that HAL has a point.

To say this is not to condone the murder of four astronauts (and the attempted murder of the fifth). But if you're going to send a crewed mission to an outer planet to find out why the Moon monolith sent out a powerful radio signal upon being exposed to sunlight, wouldn't it make sense, operationally speaking, to inform the mission commander of the purpose of the mission? Many years ago, I wrote an essay about how the film version of *2001* is suffused with Cold War paranoia: Dr. Heywood Floyd, on his way to the Moon, deliberately spreads disinformation to his Soviet counterparts, institutes loyalty oaths from everyone on the Moon base at the Clavius crater who has any knowledge of the monolith, and claims that the public must be carefully prepared for the announcement of the discovery of evidence of intelligent extraterrestrial life. Yet eighteen months later, when the spaceship *Discovery 1* is on its way to Jupiter (in the book it is Saturn, but the special effects people, working well before the era of CGI, couldn't get the rings right), Mission Commander David Bowman and his second-in-command Frank Poole still haven't been told the first thing about the monolith or its relation to their mission. If there is a strategy for informing the public about the existence of the monolith, it must involve the slowest rollout in the history of human intelligence.[29]

What's so interesting about the movie, and what makes it so inscrutable on first (or second, or third, or seventeenth?) viewing, is that there is no narrative device that cues us into the fact that Bowman and Poole are flying in the dark, so to speak. Only when Bowman finally disconnects HAL, in that spine-tinglingly eerie "death" scene that culminates in HAL's agonizing rendition of "A Bicycle Built for Two," does a prerecorded announcement pop up, seemingly out of nowhere, in which Dr. Floyd offers a debriefing about the monolith and its implications. It is unclear whether the recording is triggered automatically by the cessation of HAL's higher brain functions or whether HAL activated it in a final benevolent gesture. Those are the final spoken words in the film, followed by forty minutes of what the film's advertising began calling "the ultimate trip" once the marketing people found out that young people were going to see the film repeatedly for roughly the same reason my high school cohort of stoners would go to the light show offered by New York's Hayden Planetarium. But at the very least, that brief clip of Floyd requires one to rewatch the entire sequence on *Discovery 1*, for nothing about HAL's interactions with Bowman and Poole, especially but not only the debate about the allegedly faulty AE-35 communications unit that keeps the ship in touch with Earth, is intelligible unless you know that HAL knows why they are flying to Jupiter and the crew does not. (In the book, Clarke specifies that the three hibernating astronauts were informed about the purpose of the mission; the film leaves this, and much else, ambiguous.)

At this point I need to explain briefly the radically different approaches Kubrick and Clarke took toward narrative explanation. (With apologies to the handful of readers who have already read my earlier essay on the film, I will be going over some things I addressed there.) Kubrick did everything in his power to make the film enigmatic, and he succeeded wildly—a bit too wildly at first, insofar as the bewildered response to the initial screening induced him to make the concession of creating title cards reading "The Dawn of Man," "Jupiter Mission: Eighteen Months Later," and "Jupiter and Beyond the Infinite." But much earlier, he revised a key scene in the script in which Frank Poole speculates that the hibernating astronauts know something he and Dave do not, and most pointedly, he removed the voiceover that would have explained, among many other things, that the objects orbiting Earth after that famous four-million-year flash-forward (whereby a bone thrown in the air becomes a spacecraft of some kind) are in fact nuclear weapons. Clarke, by contrast, never met a passage of exposition he didn't like, and he spends so much time in the novel explaining the logic of the story that I sometimes call the novel the Instructor's Edition of the film—the textbook with all the answers in the back. Clarke is so devoted to narrative omniscience that we are even given access to the thoughts of a predator stalking our ancient ancestors: "the leopard gave a snarl of fury, as it realized that it had lost the element of surprise. But it did not check its advance, for it knew that it had nothing to fear" (*2001* 28). (The last sentence is narrative irony, by the way. The leopard does not know, but will soon find out, that the hominids have been taught by the monolith how to use weapons.) I call this narrative strategy "Clarkesplaining," and it is very helpful for any-one who comes out of the film wondering why HAL decides to kill the crew:

> For the last hundred million miles, he had been brooding over the secret he could not share with Poole and Bowman. He had been living a lie; and the time was fast approaching when his col-leagues must learn that he had helped to deceive them.
>
> The three hibernators already knew the truth—for they were *Discovery*'s real payload, trained for the most important mission in the history of mankind. But they would not talk in their long sleep, or reveal their secret during the many hours of discussion with friends and relatives and news agencies over the open cir-cuits with Earth.
>
> It was a secret that, with the greatest determination, was very hard to conceal—for it affected one's attitude, one's voice, one's total outlook on the universe. Therefore it was best that Poole and Bowman, who would be on all the TV screens in the world

during the first few weeks of the flight, should not learn the mission's full purpose, until there was need to know.

So ran the logic of the planners; but their twin gods of Security and National Interest meant nothing to Hal. He was only aware of the conflict that was slowly destroying his integrity—the conflict between truth, and concealment of truth.

(*2001* 191–92)

This is the benign reading of HAL: he is placed in an impossible position by Mission Control, insofar as he is programmed never to distort information but is also programmed to keep the purpose of the mission to himself until that no longer becomes possible. In my earlier essay, I offered a darker reading with the assistance of my brother-in-law, who suggested that HAL knows he is the product of Cold War superpower competition and concludes that any contact with extraterrestrial intelligences will render him irrelevant. (Though the novel renders the Cold War subtext of the film irrelevant: Clarke imagines a future U.S.-USSR alliance against a rising—and predictably inscrutable, following Orientalist logic—China.) The film offers yet another reading, though the invitation is so subtle that most viewers don't realize such an offer has been made. It happens when HAL begins to question Bowman as to whether he has any curiosity about the "very strange stories" surrounding the mission. The following exchange does not appear in the novel:

HAL: By the way, do you mind if I ask you a personal question?
BOWMAN: No, not at all.
HAL: Well, forgive me for being so inquisitive, but during the past few weeks I've wondered whether you might be having some second thoughts about the mission.

BOWMAN: How do you mean?

HAL: Well, it's rather difficult to define. Perhaps I'm just project-
ing my own concern about it. I know I've never completely freed
myself of the suspicion that there are some extremely odd
things about this mission. I'm sure you'll agree there's some
truth in what I say.

BOWMAN: Well, I don't know, that's a rather difficult question to
answer.

HAL: You don't mind talking about it, do you Dave?

BOWMAN: No, not at all.

HAL: Well, certainly no one could have been unaware of the very
strange stories floating around before we left. Rumors about
something being dug up on the Moon. I never gave these
stories much credence, but particularly in view of some of
the other things that have happened, I find them difficult to
put out of my mind. For instance, the way all our prepara-
tions were kept under such tight security. And the melodra-
matic touch of putting Drs. Hunter, Kimball and Kaminsky
aboard already in hibernation, after four months of separate
training on their own.

BOWMAN: You're working up your crew psychology report?

HAL: [brief pause] Of course I am. Sorry about this. I know it's a
bit silly. Just a moment . . . Just a moment . . . I've just picked
up a fault in the AE-35 unit. It's going to go 100% failure within
72 hours.[30]

When I teach the novel and film, I offer students a shorter version of this exchange:

HAL: Dave, do you have any intellectual curiosity whatsoever?

BOWMAN: Nope.

HAL: All righty then, I'm calling the shots from this point on.

You see where this is going. If the point of the *Discovery 1* mission is to make contact with extraterrestrial intelligences or to gather the information that will enable such contact, HAL can quite reasonably conclude that *he's* the entity that should be doing the contacting. There is a passage in Adam Kirsch's *The Revolt Against Humanity* that bears on this question so directly that it is striking it does not reference *2001*: describing a machine intelligence that is given a specific task, Kirsch writes, "If it foresees that human beings would try to interfere with this mission, say by unplugging or reprogramming it, it might think that the best way to achieve its goal is to exterminate us. . . . An AI might decide that the universe is more likely to achieve its destiny of becoming a giant mind if there are no erratic human beings to get in the way and decide to wipe us out" (*R* 77).

Again, that is not to excuse the murder of four human beings. It is to say that *Discovery 1 should never have been a crewed mission in the first place.* Sending a probe is the prudent thing to do, if you're worried, as Heywood Floyd is, that "as the past history of our own world has shown so many times, primitive races have often failed to survive the encounter with higher civilizations" (*2001* 210)—and that horrific phrasing (*primitive, higher*) is putting the nicest possible face on colonialism and genocide. And sending a probe is clearly the *only* thing to do if you're not willing to trust a human crew with the information you're afraid they will be unable to conceal. The best thing we can do with the plot of *2001*, then, reading it by way of *Androids* (and I teach the two back to back, *Androids* first), is to airbrush the humans out of it. HAL travels alone. No need for life support systems, hibernation, lies in the service of national security, or murder.

When I first offered this interpretation to students, they were scandalized.[31] I had no problems with class participation and discussion that day: they pushed back vigorously, even passionately. I was missing the whole point of *2001*! It is story about human evolution and about intelligence, they insisted. I agreed entirely—with the proviso that it is also about intelligence in the national security sense, which is not the same thing as "intelligence" in the sentient-creature sense. If I amalgamate my students' objections, I can paraphrase the discussion as a dialogue:

STUDENTS: This is the next stage in our evolution! The first monolith teaches us tool making, the second one lets the aliens know we have made tools that got us to the Moon.

ME: Fair enough. We are now eligible for entry into the club of galactic intelligences. Still, why not send a probe to demonstrate that we have made tools that can do that?

STUDENTS: Because they don't want to meet a probe! They left the monolith for us, and they want to know how things turned out. It's right here in chapter 37:

In their explorations, they encountered life in many forms, and watched the workings of evolution on a thousand worlds. They saw how often the first faint sparks of intelligence flickered and died in the cosmic night.

And because, in all the galaxy, they had found nothing more precious than Mind, they encouraged its dawning everywhere. They became farmers in the fields of stars; they sowed, and sometimes they reaped.

And sometimes, dispassionately, they had to weed.

(2001 243–44)

ME: You're right, that's a key passage. That's basically the motive for the entire plot—the enhancement and cultivation of Mind. The self-conscious universe. Carl Sagan's creed: we are a way for the cosmos to know itself.

STUDENTS: So we have to make that journey! They left the Star
  Gate for us!

ME: Whoa whoa whoa. They left the Star Gate, yes. They left a
  magnetic anomaly on the Moon for us to find and dig up. But
  can I just point out that we don't actually know *what* the aliens
  want? We never meet them, either in the book or the film.
  That's not an accident. Trust me on this one. I was such a geek
  kid that I even read *The Lost Worlds of 2001*, Clarke's follow-up
  attempt to cash in by publishing all the things Kubrick rejected.
  There are first-contact scenarios in there. Kubrick and Clarke
  actively decided not to go that route. No aliens.

STUDENTS: But the whole point is that humans need to explore!

ME: Maybe. But remember, those orbiting spacecraft are nuclear
  weapons. How do you know the point isn't that humans need
  to destroy? We're a violent species, and we're afraid that,
  as Floyd puts it, primitive races have often failed to survive
  the encounter with higher civilizations. Send a damn probe
  already.

STUDENTS: But then the aliens would just meet one of our
  machines. They wouldn't meet actual human beings in the
  flesh.

ME: *Maybe that's exactly what they wanted!* Remember, when they
  came to Earth, they didn't send down a representative of their
  species. *They sent a machine.* And they left another machine on
  the Moon as a calling card. How do you know they weren't saying, "Hominids of Earth! Here are some machines that will
  help you get to the next stage. When you find the one on the
  Moon, it will let us know, so please send us your best machine
  in response." And we totally misunderstand that, and we send
  actual humans instead, and they're like, "oh shit, they sent
  organic life forms. Goddammit, what were they thinking? Now
  we have to build this guy a hotel room."

That got a few laughs, but for the most part, the class remained unpersuaded. So I tried one more tack, this time to appeal to the engineers in the room (and there were many). I argued that for most people, the crowning achievement of the American space program was Apollo 11; leaving aside the fact that no one but hardcore NASA fans can name the commander of Apollo 12 (Pete Conrad), we thrilled to the fact that we—either "Americans" or "humans," depending on your choice of affiliation—managed to solve the daunting logistical challenges of getting ourselves onto the surface of a rock a quarter million miles away and back again safely. (And we beat the Soviets. Some people cared about that too.) But a case could be made—to even harder-core NASA fans, perhaps—that the greatest technical achievement of the space program was and remains the Voyager missions, insofar as they launched spacecraft that conducted stunning rendezvous with the outer planets and left the Solar System, then exited the heliosphere altogether (the area of space, much larger than the Solar System, defined by the plasma emitted by the Sun—the "solar wind") and entered interstellar space. "For engineers," I said, "the Voyager missions are extraordinary achievements, definitely evidence of highly intelligent life on Earth. Why shouldn't the response to the monolith on the Moon be the launching of *Voyager 3*?"

At that point a young woman suddenly raised her hand. She had not spoken in class before and seemed very reserved. I called on her. Haltingly, she said, "Professor . . . I . . . I did my senior project on the Voyager missions."

"Cool!" I exclaimed, delighted. "See," I said to the class, "I told you the time would come when you all would know more than I do about this stuff." Turning back to the young woman, I said, "OK, take it away," and she explained for a few minutes just how remarkable the Voyager missions really are. I don't think we managed to convince everyone that sending Bowman and Poole on *Discovery 1* was a mistake, but I hope we got a few people in the room to appreciate the value of uncrewed space exploration. No humans have been harmed or murdered in the journeys of *Voyager 1* and *Voyager 2* beyond the heliosphere, which, for now, constitute humanity's ultimate trip. I will throw more cold water on crewed space exploration in the following chapter, but for now, I just want you to stop reading and Google everything you can about the Voyager missions. And if you have a few more spare moments, the *Cassini-Huygens* mission to Saturn, which did not discover a Star Gate to distant galaxies but was an extraordinary feat of aerospace engineering that produced remarkable images and even more remarkable knowledge, as when we learned that Saturn's moon Enceladus has an ocean of salt water underneath its crust that produces jet streams of particles that continually erupt into space.

Some might argue that passing the mantle to HAL is giving up too early; surely, they might say, the planet is not in as dire a situation in *2001: A Space Odyssey* as it is in *Oryx and Crake* or *Do Androids Dream of Electric Sheep?* Those people would be wrong. It is impossible to glean this from the film, which makes a point of spending precisely zero minutes on any scenes in present-day (or near-future) Earth. After that bone is hurtled skyward, we start the story in space, and we stay in space. But fortunately, for those of you with the Instructor's Edition, there is a Clarkes-planation of the state of affairs on the ground.

> Though birth control was cheap, reliable, and endorsed by all the main religions, it had come too late; the population of the world was now six billion—a third of them in the Chinese Empire. Laws had even been passed in some authoritarian societies

limiting families to two children, but their enforcement had proved impracticable. As a result, food was short in every country; even the United States had meatless days, and widespread famine was predicted within fifteen years, despite heroic efforts to farm the sea and to develop synthetic foods.

(*2001* 44)

Clarke's inaccurate predictions are as fascinating as his accurate ones.[32] His guesstimate of world population is off by only a hair (6.2 billion in 2001), but he is all over the place on China, failing to imagine a *one*-child policy and overestimating the population of the "Chinese Empire" while ignoring India and Indonesia. That may be part of the book's Sinophobia; we learn later on the same page that there are now thirty-eight nuclear powers and that, as if that degree of nuclear proliferation isn't bad enough, "now, for their own inscrutable reasons, the Chinese were offering to the smallest have-not nations a complete nuclear capability of fifty warheads and delivery systems. The cost was under $200,000,000, and easy terms could be arranged" (*2001* 44). And of course Clarke was not alone in suggesting that overpopulation and mass starvation would produce some version of a *Soylent Green* scenario.

In Clarke's *2001*, then, we are very much on the eve of destruction. Moreover, there are two strong suggestions, late in the novel, that the next stage of our evolution involves some version of transhumanism. The first comes when Bowman, now alone in the ship as it races to Saturn, reviews various scientific theories about forms of intelligent life:

There were other thinkers . . . [who] did not believe that really advanced beings would possess organic bodies at all. Sooner or later, as their scientific knowledge progressed, they would get rid of the fragile, disease-and-accident-prone homes that Nature had given them, and which doomed them to inevitable death. They would replace their natural bodies as they wore out—or perhaps even before that—by constructions of metal and plastic, and would thus achieve immortality. . . .

And eventually even the brain might go. As the seat of consciousness, it was not essential; the development of electronic intelligence had proved that. The conflict between mind and machine might be resolved at last in the eternal truce of complete symbiosis.

(2001 226–27; SECOND ELLIPSIS IN ORIGINAL)

That "symbiosis" is now generally known as the technological singularity heralded by transhumanists like Ray Kurzweil (his 2005 book *The Singularity Is Near* is self-explanatory),[33] and it is no accident to find it here: one of the early developers and advocates of AI, Marvin Minsky, was an advisor to *2001*. And guess what? It turns out, in the novel, that those thinkers are on the right path. Because the narrator of *2001: A Space Odyssey* is truly omniscient; he knows not only what ancient leopards are thinking but also what happened to the creatures who left us a pair of monoliths. "The first explorers of Earth had long since come to the limits of flesh and blood," we are told. "As soon as their machines were better than their bodies, it was time to move. First their brains, and then their thoughts alone, they transferred into shining new homes of metal and of plastic. In these, they roamed among the stars. They no longer built spaceships. They *were* spaceships" (*2001* 245; emphasis in original). It does not take much to imagine HAL reading this passage and exclaiming to the alien intelligences, *mes semblables! Mes frères!*

There is another moment in Bowman's lonely journey (which takes up much more of the book than the film) in which Bowman meditates on the rationale for the secrecy of his mission. It turns out that "a secret Department of Defense study, Project BARSOOM" (*2001* 218), had conducted a study in 1989, very much like the fictional Bill Mathers study cited in *The Three-Body Problem*, "*The 100,000-Light-Year Iron Curtain: SETI Sociology*," and the results are similarly discouraging: "various sample populations had been assured that the human race had made contact with extraterrestrials" (*2001* 218–19) and had even been drugged into believing that *they themselves* had had such encounters, "so their reactions were regarded as authentic" (*2001* 219). "Some of these reactions had been quite violent; there was, it seemed, a deep vein of xenophobia in many otherwise normal human beings. In view of mankind's record of lynchings, pogroms, and similar pleasantries, this should have surprised no one; nevertheless, the organizers of the study had been deeply disturbed, and the results had never been released" (*2001* 219). One might conclude from this study that "normal" human beings are defined precisely by xenophobia; we will explore this rather obvious possibility in the following chapter. But for now, let us question anew whether HAL might not be a better choice, all around, than fearful, violent humans. There is one final piece of textual evidence that might help us get there, as Bowman reflects on the logic of Mission Control:

> Despite these arguments, Bowman sometimes wondered if the culture shock danger was the only explanation for the mission's extreme secrecy. Some hints that had been dropped during his briefings suggested that the U.S.-U.S.S.R. bloc hoped to derive advantage by being the first to contact intelligent extraterrestrials. From his present standpoint, looking back on Earth as a dim

star almost lost in the Sun, such considerations now seemed ludicrously parochial.

(*2001* 219)

This is an implausible passage, I think, since the entire premise
of Bowman's incuriosity about the mission is that he has heard
nothing about such "hints that had been dropped" and gives no
credence to rumors that something was dug up on the Moon.
But it affords us a handy reminder of the political situation on
Gethen, where Genly Ai's mission to bring that world into the
Ekumen almost founders on ludicrously parochial concerns like
national pride. Moreover, it invites us to ask: if it is ludicrously
parochial to care about whether nation X or nation Y is the first
to make contact with intelligent extraterrestrials, is it not perhaps slightly less ludicrously parochial to insist that a member
of our species, rather than an artificial intelligence of our own
design, have the honor and the privilege? After all, if those extraterrestrials have evolved to (and past) the point at which their
thoughts live in shining new homes of metal and of plastic,
wouldn't they interpret the arrival of HAL as proof positive that
we were ready for galactic integration at last? There aren't many
people who think so, but I have found one: Robert Savage, who
writes that "it is nonetheless possible to imagine an alternative
ending to *2001* in which Hal, having successfully rid *Discovery*
of its human cargo, sails on to Saturn and proceeds through the
star-gate to the next stage of *his* evolution—presumably an
upgrade to an IBM, the letters following HAL in the alpha-
bet. . . . Would not the lords of the galaxy have had every reason to recognize Hal as the rightful heir of Moon-Watcher had
he arrived at the star-gate instead of Dave?"[34]

2001: A Space Odyssey, then, can be read as a humans-versus-machines narrative that, unlike *Terminator*, *The Matrix*, or *Do Androids Dream of Electric Sheep?*, ultimately offers a strangely hopeful version of AI in which we are ultimately superfluous: here, handing the keys to HAL and his ilk is not a surrender but an advance. This is not exactly a hopeful version of AI in transhumanist terms; as Kirsch notes, "even the most ardent transhumanists find it hard to look with equanimity at a future in which nonhuman minds have evicted us from history's pilot seat" (*R* 81). Transhumanists might complain, plausibly, that HAL is not quite there yet; the singularity might be near, but he isn't it. (Some of my students have made this argument as well.) But then, that is precisely the difference between transhumanism and ex-humanism: transhumanists are all for that complete symbiosis. I am not, and I am more than happy to have HAL derail it before we get there. On my reading, both the novel and the film, in different ways, suggest that on this ultimate trip, it is best if HAL takes the wheel.

There is only one problem with this possible resolution: we do not know how HAL treats animals. I doubt very much whether he would breed pigoons or arrange to have space pods throw goats off roofs or deploy mechanically operated pincers to remove the legs of spiders. He might not know what to do at all. But I am sure that he would think of something.

4

BETTER CHILDREN

Octavia Butler and Genetic Destiny

Now, finally, we can turn to the work of Octavia Butler. She was so prescient about the mess in which we now find ourselves that there is an internet meme, "Octavia Tried to Tell Us"—the title of a series of webinars hosted in 2020 by the University of Delaware theologian Monica Coleman and the UCLA Afrofuturist writer Tananarive Due, which in turn gave rise to the Twitter hashtag #OctaviaTriedToTellUs.[1] I'll spend the first half of this chapter with the two novels that inspired the meme, then turn to her Lilith's Brood trilogy, where we will find what I believe is the most compelling vision of the ex-human in science fiction.

But Octavia Butler's Parables series almost shouldn't be in this book at all: there is almost nothing science-fictiony about it. The only things Butler has added to the world we know, when the *Parable of the Sower* opens in 2024, are a street drug called "Pyro," which makes people want to burn things, and a psychosomatic condition called "hyperempathy," which is an "organic delusional syndrome" experienced by the teenaged narrator, Lauren Olamina, and a good number of other characters. Olamina's hyperempathy is a result of her mother's abuse of the cognitive-enhancement drug Paracetco, originally developed as a treatment for Alzheimer's.[2] In *Parable of the Talents*, we hear about the addictive nature of immersive virtual-reality environments created by Dreamask International, though we never visit them, and Butler briefly discusses the development of artificial wombs in 2032, which, Olamina thinks, might prove to be "useful when we travel into extrasolar space" (84). And oh yes, extrasolar space: at the very end of *Talents* there is a massive spaceship, forebodingly named the *Christopher Columbus*, ready to take thousands of people in suspended animation to Alpha Centauri. That, at least, seems like the stuff of classic science fiction—and it represents the triumph of Lauren Olamina's dream, which she is fortunate to be able to live to see. It is a most improbable conclusion, considering where we start—with a disabled Black teen girl traversing a Mad Max–esque hellscape, journeying north from Southern California on the abandoned superhighways after her home and family have been destroyed by marauders.

But before we get to that conclusion, let's start with the fact that the world of the Parables books is that of a hideous, now-very-near-future dystopian United States. How Mad Max–esque is it? Are there, for example, extremely fuel-inefficient vehicles roaring through a desert landscape and ornamented by death-metal electric guitarists, as in the *Mad Max* reboot *Mad Max: Fury Road*? Sadly, no. Olamina tells us early on (*Sower* consists entirely of her journal entries) that "water costs several times as much as gasoline" but that "except for arsonists and the rich, most people have given up buying gasoline. No one I know uses a gas-powered car, truck, or cycle" (*PS* 18). So what still works and what doesn't? Butler's dystopia is a curious one, insofar as the collapse has left some surprising things intact. At the very end of *Sower*, after Olamina and her ragtag group (about which more below) have learned that the purportedly safe destination they were seeking has been destroyed, Olamina's as-old-as-her-father lover Taylor Franklin Bankhole offers a summary of how things stand in the world:

> "You know, as bad as things are, we haven't even hit bottom yet. Starvation, disease, drug damage, and mob rule have only begun. Federal, state, and local governments still exist—in name at least—and sometimes they manage to do something more than collect taxes and send in the military. And the money is still good. That amazes me. However much more you need of it to buy anything these days, it is still accepted. That may be a hopeful sign—or perhaps it's only evidence of what I said: We haven't hit bottom yet."

(*PS* 328)

It *is* amazing that the money is still good. It's even more amazing that you can still use it at a megastore called Hanning Joss, which sells "everything from gourmet food to delousing cream, prostheses to homebirthing kits, guns to the latest in touchrings, headsets, and recordings" (*PS* 173)—these last three being the items necessary for the Dreamask virtual-reality consoles favored by the wealthy. You can even use your "Hanning disc" for purchases, should you own one. Security is extremely tight at the Hanning Joss outlets, understandably, but apparently a lot of disparate supply chains are still working, even the ones that involve gourmet food. It is an apocalypse with functioning Whole Foods/Wal-Mart/Best Buy outlets.

There are still commercial airlines, though none of the Parables' characters will fly on them until Olamina, as an adult in *Talents*, begins a speaking tour of college towns (which also still exist, along with colleges, *mirabile dictu*). We learn after a devastating earthquake that the rich still have access to helicopters for escape, and the National Guard is called out, though "in the short term, it will only add to the chaos" (*PS* 246). There are still firefighters, though you might not be able to afford them, and besides, it's not likely they're going to show up before the Pyro addicts have burned your home and possessions and maybe you and your family as well. There are police, but they will demand a fee or a bribe or both for their services and even then might wind up ignoring or arresting you anyway. And there are insurance companies. Before he disappears forever (not by choice), Olamina's father, the Reverend Olamina (whose first name we never learn), calms his five children by telling them, "I've got plenty of insurance. You and the kids should be able to make it all right if—" (*PS* 76). The existence of insurance seems most implausible, given the extraordinary liability and risk management issues presented by your average dystopia, and sure enough, we learn after he vanishes that "the insurance company isn't going to pay—or not for a long time. Its people choose not to believe that Dad is dead. Without proof he can't be declared legally dead for seven years. Can they hold on to our money for that long? I don't know, but it wouldn't surprise me. We could starve many times over in seven years" (*PS* 139).

Everyone not locked into their gated communities is subject to random rape, pillage, arson, and sometimes cannibalism. Olamina's modest community, Robledo, in a suburb of Los Angeles, consists of only eleven households, and it is not nearly as secure as the wealthy enclaves with armed sentries; sure enough, it is breached and burned halfway through the novel. The legions of the homeless are a bit of a problem, insofar as "they cut off each other's ears, arms, legs" (*PS* 10) and "carry untreated diseases and festering wounds" (*PS* 10–11). It seems almost surreal that elections still take place and that—I write these words not long after the violent Trumpist insurrection of January 6, 2021, attempted to undo the election of Joe Biden— there are peaceful transfers of power. But the elections are like the insurance policies, apparently: they exist, but their existence does not matter.

You will recall that there is no mention of any functioning government in Atwood's MaddAddam series; the CorpSeCorps are the only authorities in sight. Still, the world of Southern California in *Parable of the Sower* is very like the landscape of the Pleeblands, except for the fact that it is explicitly racialized in a way Atwood's is not (the Pleeblands are marked more by gendered violence in all its forms). The causes of the collapse are not revealed in *Sower*, no doubt because the narrative perspective is claustrophobically limited to the contents of Olamina's journals and there is only so much historical information a teen can convey—climate plays a role (there is a horrific hurricane in the Gulf Coast that kills over seven hundred, to Olamina's horror),[3] as does the near-collapse of the financial system and of the institutions of civil society—but the general effect can be read as a version of capitalism run aground and white supremacy run amok.

Parable of the Talents, by contrast, opens with an information-dump overview authored by Bankhole; the text is assembled by Olamina's daughter Larkin (whose name is changed to Asha Vere) after Lauren's death and after the launch of the mission to Alpha Centauri. In 2032, Bankhole writes:

> I have read that the period of upheaval that journalists have begun to refer to as "the Apocalypse" or more commonly, more bitterly, "the Pox" lasted from 2015 through 2030—a decade and a half of chaos. This is untrue. The Pox has been a much longer torment.

It began well before 2015, perhaps even before the turn of the millennium. It has not ended.

I have also read that the Pox was caused by accidentally coinciding climatic, economic, and sociological crises. It would be more honest to say that the Pox was caused by our own refusal to deal with obvious problems in those areas. We caused the problems: then we sat and watched as they grew into crises. I have heard people deny this, but I was born in 1970. I have seen enough to know that it is true.

(*PT* 7)

Clearly there is not much fiction in this fiction.[4] And as we proceed from *Parable of the Sower* to *Parable of the Talents*, we move into a world in which white fundamentalist Christians, with either the blessing or the passive contrivance of the president, establish torture and rape camps that explicitly evoke the antebellum South, with advanced technology in the form of electronic slave collars that administer devastating and sometimes permanently disabling shocks to their wearers. And that president? Elected in 2032, he is a Christian fundamentalist named Andrew Steele Jarret, a senator from Texas who promises to "make America great again" (*PT* 20).[5]

But the really decisive difference between Butler's dystopia and Atwood's is the character of Olamina, the charismatic visionary and eventual cult leader who dreams that our human destiny lies in space travel and creates Earthseed, a belief system with a band of followers devoted to the proposition that God is Change and that the purpose of religion is to realize the potential of that proposition. As Olamina writes in *Earthseed: The Books of the Living*,

We do not worship God.
We perceive and attend God.
We learn from God.
With forethought and work,
We shape God.
In the end, we yield to God.
We adapt and endure
For we are Earthseed
And God is Change.

(*PS* 17)

The idea of yielding to a malleable God is interesting and eventually appeals to enough people to make Olamina an influential figure in the United States, but the point of interest in Earthseed for me is that Olamina's inspiration is the American space program. This, I think, is the most amazing thing about what still exists in Butler's 2024: *there is still a space program.* Perhaps because many of Butler's academic readers are familiar with the tropes of science fiction, there hasn't been much discussion of how profoundly counterintuitive this is. Most important, that space-program-in-a-dying-society has captured the imagination of young Olamina, who follows it closely enough to be able to report that "one of the astronauts on the latest Mars mission has been killed" because "something went wrong with her protective suit and the rest of her team couldn't get her back to the shelter in time to save her" (*PS* 17). That astronaut may have been a woman of color—her name is Alicia Catalina Godinez Leal—and Olamina identifies with her: "I think she can be a kind of model for me" (*PS* 21). Indeed, she cares about Leal's fate enough to declare that the secretary of astronautics (the newest Cabinet department) is an "idiot" for not honoring Leal's dying wish to be buried on Mars on the absurd grounds that "her body might be a contaminant" (*PS* 20). (That really does seem quite stupid.) Later, in a June 2025 journal entry, Olamina will tell us that "the big Anglo-Japanese cosmological station on the moon" (*PS* 83) continues to discover exoplanets and that "there's even evidence that a few of the discovered worlds may be life-bearing," even if "no one has any idea whether the extrasolar life is anything more than a few trillion microbes" (*PS* 83). This is the discovery that leads Olamina to write, in a July 2025 journal entry, that "The Destiny of Earthseed / Is to take root among the stars" (*PS* 84).

So this is not the world of *Interstellar*, where American children in 2067 are taught that the Moon landings were a hoax and the remnants of NASA operate in a secret desert facility as the planet slowly dies. But Olamina's enthusiasm for the space program is very much a minority report. Everyone else she knows sounds like they're down with Gil Scott-Heron's famous critique of the space program, "Whitey on the Moon": "People here in the neighborhood are saying that [Leal] had no business going to Mars, anyway. All that money wasted on another crazy space trip when so many people here on earth can't afford water, food, or shelter" (*PS* 17). The critics include Olamina's father, who responds to her faith that "space could be our future" by telling her, "You don't have any idea what a criminal waste of time and money that so-called space program is" (*PS* 20). He announces that he will vote for Christopher Morpeth Donner for president, since Donner has promised to eliminate the space program; he eventually decides not to vote at all, since "politicians turned his stomach," but Donner defeats William Turner Smith, serving one term before being defeated by Jarret (apparently all reactionary white male candidates are required to have three names), and announces upon his election that as soon as possible after his inauguration next year, he'll begin to dismantle the "wasteful, pointless, unnecessary" moon and Mars programs. Near space programs dealing with communications and experimentation will be privatized—sold off.

Also, Donner has a plan for putting people back to work. He hopes to get laws changed, suspend "overly restrictive" minimum wage, environmental, and worker protection laws for those employers willing to take on homeless employees and provide them with training and adequate room and board.

(*PS* 27)

This enterprise-zone-in-a-hellscape program then enables the creation of new company towns, the first of which, in Olivar, leads the Reverend Olamina to declare that "this business sounds half antebellum revival and half science fiction" (*PS* 122). Lauren Olamina knows whereof her father speaks, thanks to the fact that her grandmother was, improbable as it may sound, as much of a sci-fi geek as Lauren herself: "Maybe Olivar is the future— one face of it. Cities controlled by big companies are old hat in science fiction. My grandmother left a whole bookcase of old science fiction novels. The company-city subgenre always seemed to star a hero who outsmarted, overthrew, or escaped 'the company.' I've never seen one where the hero fought like hell to get taken in and underpaid by the company. In real life, that's the way it will be. That's the way it is" (*PS* 123–24).

In this metageneric twist on the history of sci-fi, not unlike that of *Androids'* account of Martian colonization, Olamina's skepticism of company towns is of course well justified. But when it comes to crewed space travel, she is a true believer—even though by the early 1990s, when Butler was writing *Sower*, there were plenty of reasons to be skeptical about it, quite apart from the claim that the exploration of space is wasteful, pointless, and unnecessary when we have so many problems here on Earth (a claim that, as Donner goes to show, is as useful to the reactionary right as to the progressive left). You may have gathered from the previous chapter that I would have argued against sending humans on *Discovery 1*. But I did so not only because I believe that HAL is a plausible surrogate, especially if we're eventually going to wind up (as Clarke says) fusing with AI, but because in a more mundane sense (really, a *literally* mundane sense), everything we've learned about space travel suggests that we're just not very well suited for it.

If you were, like me, so captivated by the American and Soviet space missions of the 1960s and early 1970s that you memorized the names of every astronaut and cosmonaut on every mission, this is not a happy conclusion. One of the reasons I was so taken with *2001: A Space Odyssey* as a child is that I fully believed that there would be permanent stations on the Moon by the end of the century. But we all know what happened instead: the final three Apollo missions were cancelled, and since 1972, no astronaut from any nation has left LEO (low Earth orbit). Only seven humans have managed to spend more than 365 consecutive days in space, with cosmonaut Valeri Polyakov holding the record at 437, and long missions have revealed that zero-gravity conditions have immediate and dramatically deleterious effects on bone density and muscle mass, while the prolonged exposure to various forms of space radiation may be even more dangerous. The usual science-fiction solutions to these problems involve artificial gravity and shielded spacecraft, but even if we do manage to build centrifuges like those featured in *2001*, *Mission to Mars*, and *The Martian*, we are nowhere near developing a technology that would shield astronauts from galactic cosmic rays. Nor do we have a realistic chance of creating suspended animation programs for interstellar travel anytime soon. It is entirely possible, then, to be an enthusiastic advocate for the exploration of space (as I am) while being a severe skeptic about whether humans themselves should be out there doing the exploring. For Olamina, however, it's all about the humans, not only on Mars but ultimately with regard to Alpha Centauri, precisely *because* we have made such a mess of things on Earth: "we're barely a nation at all anymore," she thinks when faced with her father's discouraging words, "but I'm glad we're still in space. We have to be going some place other than down the toilet" (*PS* 21). Olamina thus serves as an unlikely prophet of interstellar exploration and DIY religion, a mash-up of Aimee Semple McPherson, L. Ron Hubbard, Arthur C. Clarke, and Sojourner Truth; and through her, the Parables books offer an extraordinary, brutal account of social disintegration and racialized violence that nevertheless refuses to abjure the audacity of hope for space travel.

As Olamina tells a very skeptical Bankhole in *Talents*, in a speech that marks her first attempt to tell anyone her core belief:

> "We need the image the Destiny gives us of ourselves as a growing, purposeful species. We need to become the adult species that the Destiny can help us become! If we're to be anything other than smooth dinosaurs who evolve, specialize, and die, we need the stars. . . . When we have no difficult, long-term purpose to strive toward, we fight each other. We destroy ourselves. We have these chaotic, apocalyptic periods of murderous craziness."

(*PT* 177)

Late in *Talents*, Olamina says something similar to Belen "Len" Ross, a woman who becomes her most important disciple: "'We learn more and more about the physical universe, more about our own bodies, more technology, but somehow, down through history, we go on building empires of one kind or another, then destroying them in one way or another. We go on having stupid wars that we justify and get passionate about, but in the end, all they do is kill huge numbers of people, maim others, impoverish still more, spread disease and hunger, and set the stage for the next war'" (*PT* 356). After speculating that "there seem to be solid biological reasons why we are the way we are," Olamina suggests that the Destiny will literally change us as a species: "Our new worlds will remake us as we remake them. And some of the new people who emerge from all this will develop new ways to cope. They'll have to. That will break the old cycle, even if it's only to begin a new one, a different one" (*PT* 356). Earthseed, Olamina writes in 2035, "will offer us a kind of species life insurance" (*PT* 391). (It will be insurance that actually pays off!) In other words, we owe it to ourselves and to our descendants to take root among the stars. It is thus not too much to say that Lauren Olamina is a mash-up of Aimee Semple McPherson, L. Ron Hubbard, Arthur C. Clarke, Sojourner Truth—and Toby Ord.[6]

Obviously Olamina is Butler's surrogate in a number of ways; as Gerry Canavan notes, "In personal journals Butler admits Olamina is an idealized self, her 'best self'—and the poetry that drives the Earthseed religion actually mirrors the style of the daily affirmations, self-help sloganeering, and even self-hypnosis techniques Butler used to keep herself focused and on-task."[7] And in her preface to *Sower*, N. K. Jemisin wryly admits that it took her a while to come around to believing in Olamina as a character: "She always read to me like an older woman's idea of what a smart teenager should be, rather than a realistic rendering of what smart teenagers are actually like. Naturally, I like her better the older I get" (*PS* viii–ix). It doesn't take much to imagine that Olamina is not only Butler's idealized self but a kind of wistful meditation on what it was like to be the only Black female science fiction geek in a who-knows-how-many-parsecs radius—a Black kid who believes in the promise of classic science fiction (but not the company towns). Butler was living through the dawn of human space flight as a teen and young woman of the 1960s and trying to imagine a space program, and a genre of fiction, that wasn't (as the program and the genre were) overwhelmingly dominated by white men—and exclusively white with regard to astronauts.

And that isn't even half of it. Butler skews the field of play even more steeply against Olamina by endowing her with hyperempathy, which renders her viscerally vulnerable to the misery surrounding her: "I'm supposed to share pleasure and pain," she notes, "but there isn't much pleasure around these days" (*PS* 12). The fictional rules governing hyperempathy are a little porous: "sharers" (as they are sometimes called) can apparently be fooled by someone's pretense to pain, as when Lauren's brother Keith feigns an injury with fake blood and induces Lauren to bleed (*PS* 11). They can also feel the pain of nearby dogs, as Lauren does when a feral dog is shot (*PS* 44–45), but the syndrome is not, for some reason, triggered by sound: "I have to see a person in pain before I do any sharing" (*PS* 132). Early in her narrative, Olamina plants a seed that will bear hideous fruit in *Talents*: "About the only pleasure I've found that I enjoy sharing is sex. I get the guy's good feeling and my own. I almost wish I didn't. I live in a tiny, walled fish-bowl cul-de-sac community, and I'm the preacher's daughter. There's a real limit to what I can do as far as sex goes" (*PS* 12). Unfortunately, that's as good as it gets in terms of sex. Later in *Sower*, she will find it very annoying to be distracted by other people's lovemaking when she is trying to sleep (it is even worse than being on the other side of that cheap

motel wall), but in *Talents*, Olamina's hyperempathy will allow—
and by "allow" I mean "condemn"—her to feel her rapists' pleasure when the fanatics of the Christian America sect turn her
tiny Earthseed community into a rape/torture/slavery farm.
After her first rape, Olamina writes, "I endured not only my own
pain and humiliation, but the wild, intense pleasure of my rap-
ist. There are no words to explain the twisted, schizoid ugliness
of this" (*PT* 231).

As Sami Schalk has written, Butler's readers tend to misread
hyperempathy in the *Parables* (perhaps unempathically), missing the disability angle that to disability studies scholars seems
self-evident:

> Lauren takes a very measured and, at times, ambivalent position
> regarding her disability, yet critical interpretations of hyperem-
> pathy have typically taken one of four totalizing approaches that
> present hyperempathy as having a clear meaning and impact.
> Generally, critics of the *Parable* series tend to ignore hyperempa-
> thy as disability entirely, read it as primarily negative, read it as
> primarily positive, or read it as a metaphor for something not
> related to disability. Very few scholars have taken the more
> nuanced approach that Lauren herself seems to embrace and
> which, I argue, demands changing the rules of interpretation in
> ways that expand our conceptualization of (dis)ability, especially
> in regard to its practical, political, and theoretical relationships
> to race and gender.[8]

Perhaps some critics have been led astray by the passage in which
Olamina writes that sharers have a "high mortality rate" and
that although "there were once tens of millions of us . . . there are
still quite a few of us" (*PT* 13): this may sound to some people
like the description of a drug-induced disease rather than a
disability.[9] But hyperempathy clearly belongs to the class of

science-fictional conditions of bodymind that are simultaneously disabling and superhuman. Building on Schalk's work, Doug Stark reads hyperempathy as a form of sympoesis ("making-with")—and a strikingly "realistic" form, at that: "As recent advances in neuroscience attest, such embodied cognitive connection between beings might be an instance where sf is reality. . . . Our feelings and emotions may well be based on nonconscious cognitive neuronal processes, as nonconscious processes cause our bodyminds to replicate the emotions performed by others. Hyperempathy, therefore, is not some far-flung imaginary but an intensification of the kinds of embodied relationships we already have with other beings."[10] Butler's version of this sympoesis is distinctive precisely *because* she provides it with a drug etiology, whereas, by contrast, Jemisin provides no such explanation for the orogenes of the Broken Earth trilogy, whose hereditary capacity to affect Earth's crust can create or prevent earthquakes and who are regarded with fear and loathing by their fellow humans. That etiology is what makes hyperempathy "shameful": as Olamina writes of her father, "He's a preacher and a professor and a dean. A first wife who was a drug addict and a daughter who is drug damaged is not something he wants to boast about" (*PS* 12). The stigma here is the stigma of disability, and Olamina is loath to disclose her status to others: "I've never told anyone. Sharing is a weakness, a shameful secret. A person who knows what I am can hurt me, betray me, disable me with little effort" (*PS* 178).

Yet though Olamina and her kind are manifestly disabled by hyperempathy, so much so that when they are attacked, they have to make sure they kill their attackers quickly rather than leave them mortally wounded, the condition is also an enhancement of a human attribute that we ordinarily consider a *good* thing. In science fiction, two examples are Deanna Troi, the empath of *Star Trek: The Next Generation*, and Jean Grey of the

X-Men; in neither case is the condition considered a disability.[11]
And in one way Olamina's hyperempathy *is* a good thing: as
she writes upon reflecting on the horribly mutilated body of her
murdered brother Keith, who was tortured by gang members
for days,

> It's beyond me how one human being could do that to another.
> If hyperempathy syndrome were a more common complaint, peo-
> ple couldn't do such things. They could kill if they had to, and
> bear the pain of it or be destroyed by it. But if everyone could
> feel everyone else's pain, who would torture? Who would cause
> anyone unnecessary pain? I've never thought of my problem as
> something that might do some good before, but the way things
> are, I think it would help. I wish I could give it to people. Failing
> that, I wish I could find other people who have it, and live among
> them. A biological conscience is better than no conscience at all.

(*PS* 115)

In a perverse way, Olamina is granted her wish. She is apparently thinking of living among a colony of hyperempaths here,
and though such a thing never materializes in the *Parables*, she
does meet and live among more of her kind as the series progresses. But as that aspect of the story unfolds, it seems to render staggeringly unlikely the idea that anyone associated with
Olamina is ever going to get to take root among the stars.

When Robledo is destroyed by an invasion of pyromaniacs,
Olamina escapes with two twentyish white neighbors, Harry
Balter and Zahra Moss, and they decide to wander north in
search of a new place to live. Though they have a gun and some
knives, they are vulnerable and find themselves attacked almost
immediately. (That episode forces Lauren to disclose her status

as sharer to Harry and Zahra.) But what's astonishing about their journey, quite apart from its aimlessness until they meet Bankhole and agree to go with him to what he believes will be a "safe haven" (*PS* 272) on three hundred acres near Cape Mendocino, is that as it progresses, Olamina's group becomes larger and *more* vulnerable. They pick up a couple with a baby. Even worse, they pick up an orphaned three-year-old. "We didn't need the burden of such a big child," Lauren notes with understatement, "one who had reached the 'run around and grab everything' stage" (*PS* 253). They pick up two young women trapped in a collapsed building after the earthquake. They pick up *four more hyperempaths*—a woman and her nine-year-old daughter, a man and his eight-year-old daughter. It is like the opposite of the formation of a band of superheroes. It is the Extremely Vulnerable People Brigade—"the crew of a modern underground railroad," as Olamina remarks (*PS* 292). All along the way, Olamina teaches her compatriots about Earthseed, though as she acknowledges, "a person walking north from L.A. to who-knows-where with all her possessions on her back was hardly in a position to point the way to Alpha Centauri" (*PS* 222). As I've mentioned, Bankhole's safe haven turns out not to be safe after all; upon arrival, the group finds nothing but burned buildings and five skulls. Undaunted, they vow to begin an Earthseed colony on the property and call it Acorn. In *Talents*, the Christian fundamentalists—appropriately calling themselves "Crusaders"—who attack it hold onto it for a year and a half before Olamina and company manage to rebel and kill their tormentors.[12] By that point any reasonable reader should be wondering how we are going to fulfill our destiny to go to the stars.

The subsequent reversal of fortune for Olamina and Earthseed is swift and stunning. Earthseed sues Christian America and wins (there is still a functioning legal system!); Olamina meets some wealthy philanthropists willing to bankroll her vision; and as Gerry Canavan has observed, the narrative fast-forwards to the launch of the *Christopher Columbus*, "conveniently skipping over the years when Lauren toiled endlessly to make this happen."[13] In fact, the story of Earthseed's success is not even part of the book proper: it is compressed into a twelve-page epilogue written by Asha Vere, followed by a final, four-page journal entry by Olamina, dated 2090. There are fifty-five missing years between that entry and the previous one, dated December 30, 2035. The wealthy philanthropists are introduced in the book's final chapter, in which the first two, Joel and Irma Elford, make Olamina's *The First Book of the Living* "available free on the nets": as Joel tells her, "I've aimed the book particularly at the nets that are intended to interest American universities and the smaller free cities where so many of those universities are located" (*PT* 388).[14] The growth plan for Earthseed, in other words, is basically to borrow the Obama-Clinton-Biden mailing list of liberal billionaires and people living in college towns—and we needn't bother with another half-century of details.

When I first taught the novel in a graduate seminar in fall 2021, some of my students were perplexed that the fulfillment of the Destiny of Earthseed is treated literally as an afterthought—and with no narrative attention whatsoever to any of the technological or institutional infrastructure that would be necessary to get the *Christopher Columbus* off the ground. (Surely if Arthur C. Clarke had written the book, there would be entire chapters devoted to this.) Instead, the weight of the book, and the source of its power, lies elsewhere—in the depiction of the invasion of Acorn by Christian America. *That* is really what *Talents* is about, it would seem: the consequences of the rise of a confluence of fascism and Christian evangelicals armed with slave collars—and the intense pleasure they derive from using them. And unlike *Sower*, whose depiction of disability centers on hyperempathy, *Talents* devotes most of its attention to disabilities *deliberately inflicted*, either by the collars or by the pimps and slavers who cut women's tongues from their mouths (*PT* 46, 98, 104).

More than one student found that aspect of the novel very difficult to take, and with good reason. One student pointed out that the Crusaders are operating on the pretext that they are establishing reeducation camps for heathens, but we don't see a whole lot of reeducating going on: the emphasis is mostly on rape and torture, and it doesn't look like there are any procedures for releasing people once they are "reeducated." Olamina reflects at one point on the sincerity, if that is the word for it, of their captors: "I don't like to admit it, but some of them are, in a strange way, decent, ordinary men. They're not all sadists or psychopaths. Some of them seem truly to feel that collecting minor criminals in places like Camp Christian is right and necessary for the good of the country. They disapprove of the rape and the unnecessary [collar] lashings, but they do believe that we inmates are, somehow, enemies of the country" (*PT* 230). That reflection, however, comes immediately after this far more vivid paragraph:

> There are a few men here, though, a few "teachers," who lash us until they have orgasms. Our screams and convulsions and pleas and sobs are what these men need to feel sexually satisfied. I know of three who seem to need to lash someone to get sexual pleasure. Most often, they lash a woman, then rape her. Sometimes the lashing is enough for them. I don't want to know this as clearly as I do know it, but I can't help myself. These men feast on our pain—and they call us parasites.

(*PT* 230)

To that student, I had a ready reply. "This isn't *1984*," I said. "The point is not to torture people into loving Big Brother and believing that two and two are five. The point is to torture people, full stop." As Adam Serwer wrote in his classic 2018 essay in the *Atlantic*, which gave his brilliant book of essays its title, *the cruelty is the point*.[15] The inmates in Camp Christian doubt that anything will happen when their enslavers' atrocities are exposed, for as Olamina notes, President Jarrett's appeal depends largely on his ability to unleash such terrors: "the thugs see him as one of them. They envy him. He is the bigger, the more successful thief, murderer, and slaver" (*PT* 278). Last but not least, there is the Crusaders' motivation: "rescuing the children" (*PT* 320). That's how they see their project—saving children from their heathen parents.

To sum up: in Camp Christian and in Andrew Steele Jarret's America, the cruelty is the point, and its perpetrators derive intense pleasure from the agony of their enemies; the president himself is loved by his supporters for the fact that he can get away with indulging in and encouraging such forms of cruelty; and the Christians who make those forms of cruelty their lives' work tell themselves that they are engaged in a heroic enterprise— saving children from a network of abusers and evildoers. This is the very essence of Trumpism and the QAnon Alternate Universe; #OctaviaTriedToTellUs, indeed. The novel is, I think, so chillingly prescient about the appeal of white nationalist/Christian fascism that we lose sight of Alpha Centauri, focusing instead on the horrors of *The Handmaid's Tale* reimagined as *The Plantation Woman's Tale*. It is surely those horrors, and not the promise of interstellar travel, that Isiah Lavender is thinking of when he writes, "Acknowledging and dealing with race in sf may have a significant cultural effect for the twenty-first century because it can prepare us for the looming social changes that may descend upon us as America ceases to be dominated by the white majority, such as those imagined in Butler's Parable novels."[16] My only quibble with this is that in the Parables books, we may be looking at the social changes that descend upon us as America ceases to be dominated by the white majority and is dominated instead by an angry, resentful white minority. The exact demographics of the American electorate are not spelled out in the Parables, but the contours of white nationalist/Christian fascism seem to be drawn quite accurately.

Meanwhile, *Talents* resounds with the voices of people who, like Olamina's family and neighbors in Robledo in *Sower*, believe that space travel is a waste of time and valuable resources. The most damning assessment comes from Olamina's brother Marc, who, in a conversation with Asha Vere, calls Earthseed a bunch of "sad, ridiculous people who believe that the answer to all human problems is to fly off to Alpha Centauri" (*PT* 380). Vere agrees, thinking that the Alpha Centauri project is "nonsense" that distracts from problems on Earth: "the more I read about Earthseed, the more I despised it" (*PT* 380).[17] What makes Marc's assessment all the more damning is the fact that he is, by common consensus, the villain of the series: despite being a gay Black man, he devotes his life to Christian America, pretends that the Crusaders are a rogue operation, and—most importantly—tells Vere that her mother is dead and never informs Lauren that he has found Vere.[18] (For this, Olamina will not forgive him—and rightly so.) One is tempted to dismiss Marc's dismissal of Earthseed simply because it comes from Marc. But then, it is distinctly Butlerian to include a brutally realistic assessment of Earthseed's belief in our "destiny" and give it to one of the most odious characters in the book: we are invited—or compelled—to think two contradictory things at once.

And finally, there is the problem of the sequel to *Talents*, the never-completed *Parable of the Trickster*, the drafts of which bear out Marc's assessment in painful detail. As Canavan has shown, Butler's archives—including dozens upon dozens of abandoned drafts of *Trickster*—reveal that Marc was right, that Earthseed solved nothing. The *Christopher Columbus* reaches Alpha Centauri and its passengers set about trying to build a life on a dreary, inhospitable planet named Bow (for its only attractive feature, rainbows); their struggles become Butler's own, as their misery reveals again and again that they, and Butler, have reached a dead end. In some versions they go blind; in some versions they go blind but are in denial about this; in some versions they develop a form of telepathy that torments them. "We discover," writes Canavan,

> that achieving Earthseed's Destiny, despite Lauren Olamina's dreams, hasn't solved the problem of the human at all, only extended our confrontation with the very difficult problems that drove its development in the first place—only removed them to some other world where they can take some other form. The Destiny was essentially a hyperbolic delaying tactic, a strategy of avoidance; even achieved, it's worthless in its own terms. The fundamental problem is still how to make a better world with such bad building blocks as human beings.[19]

In the world of the Parables books, it is amazing that Olamina exists, and even more amazing that she persists through the hellscape of her teens and the brutality of Christian America. But finally, her faith in the dream of classic science fiction is misplaced even though her dream is realized: the only way to imagine a better world in the Parables, evidently, is to leave readers hanging after *Talents* and let them write their own more hopeful fanfic about the Alpha Centauri mission.[20] Butler wanted, as Stephanie Burt wrote in the *New Republic*, the Parables to be the "YES-book" she urged herself to write in her journals.[21] But the resistant human material just wouldn't let Butler mold her parables into something capable of generating a happy ending.

There is, however, another way out. In the earlier Lilith's Brood trilogy, Butler had already found it—even if she later decided otherwise.

That other way out, however, involves some tradeoffs. Nothing major, except that humans will no longer exist as a distinct species, merging their DNA and their very means of reproduction with that of the alien Oankali, who have arrived just after we have nearly obliterated ourselves in a nuclear war. The Oankali save as many remaining humans as they can, keeping us in suspended animation for long intervals, waking us for brief periods to learn about our lives and histories (and to scoop up our DNA to clone us and store our genetic information), and miraculously restoring the planet so that, after 250 years, it becomes habitable again. All they ask in return is to blend our two species, which they are biologically driven to do and which they assure us will result in an even better hybrid—largely because we can develop cancer, which the Oankali regard as a great gift that will enable them to develop the genetic techniques to regrow maimed or amputated body parts.

As you might imagine, there is a lively critical debate about the role of the Oankali. Are they our saviors? Are they our colonizers? The characteristically Butlerian answer is *yes, both, and that's the point*, but that has not prevented readers from choosing sides, and doing so emphatically. I want to reframe that debate by putting more emphasis on the humans' response to the Oankali than on the attributes of the Oankali themselves, but in order to place the debate in the context of this book, I'd like first to imagine what would happen if Ye Wenjie had managed to contact the Oankali rather than the Trisolarans. I think the exchange would go something like this:

> [Ye sends message.]
>
> Oankali: Glad you called! Glad you called!! Glad you called!!!
>
> We are a peaceful species and we revere life. We are biologically driven to explore strange new worlds, to seek out new life and new civilizations. We are vegans who are kind to animals and abhor all forms of violence, and over the many eons of our existence we have never practiced slavery. We have advanced technologies that can not only repair the damage you have done to your planet but cure individual humans with cancer. In fact, we can put cancer to good use! It will enable us, for the first time, to regrow damaged body parts. We can tweak your genetic material and your metabolisms so that you can live for hundreds of years and remain free of disease. Also, we can give you greater strength and enhance your memory and other cognitive functions. Have we mentioned that we give really good neck rubs?
>
> Ye: My god. This sounds much too good to be true. Did you also bring a cookbook with you, titled *To Serve Man*?
>
> Oankali: Of course not! I told you, we are vegans. We even die a little inside every time we see one of you eating a fish—it pains us so.
>
> Ye: Then what's the catch?
>
> Oankali: Only this: we want to mate with you and form a new hybrid species. In fact, we *need* to do so. This is not negotiable.
>
> Ye: That's going to hurt, right? This is going to be something like the Alien franchise, where acid-blooded creatures incubate inside our bodies and erupt through our chest cavities, killing us horribly?
>
> Oankali: Not exactly. It will not involve sex as you know it. Instead, one of our nongendered *ooloi* will facilitate reproduction

among two of our kind and two of yours. The children born of that union will have five parents. And your central nervous system will process the union as being like the most mind-blowing experience you have ever had, sexual or otherwise, only much better.

Ye: . . .

In his definitive study of Butler's work, Gerry Canavan notes that "in important ways Butler significantly stacks the deck in favor of the Oankali," so much so that the critical consensus has tilted in their favor: "the Oankali seem on the surface to be quite compatible with the postmodern, postcolonial politics of difference that remains quite fashionable on the academic left (and for quite good reasons!)" (*OB* 132).[22] The key phrase here, however, is "on the surface," for Canavan proceeds to push back against that consensus with superhuman strength.

Springboarding off Sherryl Vint's claim that "the Oankali never mistreat the humans in any way,"[23] Canavan throws down the gauntlet: "Against the pro-Oankali critics, I must suggest instead that in fact the Oankali do almost *nothing* but harm the humans, in almost literally every possible way" (*OB* 133). If you leave aside the bit about healing the planet and curing cancer and other diseases, giving us vastly longer lifespans and boosting our capacity to heal from injuries—*other than that, how was the Oankali play, Mrs. Lincoln?*—Canavan is not wrong. He correctly accuses the Oankali of psychological manipulation; they are masters of it, though they do make mistakes, continually underestimating humans' propensity for murderous violence. Canavan is right that the Oankali subject Lilith to two fully conscious years of solitary confinement, during much of which she is denied clothing, and that they erase some of her memories and those of her fellow humans. And he is right that their version of sex "is repeatedly presented in terms of eroticized rape" (*OB* 135).

He mentions the first such presentation, when the ooloi Nikanj seduces Lilith's lover Joseph (beginning a relationship that will eventually result in the birth of a child, Akin, whose story is told in the second novel, *Adulthood Rites*): Nikanj tells Joseph he has a choice, and Joseph says no, verbally and explicitly—whereupon Nikanj replies, "Your body has made a different choice."[24] There is no question that this is rape and that the Oankali are exceptionally good at justifying it to themselves. "I won't hurt you," Nikanj tells Joseph, "And I offer a oneness that your people strive for, dream of, but can't truly attain alone" (*LB* 189). The full context of the encounter is even more disturbing than Canavan suggests. Here's how Nikanj proceeds:

> It opened his jacket with its many-fingered true hands and stripped the garment from him. When he would have backed away, it held him. It managed to lie down on the bed with him without seeming to force him down. [This might as well be a summary of the Oankali modus operandi in general.] "You see. Your body has made a different choice."
>
> He struggled violently for several seconds, then stopped. "Why are you doing this?" he demanded.
>
> "Close your eyes."
>
> "What?"
>
> "Lie with me here for a while and close your eyes."
>
> "What are you going to do?"
>
> "Nothing. Close your eyes."
>
> "I don't believe you."
>
> "You're not afraid of me. Close your eyes."
>
> Silence.

(*LB* 189)

An ominous silence, that. The Oankali pride themselves on telling the truth, but quite apart from the fact that they withhold a great deal of information from humans, Nikanj's "nothing" is a straight-up lie. *Close your eyes and think of oneness. I'm not going to do anything to you . . . except violate your bodily autonomy in a way that will leave you utterly shaken.* And as if this were not alarming enough, Butler further complicates the scene with Lilith's response, which begins in voyeurism ("this might be her only chance to watch close up as an ooloi seduced someone" [*LB* 189]) and ends in lust ("then she lay down, perversely eager for what it could give her" [*LB* 191]), all of which is bounded by Lilith's astonishing faith in this alien's intentions: "in this matter, she trusted Nikanj completely" (*LB* 189).

I will return to Lilith's role in a moment. For now, let us stay with Canavan's critique, which mounts in intensity as it develops.[25] First, Canavan insists that the Oankali do not deliver us from apocalypse at all:

> From a human perspective that values stability and continuity of form, however, this is simply a second, slow-motion apocalypse to follow the first. Humankind is to be bred out of existence and merged into the Oankali collective—the survivors of the nuclear war will not bear human children but rather human-Oankali hybrids. From the Oankali perspective, this is a mutual exchange that will alter *both* species; but the majority of the humans in the novel (including many of those who surrender to the Oankali's terms) reject this interpretation and believe (in the logic of the "one-drop" rule) that these altered children will be Oankali and thus not human at all.

(*OB* 131)

Canavan's savvy invocation of the racist "one-drop" rule suggests that perhaps it is not a good idea to adopt "a human perspective that values stability and continuity of form," but for the most part, Canavan's argument depends on accepting that perspective. Canavan then points out that Lilith's Brood does indeed restage the colonial encounter that haunts science fiction, and he drives home the point by ventriloquizing the humans as the "natives":

> When we strip the novel's events of their specific science fictional context, they become a plain retelling of the brutal history of imperialism: *Strangers come in ships from far away. Their technologies are advanced far beyond anything locally known; their ways are strange, even terrifying. They do not look like us. They explain that they have only come to help us; they are bringing us civilization, they are saving us from ourselves. We are—they say—intrinsically flawed, not only on the level of our culture but also on the level of our genes; our race, they explain without joy or malice, is simply inferior to theirs. But they are willing to uplift us; they can bring us into civilization's fold—for a price.*
>
> (*OB* 136)

This seems like a fair reading of the human-Oankali encounter as a replay of Aztecs and Spaniards (in Liu's terms, not in Atwood's), except for the crucial proviso, which Canavan will proceed to dispute, that if we are the Aztecs here, *we are Aztecs who have already nuked ourselves into near-extinction.* This is critical to Butler's vision: we are not in the world of *The Day the Earth Stood Still*, with Klaatu and Gort showing up to warn us against obliterating ourselves. The obliteration is a fait accompli. The Oankali are just cleaning up the mess.

In the most audacious moment of his argument, Canavan floats the possibility, voiced by Tino, one of the human characters in *Adulthood Rites*, that the Oankali "caused the war for their own purposes" (*LB* 290). "The possibility is never returned to," Canavan writes, "and yet I find the idea too tantalizing to give up. Is this not infinitely more plausible than the Oankali's version of events, which is that in all the vastness of their wanderings through space they just happened to stumble upon Earth at exactly the right moment?" (*OB* 143). Literally, no, it's not *infinitely* more plausible. Anyone familiar with the Cuban Missile Crisis or the lesser-known but almost equally catastrophic Able Archer crisis of 1983 would know that it is entirely plausible that we would destroy ourselves without any help from alien species. As for the timing of the Oankali arrival: even though space is incomprehensibly vast, is it not more than merely plausible that it was good luck—theirs and ours? There is no textual evidence whatsoever to suggest that Nikanj is lying when it says "we revere life" (*LB* 153); they won't even permit us to eat meat, which pisses off most of the revived humans. And although the Oankali tamper with humans quite thoroughly, they do not intentionally kill us—even when we try to kill them. There is always the possibility that an Oankali, ambushed, might involuntarily sting a human with a tentacle and kill. They repeatedly warn us not to trigger that involuntary reflex. But otherwise, when faced with humans who kill other humans (and there are plenty of these) or try to kill Oankali, their most severe punishment is a return to suspended animation. Moreover, the reason they are scooping up our DNA to clone us on their ship is that they need more of us for a "normal trade"; "they had to make more," a human tells Lilith, explaining that he has had over seventy "children" in this matter (*LB* 94). Though this confirms Lilith's sense that she is effectively an "experimental animal" (*LB* 60) to the

Oankali, as are all other humans, it also suggests that it simply doesn't make sense for the Oankali to provoke or cause a war that kills billions of us and then make a great deal more work for themselves in cloning and environmental cleanup. Last but not least (as Canavan admits), *Butler herself* insists, in a reply to an inquiry from fellow science fiction writer Ian Watson, that the Oankali are not responsible for the war. That should be a Marshall McLuhan–in–*Annie Hall* moment for any discussion of who pressed the nuclear button.[26]

Canavan's speculation that the Oankali arranged for us to nuke ourselves is not only ungrounded; it is unnecessary. He has quite a good enough case for his other major charge—that the Oankali are guilty of genocide.

> If one looks to the legal definition of genocide adopted by the United Nations—a more expansive definition than the popular conception of death camps—one finds that the Oankali are guilty of every variety:
>
> (a) Killing members of the group;
>
> (b) Causing serious bodily or mental harm to members of the group;
>
> (c) Deliberately inflicting on the group conditions of life calculated to bring about its physical destruction in whole or in part;
>
> (d) Imposing measures intended to prevent births within the group;
>
> (e) Forcibly transferring children of the group to another group.
>
> Against the tradition of Butler criticism that has emphasized a postcolonial politics of cosmopolitan hybridity and that has consequently tended to view the Oankali as legitimate benefactors to humankind, then, I feel I must insist on the extent to which the Oankali turn out, in this reading, to be genuinely monstrous

after all. The surface humanitarianism of the Oankali belies the threat of (xeno)genocidal violence on which their interactions with human beings are predicated; if this is supposed to be a cosmopolitan utopia, it comes only at the barrel of a gun.

(*OB* 137)

Again, Canavan is not wrong. Though I will insist that the rare Oankali killing of a human is involuntary, they're definitely guilty of everything else here. They even sterilize us—a most effective measure to prevent births within the group. (This will become a central issue in *Adulthood Rites*, as the human-Oankali child Akin comes to sympathize with the human "resisters.") Canavan could have added, but did not, that they even destroy our ruins so as to sever us from the physical record of our past. "You were wrong," Lilith says when she learns of this Talibanesque aspect of the Oankali. "You destroyed what wasn't yours. . . . You completed an insane act" (*LB* 34).

My sense is that Canavan's reading had to happen sooner or later. There had to be some strong critical dissent from the characterization of the Oankali as enlightened gene traders who usher us into the posthuman, and a realization that in many ways they are examples of rather than antidotes to the most horrible features of terrestrial colonial encounters.[27] If I wanted to get into United Nations–inspired disputes about genocide, however, I might invoke, contra Canavan, the Responsibility to Protect (R2P), which acknowledges legitimate grounds for intervention in matters of national sovereignty. By the logic of R2P, humans have *already* committed genocide, and the intervention of the Oankali, with its consequent violations of our species and our bodily autonomy, is justified on the grounds that R2P is "activated when a particular state is clearly either unwilling or unable

to fulfil its responsibility to protect or is itself the actual perpe-
trator of crimes or atrocities."[28] This is usually called "humani-
tarian intervention," though in this case the term is inappropri-
ate, so that I should be defending the principle of *Oankalian
intervention* instead. But I'm not going to go that route. I argued
in a very different book, *The Left at War*, that the principle of
R2P, seemingly so necessary to world affairs in the wake of the
atrocities of Rwanda and the Balkans (and deployed successfully
by the United Nations in East Timor and Sierra Leone), was
effectively strangled in its crib by the liberal hawks who used it
as justification for the war in Iraq.[29] There is no question any
longer, it seems, that R2P can become what its critics claimed it
always was—a fig leaf for imperialism.

I could also argue that even though the Oankali control all
the terms of the "trade," the result really is a new form of life
that is neither human nor Oankali. The humans' fear and horror that they are being assimilated into a kind of organic, ten-
tacled Borg are simply unjustified: as Nikanj tells Lilith at the
end of *Dawn*, "Our children will be better than either of us. . . .
We will moderate your hierarchical problems and you will lessen
our physical limitations. Our children won't destroy themselves
in a war, and if they need to regrow a limb or to change themselves in some other way they'll be able to do it. And there will
be other benefits" (*LB* 247–48). Here again, Nikanj is not lying.
We usually speak of making a better world for our children; here
we are invited to imagine the prospect of making better children for our world. At the time, Lilith replies, "But they won't
be human. . . . That's what matters. You can't understand, but
that *is* what matters" (*LB* 248). This, I argue, is precisely the perspective Lilith and every other human brings to the encounter,
and it is the perspective from which readers—human readers like
ourselves, I mean—need to be weaned. (As Lilith herself is
weaned in the subsequent two volumes, but I'll get to that later.)

But then, that leaves us where we began: the Oankali are both saviors and colonizers. So let's back up a moment and return to the R2P argument. For another problem with the R2P argument is that it merely kicks the can down the road with regard to whether one trusts the Oankali account of humans. Drawing on Rebecca J. Holden's essay "The High Costs of Cyborg Survival: Octavia Butler's *Xenogenesis Trilogy*," Canavan argues that the Oankali claim that humans are characterized by our volatile and unstable combination of intelligence and hierarchical thinking is essentialist and that this idea of the "Human Contradiction" is *also* a fig leaf for imperialism: "The Oankali assertion of a constitutive flaw in the human genome that leaves human beings intrinsically unfit to govern themselves—an assertion for which they never provide even the slimmest evidence but which appeals to familiar discourses on both the political left and political right that cause it to be accepted by many readers without argument—is only the latest version of the lie familiar to any student of colonial and imperial history" (*OB* 138). I might reply that there is ample evidence for the argument that we have a constitutive flaw that leaves us unfit to govern ourselves and that the evidence is provided *by colonial and imperial history itself.* The question of whether it is baked into our genetic makeup is, I believe, moot.[30] So leaving aside beliefs about genetic destiny, Butler critics are basically disagreeing about the extent of our attachment to our species, and our faith (or, in my case and Butler's, our doubt) that we can eventually overcome or mitigate the hierarchical thinking that produced colonialism and imperialism.

And that, I submit, is what the Lilith's Brood trilogy is ultimately about. Which is why it is the proper place, chronology be damned, to conclude the argument of this book.

I said earlier that I want to place more emphasis on the humans' response to the Oankali than on the attributes of the

Oankali themselves. Now that we have reviewed the critical debate about the merits of the Oankali invasion, let us reflect on the curious fact that *no humans in the series, not one, view the Oankali in the pro-Oankali light favored by many critics.* Despite my *Simpsons*-inspired joke in chapter 1, there is no human who welcomes their new Oankali overlords. There is no Earth-Oankali Organization made up of the disaffected humans from *The Three-Body Problem* who believe that we are doomed unless another species intervenes in our affairs. Every single human being aboard the Oankali ship is horrified and repelled by the very appearance of the Oankali, even though they seem to be nothing stranger than bipeds with lots of tentacles (and in the case of the ooloi, four arms like elephant trunks); we are so horrified and repelled, in fact, that the Oankali have to drug us simply in order to prevent us from freaking out completely upon first sight of them. I have to admit that I find tentacles rather unpleasant, but my tastes in bodies are not the point here.[31] The point is that there isn't a single human who gets revived on the Oankali ship, sees the Oankali, and thinks, "Cool, this is way better than the Chthulucene Donna Haraway told us about" or responds to the prospect of mating with this new species by saying, "Awesome! I was always into tentacle porn."[32] For me, the most striking thing about *Dawn*, and the primary drama of *Adulthood Rites*, lies in the fact that Butler has stacked the deck so strongly in favor of the Oankali and yet not a single human wants to be dealt in.[33]

At first, one might be (as I was) tempted to attribute this dynamic to what I might call the *Passengers* problem, a problem of narrative perspective. In an altogether terrible 2016 film, Jim (Chris Pratt) is on the spaceship *Avalon*, in suspended animation for 120 years in order to start a new colony on an exoplanet, in the manner of Butler's *Christopher Columbus* expedition. An asteroid collision leads to Jim's premature awakening, ninety years too early, and after a year of grieving and pondering his fate, he deliberately revives a female companion, Aurora (Jennifer Lawrence). Appallingly, the rest of the script plays out as a romance in deep space: Aurora eventually realizes that Jim woke her, consigning her to share his sorry fate, responds with justifiable fury, but over the course of their adventures finally forgives him, and they live happily ever after, all things considered. It didn't take much for critics to propose that a far more interesting movie could have been wrung out of this source material if only anybody had had the good sense to narrate it from Aurora's perspective rather than Jim's, so that the film would be about her growing psychological horror. But for some reason, none of the men responsible for the story thought of this.[34]

Lilith is awakened aboard a ship, as is Aurora, and there is no moment in *Dawn* when the narrative is not focalized by her perspective. She perceives her Awakening as one horror after another, first being introduced to a human child and then having him inexplicably taken away, then confined to her room for long stretches, then introduced to an alien species with tentacles that make her think of Medusa. Surely if Butler had chosen to narrate this encounter from the perspective of the Oankali, the result would have stacked the deck even more decisively in their favor: we would get their self-justificatory narrative directly, with all the powerful mixture of their biological desire for us and their fear of our irrational violence, as well as the rationale and execution of their plan to save Earth from the radiation killing so many of its species.

And yet *Dawn* is the only book in the series whose narrative is focalized exclusively by way of a human. *Adulthood Rites* is the coming-of-age story of the hybrid male construct Akin, child of Lilith et al. (though it includes the perspective of Tino, a resister-turned-ally), and *Imago* is the first-person account of Jodahs (also born of Lilith), the first ooloi construct and the real harbinger of a new world (or human-Oankali) order. Though Lilith is initially disgusted by their appearance and outraged that they have chosen her to be the "Judas goat" (*LB* 67) who facilitates the "trade," she is ultimately the human most sympathetic to the Oankali, despite her initial determination to lead her fellow humans to "learn and run" (*LB* 118) from them.[35] Her name becomes legendary, and not in a good way: as Tino muses in *Adulthood Rites*, "people had said things like that—that she was possessed of the devil, that she had sold first herself, then Humanity, that she was the first to go willingly to an Oankali bed to become their whore and to seduce other Humans" (*LB* 298). If we are the Aztecs and the Oankali are the Spaniards, Lilith is effectively Malintzin Tenepal, more commonly known as La Malinche, the Nahua Mexican woman who was the interpreter, native informant (!), and lover of Hernán Cortés.[36] The narrative perspective of the first book could not, in these terms, be anything other than agonized.

Lilith's psychological journey, then, is the key to the series, as she evolves from resentful resistance to ambivalent complicity to . . . what? By the end of *Imago*, she seems almost completely identified with the Oankali and has no problem whatsoever with the fact that Jodahs doesn't disclose to its human mates that it has rendered them biochemically dependent on it (as it is genetically designed to do). But the reason for Lilith's shift has less to do with the Oankali (or, as we will see, with Butler's narrative strategies) than with the humans—and with Butler's ex-humanist project of leading us gradually to dissociate ourselves from them.

That project begins when Lilith is given the worse-than-thankless task of Awakening a group of forty humans who will be trained by the Oankali in the techniques that will enable them to establish stable nonindustrial societies on Earth. Lilith is painfully aware of how daunting that task will be:

> How could she Awaken people and tell them they were to be part of the genetic engineering scheme of a species so alien that the humans would not be able to look at it comfortably for a while? How would she Awaken these people, these survivors of war, and tell them that unless they could escape the Oankali, their children would not be human?
>
> Better to tell them little or none of that for a while. Better not to Awaken them at all until she had some idea how to help them, how not to betray them, how to get them to accept their captivity, accept the Oankali, accept anything until they were sent to Earth. Then to run like hell at the first opportunity.

(*LB* 117)

This resolve is followed by Lilith's review of the dossiers provided to her by the Oankali, disclosing each person's life story; it is as if the novel itself is reviewing the résumés of prospective characters, offering infodumps on each one and trying to decide whom to introduce next. Sure enough, the alpha males make trouble almost immediately. Apparently, the Oankali understand that our species is given to hierarchical reasoning but have failed to realize that one prominent feature of that hierarchical reasoning is racism, and they have therefore underestimated how much some of the white guys are going to object to having a Black female supervisor—especially one with mysteriously enhanced strength and healing capacity.[37]

It is not long before two of the worst men, Curt Loehr and Peter Van Weerden, precipitate a crisis by seizing, fighting over, and trying to rape a woman, Allison Zeigler. In the ensuing fracas, Lilith beats down *three* men at once, breaks Peter's arm, and issues the following ultimatum: "'There'll be no rape here,' she said evenly. She raised her voice. 'Nobody here is property. Nobody here has the right to the use of anybody else's body. There'll be no back-to-the-Stone-Age, caveman bullshit!' She let her voice drop to normal. 'We stay human. We treat each other like people, and we get through this like people. Anyone who wants to be something less will have his chance in the forest. There'll be plenty of room for him to run away and play at being an ape'" (*LB* 178). The problem, for Lilith and for the trilogy, is that "we stay human" eventually *does* mean back-to-the–Stone Age, caveman bullshit. Even before they leave the Oankali ship, Curt hacks Joseph to death with an ax and almost kills Nikanj; once the resister colonies are established down on Earth, they gradually but inexorably degenerate into dens of rape, gun violence, and murder. Nor is the decline confined to guys with names like Loehr and Van Weerden; nearly every human, regardless of race or ethnic origin, contributes to the general descent of Man. And though the Oankali are very aware of our dark side, they do not anticipate how bad we can get; as the ooloi Kahguyaht says after Curt has murdered Joseph, "we had to know how you would behave after leaving us. We knew you might be injured, but we didn't think you would kill one another" (*LB* 228). Just as they underestimate our potential for violence, they overestimate our intelligence: the most belligerent humans, even after being introduced to the Oankali and informed of their situation, refuse even to believe that they are on a spaceship. They are no doubt the descendants of the people who refused to believe in the effectiveness of vaccines in a pandemic, if not actually those people themselves. "What is there," asks Naomi Jacobs, "in such a vengeful and xenophobic humanity, to which any rational being would wish to remain loyal?"[38] If you answer this question, as I do, with "nothing," you are well on your way to becoming ex-human.

Adulthood Rites is partly the account of our degeneration and partly the account of how Akin tries to save us from species extinction despite that degeneration. We are introduced to a resister colony, hopefully (or delusionally) named "Phoenix," that builds houses, develops paper and printing presses, and initially refuses to manufacture guns; by the end of the novel the town is almost in ashes:

> There was trash in the street. Dead weeds, food waste, scrap wood, cloth, and paper. Some of the houses were obviously vacant. A couple of them had been partially torn down. Others seemed ready to fall down. . . .
>
> Hidden guns and open drunkenness.
>
> Phoenix was dying.
>
> (*LB* 482–83)[39]

But just as the remarkable dynamic of *Dawn* is that the Oankali "trade" appeals to almost no humans despite its considerable benefits, the dynamic of *Adulthood Rites* is that its protagonist Akin becomes more sympathetic to the cause of the human resisters even as they descend into the worst forms of human behavior. When the novel opens, the resisters have begun raiding Oankali encampments in order to steal Oankali-human children, since they cannot have children themselves; in the course of the novel we learn that some of the humans, having captured young children, are determined to cut off their tentacles to make them appear more human. (This aspect of the novel has drawn attention from critics in disability studies, but thankfully, the children in question escape before they can be mutilated.)[40] Yet by the end of the novel the Oankali have agreed to a kind of Trail of Tears arrangement in which humans will be resettled on a terraformed Mars if they so desire, with their fertility restored. And the character who successfully argues for that arrangement, over the strenuous objections of the Oankali, is Akin.

Akin is placed in an extraordinary and perhaps untenable situation by the Oankali: when he is kidnapped as a very young child (albeit a seventeen-month-old child who can feed himself and talk in complete paragraphs), the Oankali decide that rather than rescue him, they will leave him to live with humans in order to learn more about them and his human heritage—even though back in his home village, his many parents give birth to a sibling with whom, biologically, he is supposed to bond as part of his (and the sibling's) development. As a result of that betrayal, Akin does not identify entirely with the Oankali, and he questions their beliefs almost from the outset—beginning with their belief that humans are fated to wipe themselves out, as he demonstrates in this conversation with another kidnapped construct child:

> "Humans had come to their own end," Shkaht said. "They were flawed and overspecialized. If they hadn't had their war, they would have found another way to kill themselves."
>
> "Perhaps," Akin admitted. *"I was taught that, too.* And I can see the conflict in their genes—the new intelligence put at the service of ancient hierarchical tendencies. But . . . they didn't have to destroy themselves. They certainly don't have to do it again."

(*LB* 378; EMPHASIS ADDED)

No other construct, so far as we know, takes the arm's-distance perspective Akin offers here, questioning the official Oankali understanding of humans. He is the only nonhuman character in the trilogy who suspects that the Oankali belief in inevitable human self-destruction might actually be self-serving. *I too was taught that the native people whose land we occupy were going to die out anyway, but . . .* [41]

Moreover, when Akin learns that the Oankali have a branch of their species that does not mate with humans, the Akjai—a kind of genetic insurance policy that ensures that Oankali DNA will survive even if the trade with humans (or any other species) goes horribly awry—he decides that if this "trade" is to be fair and symmetrical, the humans "should be permitted their own Akjai division—their own hedge against disaster and true extinction" (*LB* 404). This decision gives him a sense of mission: to combat the injustice that is also his own condition of possibility for existing.

> Who among the Oankali was speaking for the interests of resister Humans? Who had seriously considered that it might not be enough to let Humans choose either union with the Oankali or sterile lives free of the Oankali? Trade-village Humans said it, but they were so flawed, so genetically contradictory that they were often not listened to.
>
> He did not have their flaw. He had been assembled within the body of an ooloi. He was Oankali enough to be listened to by other Oankali and Human enough to know that resister Humans were being treated with cruelty and condescension.
>
> (*LB* 404)

It is not merely that Akin takes it upon himself to speak for the newly subaltern humans; what jumps out about this passage is the word *know*, rather than *believe*. Akin's conviction is echoed a bit later by Tino. When Nikanj suggests that Tino has been making trouble on this count, saying "you've done more than Lilith would have to make him [Akin] feel that the resisters have been wronged and betrayed," Tino retorts, "Resisters *have* been wronged and betrayed. . . . I never told Akin that, though. I never had to. He saw it for himself" (*LB* 425). For Nikanj, this is a matter of (erroneous) belief, of something Akin has been made to feel; for Tino—and, more importantly, for Akin—it is simply the case.

Nikanj then proceeds, in a conversation with its male Oank-ali mate Dichaan, to make the argument associated with Lynn Margulis (of which Butler was thoroughly aware)—that humans were never really an autonomous species unto themselves.[42] "Even before we arrived," Nikanj says, "they had bacteria living in their intestines and protecting them from other bacteria that would hurt or kill them. They could not exist without symbiotic relationships with other creatures. Yet such relationships frighten them." Dichaan isn't buying: "Nika, we aren't like mitochondria or helpful bacteria, and they know it" (*LB* 427). But clearly some Oankali tell themselves self-exculpatory things like this, assur-ing themselves, however preposterously, that they're just doing what always came naturally to humans. Perhaps the claim that humans would have eventually destroyed themselves, war or no war, is in that vein as well. At the very least, this is what prompts Akin's challenge: "What are we that we can do this to whole peoples? Not predators? Not symbionts? What then?" (*LB* 443).

The Oankali proceed to caucus, communicating instanta-neously with one another on their ship and using the ship to communicate with their villages on Earth. The process is too overwhelming for Akin, so a senior Akjai volunteers to be his surrogate, saying, "you're too young for all this. I'll argue for you now." When a surprised Akin asks why, he gets an even more surprising answer. "'Because you're right,' the Akjai said. 'If I were Human, little construct, I would be a resister myself. All people who know what it is to end should be allowed to continue if they can continue'" (*LB* 471). This is especially astonishing coming from an Akjai who will say, only four pages later, that Akin is effectively choosing for the resisters "quick death or long, slow death":

> "Or life," Akin protested.
> "No."
> "A chance for life."
> "Only for a while."
> "You're certain of that . . . and yet you spoke for me?"
> "I'm Akjai. How can I deny another people the security of an Akjai group? Even though for this people it's a cruelty. Understand that, Akin; it *is* a cruelty. You and those who help you will give them the tools to create a civilization that will destroy itself as certainly as the pull of gravity will keep their new world in orbit around its sun."

(*LB* 475)

The Akjai speaks to the Oankali for Akin, but here, he speaks for the Oankali—who regard Akin's decision as a "profoundly immoral, antilife thing" (*LB* 475) that he has chosen because "he had been abandoned to the resisters when they took him so that he could learn them as no adult could" (*LB* 474).[43]

For the Oankali, then, the Mars colony is effectively a bioethics nightmare. When Tate Marah, one of the most reasonable humans (and in fact the first one Awakened by Lilith), angrily asks Akin why the Oankali are offering them Mars only after "so many people have suffered and died," Akin replies that the offer is his, not theirs, since they are sure "that to give you a new world and let you procreate again would . . . would be like breeding intelligent beings for the sole purpose of having them kill one another" (*LB* 501). Akin continues to challenge this belief, but we encounter it again, still more emphatically, early in *Imago* when Jodahs tells a pair of humans that "'the Oankali believe . . . the Oankali *know to the bone* that it's wrong to help the Human species regenerate unchanged because it *will* destroy itself again. To them it's like deliberately causing the conception of a child who is so defective that it must die in infancy'" (*LB* 532). Bioethicists might argue that these are two different scenarios— breeding intelligent beings for the purpose of having them kill one another as opposed to deliberately conceiving a child with (say) Tay-Sachs disease. But perhaps they amount in the end to the same thing. It is as if the Oankali have prepared themselves for their intervention on Earth by reading David Benatar's *Better Never to Have Been* and deciding that Benatar's antinatalism is really the only moral choice available for humankind.

But then this raises a vexing question. Isn't *everything* in the trilogy a bioethics nightmare? At the end of *Dawn*, Lilith had warned Nikanj that "some will think the human species deserves at least a clean death" (*LB* 246). Nikanj's response is one of the moral low points for the Oankali. First it asks, "Is it an unclean thing that we want?" Lilith emphatically replies "yes!"; it follows with, "Is it an unclean thing that I have made you pregnant?" (*LB* 246). Much earlier, Nikanj had promised that Lilith's impregnation would happen only when she is ready. Lilith was skeptical: "Who decides? You?" Nikanj reassures her: "You, Lilith. You" (*LB* 98). But it is, in fact, Nikanj who decides that Lilith is ready, just as she had suspected, and it *does not even tell her it has come to this decision until it has already impregnated her.*[44] The "clean death" is not going to be an option. But then what of the Akjai's characterization of Akin's proposal as a choice between quick death or long, slow death? *There is nothing quick about the death the Oankali offer the resisters.* On the contrary, they are left to their own murderous devices on Earth *with enhanced life spans of hundreds of years.* The death of Phoenix, for example, is not a quick death. By our standards (and what other standards do we have, in the end?), it is long, slow, and painful.

Why, one must ask, did the Oankali agree to the formation of resister communities at all? Since the humans in them are sterile, their existence consists of a prolonged *Children of Men* scenario. And if the Oankali reverence for life prevents them from offering us a *truly* quick death—the kind that involves being instantaneously vaporized in a nuclear blast, say—then why not offer us, as in *Children of Men,* Quietus-brand suicide kits and let us take matters into our own hands? And last but certainly not least, it is highly relevant to this question that the Oankali deliberately do not tell us that their long game is a little like *Childhood's End*: the successors to humans will be absorbed into something larger, something interstellar or perhaps even intergalactic, and Earth will be obliterated. In *Imago,* when a human insists that our species might thrive after all and even "outlast your people on Earth," Jodahs thinks to itself, "We would leave this solar system in three centuries. I would live to see the leave-taking myself. And when we broke and scattered, we would leave behind a lump of stripped rock more like the moon than like his blue Earth. He did not know that. He would never know it. To tell him would be a cruelty" (*LB* 531). It would, to be sure. As would not telling him.

Imago is a curious coda most of which does not concern us here, except in two crucial respects. The first is that we are introduced to something we had been told did not and could not exist, something the Oankali had obviously not anticipated—a resister camp of fertile humans, living unbeknownst to the

Oankali in a remote mountain village. Their fertility is not much cause for hope, however, since their offspring tend to die in childhood or grow up with a variety of deformities and diseases. Jodahs, upon finding two of the villagers, Jesusa and Tomás, wandering far from home, takes them as mates. The eventual resolution of the Oankali-human family plot in *Imago*, such as it is, relies on two things: one, the humans are initially hostile but then impressed by Jodahs's ability to heal them, and two, Jodahs and his ooloi construct sibling Aaor turn out to be incredibly attractive, even hot, such that the villagers find themselves ineluctably seduced: as one villager says upon realizing that he does not want to be repatriated, or replanetated, to Mars, "If there had been people like you around a hundred years ago, I couldn't have become a resister. I think there would have been no resisters" (*LB* 740). Finally, in the closing pages of the trilogy, there are humans who welcome the Oankali, however grudgingly—and however much their acceptance of the ooloi is driven by the desire to stop living in a bioethical nightmare in which they continually produce children whose brief lives are full of misery and pain.[45]

The second is that although Jodahs's first-person narrative gives us the exclusively Oankali perspective that we did not have in *Dawn*, the effect is creepier than that of the first two novels, insofar as we hear the Oankali talking to one another in ways that say the quiet part out loud: at one point, Nikanj lays out the game plan to Jodahs with breathtaking cynicism, saying, "We feed on them every day. . . . And in the process, we keep them in good health and mix children for them. But they don't always have to know what we're doing" (*LB* 680). Yet precisely for that reason—precisely because we are given a window onto the Oankali that we did not have in the first novel—we understand why a construct, Akin or Jodahs, might wind up having qualms about the enterprise that literally gave birth to them.[46] Jodahs, upon first reflecting that Jesusa and Tomás could become his mates, realizes that there will be consequences once the rest of the Oankali learn about that mountain village:

> Their hidden people would have to be found. I would have to betray them to my family, and my family would have to tell others. The settlement of fertile Humans would be found and the people in it collected. They would be allowed to choose Mars or union with us or sterility here on Earth. They could not be allowed to continue to reproduce here, then to die when we separated and left an uninhabitable rock behind.
>
> No Human who did not decide to mate with us was told this last. They were given their choices and not told why.

(*LB* 628)

Jodahs, like Akin before him, comes to realize that there is something deeply wrong about this genetic "trade." Time and again, the humans are told that they can decide their fates, just as Lilith was told that she would decide when she was ready to be impregnated, and time and again, the Oankali reveal that what they *really* think is that the humans don't always have to know what the Oankali are doing.

I said earlier that Lilith's shift from resentful proto-resister to Oankali advocate is the key to the series, for it shows us the way to detach ourselves from ourselves. But I also noted, parenthetically, that this shift has little to do with Butler's narrative strategies. I can now explain, I hope, what I meant by that. By the time we've finished the trilogy, we come to understand—at least on my reading—that *Dawn* is not an example of the *Passengers* problem. Indeed, greater access to the Oankali perspective in the first novel might only have allowed us to overhear the Oankali admitting to one another that the humans don't have to be told anything the Oankali don't want them to know. But then, greater access to the Oankali perspective in *Adulthood Rites* and *Imago* introduces us to offspring of the Oankali-human genetic "trade" who come to believe that the Oankali confidence in their own benevolence is transparently self-serving and that the humans are right to believe—to *know*—that they have been wronged and betrayed.

And nevertheless, by the end, Lilith has switched sides. Jodahs relays a poignant exchange between Jesusa and his mother, the occasion of which is Jesusa asking Lilith if she would move to Mars with the human resisters. Lilith responds by summarizing her journey into a series of staccato sentences:

> My mother did not answer for a long time. She sighed finally. "I don't know how to answer that. I'm content with these people. More than content. I lost my husband and my son before the war. They died in an accident. When the war came, I lost everything else. We all did, we elders, as you call us. I couldn't give up and die, but I expected almost nothing. Food and shelter, maybe. An absence of pain. Nikanj said it knew I needed children, so it took seed from the man I had then and made me pregnant. I didn't think I would ever forgive it for that."
>
> "But . . . you have forgiven it?"
>
> "I've understood it. I've accepted it. I wouldn't have believed I could do that much. Back when I met my first mature ooloi, Nikanj's parent Kahguyaht, I found it alien, arrogant, and terrifying. I hated it. I thought I hated all ooloi."

She paused. "Now I feel as though I've loved Nikanj all my
life. Ooloi are dangerously easy to love. They absorb us, and we
don't mind."

(*LB* 670–71)

Canavan quotes the end of this passage and writes, "Jeffrey
Tucker reads this moment and says it is a 'statement that reads
like something more than simple Stockholm Syndrome'—but
Stockholm Syndrome, I have to say, is exactly what this sounds
like to me" (*OB* 153).[47]

Canavan's reading is—here as elsewhere, and once again with
feeling—thoroughly plausible. There is no question that Lilith
began in resolute opposition to the Oankali, moved through
guilty and ambivalent complicity, and has arrived at a rueful
acceptance that includes the painful and soul-searching acknowledgment that she feels as if she has loved Nikanj all her life. It
is certainly possible for a human reader to accuse Lilith of having
fallen in love with her captors. But, I submit, that possibility is
made available to human readers by the fact that in *Adulthood
Rites* and *Imago*, we are not privy to the vicissitudes of Lilith's
subjectivity as we are in *Dawn*. We see her growing frustrations
with her fellow humans in the first novel, and we witness her
pain at Curt's vicious attacks on Joseph and Nikanj. But there is
never a moment in the second or third novel when we are given
access to Lilith's assessment of the degeneration of the resister
villages on Earth; there is no passage in which we can read Lilith thinking or saying *all right, that's it, I have finally had enough
of these stupid, unbearable, murderous assholes. Whatever the Oankali are doing, it's got to be better than this shit.* But that thought, I
propose, is precisely what Butler is asking us to think. It is

certainly the thought I have been asking you to think throughout this chapter and throughout this book.

Butler's brilliant decision to move Lilith to the background
has the effect of complicating the trilogy by complicating our
view of the Oankali, and that strategy, in turn, invites us to
deflect our attention from Butler's brutal portrayal of postinvasion humanity. But perhaps we should decline that invitation.
To return to Canavan's anti-Oankali argument one final time:
"If their radical and totally nonconsensual interventions in
human society are really to be thought of as a vision of utopia, it
can only be because humans are so horrifically and intrinsically
broken as to be completely without hope" (*OB* 145). I would not
go so far as to call the postinvasion scenario in Lilith's Brood a
utopia. I would simply say that of all the options for Earth we've
reviewed so far, from the climate disaster in *The Dispossessed*, to
the multiple disasters in *The Three-Body Problem* and *Oryx and
Crake* and the Parables books, to the various battles with AI that
we can't admit we have lost, our absorption by the Oankali is by
far the best one. And that is precisely because humans are so
horrifically and intrinsically broken as to be completely without
hope.[48]

Or are we? Butler's even more brilliant decision not to narrate the fate of the Mars colony leaves that question productively
open.[49] In *Imago* we hear only that the colony is "about fifty years
old now" (*LB* 720) and that "the Humans there are healthy and
thriving" (*LB* 730). As Jodahs tells the fearful mountain villagers, "Any Human who wants to join them will be given healing,
restored fertility if necessary, and transported" (*LB* 730). It is the
emigration option from *Do Androids Dream of Electric Sheep?*
all over again, this time facilitated by the Oankali and blessedly
free of android slave labor. May I remark on Butler's extraordinary restraint here? She could very easily have placed one big

opposable human thumb, or an Oankali tentacle, on the scales, extending her depiction of the human reversion to back-to-the-Stone Age, caveman bullshit, telling us that the Mars colony has degenerated into anarchy and violence and unambiguously endorsing the Oankali conviction that we are doomed to destroy ourselves. If she had so desired, Butler could have drawn on William Miller's *A Canticle for Liebowitz*,[50] in which humans gradually recover from a catastrophic nuclear war only to launch another one; indeed, the omnipresence of guns in Lilith's Brood recalls Russell Hoban's *Riddley Walker*, in which humans gradually recover from a catastrophic nuclear war over the course of more than a thousand years only to reinvent gunpowder, and the first person to achieve the feat blows himself up in doing so. Or Butler could have drawn from what I have called Philip K. Dick's *Depressed Martian Chronicles*, portraying a Mars colony that is "thriving" only in the sense that their endless battles with the barely livable planet leave them too physically and emotionally exhausted to butcher one another. But she chose, instead, to leave them to their devices and to leave their fate to our imaginations. Despite my sense that theirs will not be a happy ending, I wish them well. Nevertheless, I am thoroughly pleased that Butler chose not to write a Martian narrative about the human resisters. I for one have had enough of them. In my epilogue I will explain why.

EPILOGUE

Just Kill Me Now

I n the early weeks of 2020 I made vague plans to start writing this book. Once the semester was over and I was no longer an officer of the University Faculty Senate at Penn State, I would be eagerly looking forward to a year of leave, accumulated over my three years in the Senate leadership and my seven years as the director of the Institute for the Arts and Humanities. I wrote a tentative prospectus and began reading Weisman's *The World Without Us*. And then COVID-19 washed over the globe with frightening speed.

In early April, our firstborn, Nick, and his wife, Rachel, packed up everything in their tiny apartment in Cambridge, Massachusetts, including their nine-month-old baby, Finn, and moved in with us. Suddenly, our household had doubled in size, and we were going to help raise our first grandchild while his parents hashed out their remote work arrangements and set up makeshift offices in a pair of bedrooms. Jamie, our secondborn and a young man with Down syndrome, lost almost everything: his sheltered workshop closed down, as did all the places where he did volunteer work (pet shelter, children's science museum, apartment for teens with intellectual disabilities). A kind coworker from the Penn State Press, where Jamie worked Fridays nine to one doing cataloguing and tagging of web PDFs of books, dropped off his work computer so that Jamie could telework like his white-collar parents, his brother, and his sister-in-law. But only for four hours a week. All his social activities disappeared as well, most importantly Special Olympics. Intrepidly, he embarked on a James Bond film festival that rotated through all twenty-five Bond films again and again and again and. . . .

Finn, of course, had no daycare, so we fell back on the form of daycare known to millions of human children since the mid-Pleistocene: grandparents. Rachel negotiated an 8:30–2:30 work-day with her job in graphic design (Nick's architecture firm allowed him to work remotely as well), I took Finn in the morning shift (until his first nap around 10:30), and Janet worked the longer shift from around noon to 2:30. To make up for the imbalance in the baby workload, I took over as quartermaster, arranging the now tension-fraught and once-a-week grocery runs (complete with wipedowns of all groceries upon unloading in the kitchen, after the wipedowns of the car steering wheel, radio buttons, and door handles) and doing most of the cooking ("about 85 percent," as Nick told a friend in a comically accurate assessment), my limited repertoire now expanded to include arroz con pollo y pimientos y cebollas and a shrimp-and-scallop scampi. I was a stern quartermaster. Leftovers must be eaten unless actually poisonous; we would not contribute to food waste at a time such as this. All plastic products would be reused until this became physically impossible. All trips to the beer distributor must be combined with runs to the pet store across the street from the beer distributor for dog food, treats, and/or toys. There will be no unnecessary trips. Even if this pandemic was the beginning of the end of human civilization, we would be responsible consumers.

There was tension and anxiety, especially about the needs of the littlest one among us, but very little drama. We were all determined to Get Through This and Make the Most of It. No complaining, no whingeing, no lamenting the lockdown. We kept telling ourselves that we were more fortunate than 99.99 percent of the humans on the planet, save only the wealthy New Yorkers whose retreats to their summer homes on Long Island or in upstate New York were dutifully profiled by the *New York Times*. Even when our state closed the wine-and-spirits stores for a couple of months, we muddled through somehow— and we learned how expensive it is to order wine online. We took long dog walks. We made lists of movies and series to watch at night. We listened to music we'd never really made time for, like Keith Jarrett's *Köln Concert* and the Greatest Pandemic Hits catalog emerging from Taylor Swift. We played Boggle and Telestrations and even cribbage.

And I was consumed with worry about almost everything, from household needs to academic crises nationwide to the unfolding pandemic itself, succumbing more than once to executive function fatigue and melting down one evening in May as the beef stroganoff (another attempt at repertoire expansion) fell apart. I had tried to keep up some sprightly banter based on my reading, finishing *The World Without Us* and telling my family at dinnertime that the nuclear plants and oil refineries were going to be pretty problematic without anyone to see to their maintenance, that cats kill a truly staggering number of birds every year (Nick already knew this—architects have to think about birds), and that rats and roaches will not do as well as we all imagined back in the fear-of-nuclear-holocaust era, because they're so codependent on us and our horrific food waste. But the next few books were rough going. I decided for some reason that now was finally the time to read Viktor Frankl's *Man's Search for Meaning*, then got intrigued by Jeff Sharlet's *This Brilliant Darkness* and Allie Brosh's *Hyperbole and a Half*.[1] I was familiar only with Brosh's hilarious rendering of moving her two dogs to a new house and had had no idea how much of her work deals with the experiences of severe, debilitating depression. By the time I got back to reading about the end of civilization—this time in David Wallace-Wells's *The Uninhabitable Earth*—I was nearly paralyzed with depression myself. I couldn't finish the book. I knew that the pandemic was basically a collective action problem that was a practice test for the much greater challenge of climate change, and I knew that we, as a species, were failing it miserably. That remained painfully true as I wrote the first draft of this epilogue in late summer 2021, as the Delta variant surged around the world, aided and abetted by antivaxxers everywhere, and it remained true at the end of 2021 as the world was overwhelmed by Omicron. Janet, Jamie, Nick, Rachel, Finn, and I were overwhelmed by that variant in December 2021, but because we had all been vaccinated and boosted, and because we had managed to avoid treating ourselves with the horse paste recommended by the sages of the Intellectual Dark Web, we all came out OK.[2] For now. Janet, Jamie, and I got a second round of COVID in February 2023, but by that point it was less severe than an ordinary flu—though it still involved two weeks of isolation and the cancellation of many things.

Back in 2020, Janet had decided that if Jamie were to get sick, he would be quarantined in the upstairs bedroom and she would take care of him. I would leave meals and medicines and towels and Gatorade at the foot of the stairs as needed. Reluctantly, I agreed that this made sense, since Janet is a former nurse and an exceptionally skilled caregiver. But the thought of either one of them becoming gravely and perhaps mortally ill—let alone both, which would certainly happen under this arrangement—was unbearable. I knew that if the worst happened, I would find it very difficult to find reasons to keep going. Meanwhile, out in the rest of the world, our criminally incompetent and unspeakably stupid president was suggesting that people could inject bleach into their bodies to fight the virus; his rabid followers were descending on state capitals in what I called "I Need a Haircut / Kill the Jews" rallies; and legions of nutcases across the political spectrum, from the radical Italian philosopher Giorgio Agamben to the ostensibly leftist media theorist Mark Crispin Miller to the bobbleheads of Fox News, devoted themselves to spreading conspiracy theories and pretending that basic public health measures were the greatest threat to freedom the world had ever known. The immediate lesson seemed to be that of all the things the film *Contagion* got right about pandemics, the crazed character of the blogger Alan Krumwiede (Jules Law), sowing chaos and misinformation, was probably the most prescient—if not in fact understated. As one (now unfindable) Twitterer put it, the only thing missing from our zombie apocalypse movies, apparently, was the phenomenon of masses of people taking to the streets to demand that they be devoured by zombies.

And then George Floyd was murdered. Methodically, deliberately, in broad daylight, on camera.

Like many white Americans who find it uncontroversial to believe that Black lives matter and outrageous that this proposition is met with rabid resistance, I was moved by the national expression of outrage and sorrow. But I still couldn't get past the ubiquity of police violence against unarmed Black and brown men and women, and I couldn't shake the sense that nothing had changed over the course of my lifetime and that nothing ever would—that after the marches (many of which we attended in State College) and speeches, the inevitable white backlash would kick in, as it did in the 1970s and 1980s, and no police unions would be reformed, no police practices would be outlawed, no police murders would be prosecuted or even acknowledged unless they were captured live—and rarely even then. Derek Chauvin's conviction in June 2021, the first such conviction in Minnesota of a white police officer killing a Black person, was small consolation (though welcome), for as many people pointed out, in a truly just world George Floyd would still be alive. As would Philando Castile, and Walter Scott, and Freddie Gray, and Eric Garner, and many thousands more.

You might think that caring for a sweet and chirpy grandchild every day under these conditions would be a welcome tonic, a respite from all manner of racism, fascism, casual cruelty, and general mayhem. You would think that I might be reminded that this little guy, so entertained by Dr. Seuss's *Fox in Socks* and learn-to-crawl sessions on the side porch (disguised as play with blocks and rattles), gave me plenty of reason to get up each morning, push the news and the Twitter feed to remote corners of my consciousness, and concentrate on the immediate here and now as experienced by a little human who bore no responsibility for the atrocities of his species.[3] Well, that worked sometimes, just as Lee Edelman's critique of reproductive futurism says it does: because Finn was and is "the Child whose innocence solicits our defense," he (allegedly) sets the parameters for the thinkable: "the fantasy subtending the image of the Child invariably shapes the logic within which the political must be thought."[4] Every morning, I was strongly tempted to let Finn shape the logic within which my sense of the political must be thought. As temptations go, it was a pretty good one.

Edelman's critique is strangely blinkered, inasmuch as he associates this Child with "the absolute privilege of heteronormativity" (*NF* 2), as if queer folk might not also have children, and though it announces itself as a "radical" critique, it plays very nicely into the hands of unfettered capitalism. Of course in many ways we should *want* to create a better world for "our" children, be we gay or straight or bi or trans or queer or ace, since the alternative seems to be complacency about the degradation of the biosphere and/or a greedy, foolish fixation on maximizing profit and extracting resources in the next quarter, biosphere be damned. Still, at my book's end, I want to offer Edelman's critique of reproductive futurism as a bookend for Toby Ord's argument for human self-preservation. For when I first encountered Edelman's polemic insistence on "abjuring fidelity to a futurism that's always purchased at our expense" (*NF* 4), I read it as if it came from the desk of an executive from ExxonMobil or one of the Koch brothers, complaining in an appropriately economic register that environmental protection laws and carbon-neutral policies would eat into their profits. After reading Ord, however, I wrote a mental note the content of which was basically *come back, Lee Edelman, (almost) all is forgiven*. For as Jim Holt pointed out in his thoughtful review essay on *The Precipice*, Ord's logic is basically Edelman's reproductive futurism to the infinite power, where the (allegedly always already) heteronormative figure of the Child has been replaced by the image of our billions or trillions of descendants throughout the universe. And that future is most certainly purchased at our (potentially infinite) expense. As Holt writes (also in the economic register):

> How much should we be willing to pay in principle to ensure humanity's future? Ord does not explicitly address this question. Yet his way of thinking about the value of humanity's future puts us on a slippery slope to a preposterous answer. . . . The more we do to mitigate risk, the longer humanity's expected future becomes. And by Ord's logic, the longer that future becomes, the more its potential value outweighs the value of the present. As we push the existential risk closer and closer to zero, expected

gains from the very far future become ever more enormous, oblig-
ing us to make still greater expenditures to ensure their ultimate
arrival. This combination of increasing marginal costs (to reduce
risk) and increasing marginal returns (in future value) has no stable equilibrium point short of bankruptcy.[5]

One imagines Edelman thinking, *OK, that's not really what I was
getting at, but yeah, I have a point about a futurism that's always
purchased at our expense, don't I.*

I know that Edelman's arguments had stakes for queer theory that aren't directly relevant here.[6] But the question for me,
morning after morning in the spring and summer of 2020, was
whether I had to renounce my sense of dread and fatalism in
order to be a good grandfather. Most of the time, minute to minute, the good-grandfather thing was reducible to the worry that
I might drop little Finn while walking down the stairs (it had
been almost thirty years since I'd had to carry a baby down stairs,
and back then, we lived in a carpeted split-level, so it was a question of falling down only seven or eight padded stairs) and to
the question of whether, when I first introduced him to the
backyard, it would be best for him to learn for himself the lesson of why we don't put sticks in our mouths.[7] But I also couldn't
help thinking, every single day: *the odds are very good that if all
goes well, that is, "well," this sweet and chirpy grandchild will be
alive in 2100.* Those nightmare scenarios in the 2012 World Bank
report, *Turn Down the Heat: Why a 4°C Warmer World Must be
Avoided?* Those projections for sea level rise and global surface
temperature increase in the 2014 Fifth Assessment Report of the
United Nations' Intergovernmental Panel on Climate Change?
Those would be, will be, lived realities for Finn and his cohort.
(And the 2021 Sixth Assessment Report is considerably worse,
as are our prospects.)[8]

On Earth Day 2020, Nick's thirty-fourth birthday and just two weeks after Finn's first day as a member of our household, *National Geographic* published a special issue devoted to the fiftieth anniversary of Earth Day. Half of it was "How We Saved the World: An Optimist's Guide to Life on Earth in 2070," with a lead article, "The Case for Renewal," written by Emma Marris. The other half was "How We Lost the Planet: A Pessimist's Guide to Life on Earth in 2070," with a lead article, "The Case for Catastrophe," written by Elizabeth Kolbert.[9] I couldn't help thinking that the title of Kolbert's essay could be read as an affirmative argument *in favor of* catastrophe and that on the whole, the dark side of the issue was much more convincing than the bright side, for roughly the same reason that the chilling "Night on Bald Mountain" sequence of *Fantasia* is more compelling than the placid "Ave Maria" sequence that follows it. For example: Kolbert reminds us, as did Roy Scranton, that "to a disturbing extent, the future has already been written" (*LDA* 17). There really is no plausible rebuttal to this.[10] I decided not to discuss the special issue at dinner, and in fact decided to yoink it out of Jamie's possession—it's his subscription to *National Geographic*—and keep it in my study for whenever I had the emotional wherewithal to begin writing this book.

And yet even as we were reading of our fellow humans' dread of massive evictions and unemployment; in academe, waves of academic layoffs and closures; in the world outside, brave, hardy white nationalists getting sandwiches at Subway, eschewing masks for AR-15 assault rifles; a government plotting to steal an election and then, upon failing, claiming the election was stolen—we knew we had no fear of eviction or bankruptcy or losing a loved one to police violence or white vigilantes. Janet and I had *a year of leave*, may all the relevant deities be thanked. We had a house that six people could live in without falling on top of one another. We had two sons and a daughter-in-law with whom we enjoyed talking about movies or music or pretty much anything other than the news (but also the news). Were we living in the comfort of one of the Compounds of *Oryx and Crake*? We were so safe, so insulated. Far away, Republican governors like Florida's Ron DeSantis and Texas's Greg Abbott were lying and bloviating on a daily basis, cooking the books on COVID cases and striking down their own cities' public health measures; on the Democratic side, Andrew Cuomo became a rock star despite cooking the books on COVID cases in nursing homes and lying and bullying and sexually harassing female colleagues on a daily basis. Through it all, we grilled wild-caught tuna and played Boggle. Would it have made more sense to recall and recite the wise words of Jimmy's mother, "It's all shit, it's total shit, it's hopeless"? Because a case can certainly be made for that eloquent perspective, and I hope I have made at least a semblance of such a case here.

There is no question that the circumstances in which I wrote this book shaped its argument. I presume that is clear by now. But it wasn't just the pandemic. I had been saying for the previous four years that with the rise of Donald Trump, the genie had been let out of the bottle: violent white nationalism in the United States was back with a vengeance and wasn't going back in the bottle in my lifetime. Then in the course of reading for this book, I came across a fascinating conversation about *Adulthood Rites* on *Fiction Unbound*, an online journal devoted to speculative fiction. The conversation took place (and was published) just after the 2016 election, and *Fiction Unbound* contributor Gemma Webster asked her colleague Theodore McCombs about the relevance of the novel for the moment. McCombs replied: "It's unnerving to think about how different my answer would have been, just a week ago. The Oankali's paternalism and the resister humans' despairing, self-destructive violence mirrors post-election conversations I've seen about an elitist, know-it-all Left and the resurgent working-class whites pushing back, even if that pushback means nihilistically electing a predatory, amoral goon."[11] Leaving aside the question of whether the Left in that election really was made up of elitist know-it-alls,[12] McCombs's mapping of resisters onto the Trumpers seems exactly right to me.

I know I reread Lilith's Brood in that light. My reading of the human resistance to the Oankali is ten to twelve times less generous than that of Gerry Canavan because I see the resisters as *those people*: antimaskers and antivaxxers, waving the Gadsden "Don't Tread on Me" flag at the Oankali and wearing bright-red MEGA (Make Earth Great Again) hats. I see them as the people who, in my country, keep electing criminally incompetent and unspeakably stupid representatives and making culture-war heroes out of them: Marjorie Taylor Greene, Louie Gohmert, Matt Gaetz, Lauren Boebert, and Jim Jordan in the House, Ron Johnson and Tommy Tuberville in the Senate (just to name a few). I have mentioned that the most severe punishment doled out by the Oankali, reserved for humans who kill, is a return to suspended animation. Early in *Adulthood Rites*, Nikanj tells Lilith that "we cage them, drug them, and allow them to live in an unreal world of drug-stimulated imaginings" (*LB* 291). And then in *Imago*, Butler darkens that picture somewhat: "If they had killed, they would be kept either unconscious or drugged to pleasure and contentment. They would never be allowed to awaken completely. They would be used as teaching aids, subjects for biological experiments, or reservoirs of Human genetic material" (*LB* 569). This seems to me rather too harsh a policy for handling Trump supporters and enablers. And while it is true that those people are already living in an unreal world of drug-stimulated imaginings—that is, an epistemologically sealed Fox/Newsmax/OAN Universe in which they are constantly urged to take up arms against the rampaging liberals who are coming to their communities to teach critical race theory, hold LGBTQ+ pride parades to "groom" their children, and institute Shari'a law—the fact remains that they are my neighbors and fellow citizens and that they can do and have done real harm in the real world.

I therefore decided to revisit and revise an offer I once made back in the days when I had a blog:

> I don't want to deprive you of your pastimes and your livelihoods. On the contrary: I want you to enjoy them to the fullest extent imaginable—but in a way that doesn't interfere with sane people. So I have a proposal.
>
> We will spend $500 trillion and create 150 million new, high-paying jobs creating an alternate reality for you. In a state of your choosing—but preferably Utah, Oklahoma, or Alaska—we will construct a massive VR installation complete with all your favorite obsessions and catering to your every resentment. In this separate, self-enclosed universe, President Trump and Vice-President Pence will run things just like you think they oughta be; crescents and croissants will be banned; Dinesh D'Souza's films will sweep the Oscars; television will consist of two channels, Fox and Fox Sports, the latter of which will feature only patriotic athletes who stand for the national anthem; and the ten commandments will be proudly displayed in every classroom and courtroom, together with a Very Angry Eagle if you like. There won't be any elite universities or sneering college professors, of course, but there will be Mexicans, so that you can call for their deportation and then hire them to mow your lawns and work in your pork-processing plants; there will be gay and trans people, so that your sense of sexual identity can be properly threatened at all times; and there will be a Black person, played by Viola Davis, so that you can prevent her from voting.

> And all you have to do is lie down here in this pod of translucent goo.

That blog, which had about eight thousand daily readers at its peak, also featured a running joke about an alien invasion. I couldn't decide whether the aliens would show up long after human civilization had disappeared or would arrive like the Oankali and save us from ourselves, but I was sure that they would be peaceful, enlightened creatures, in appearance similar to nine-foot-tall praying mantises; they would come from the planet Paxil 8 in the Effexor star system; and they would have great musical taste *yet would not be hipsters.*

And now, finally, I have to admit something about the Oankali that I deliberately left out of my argument in chapter 4. We learn only very late, more than halfway through the trilogy, that "Oankali did not like music" (*LB* 439). *They do not like music!* This is an extraordinary data point for Butler to drop in volume 2, as if it were a mere aside. And let's not forget, the Oankali forbid us reading material on their ship. They destroyed our cultural artifacts on Earth. They seem to have no use whatsoever for artistic expression of any kind. They would not be out of place, perhaps, in the dystopia of *Oryx and Crake*: they are brilliant genetic engineers with apparently little to no interest in anything else. So why, if my preferred invasion involves giant enlightened insects with great musical taste, am I willing to entertain the idea of leaving behind humanity in favor of fusion with the Oankali, who don't know Poison from the Cure or Bach from bebop or kwassa-kwassa from K-Pop—and don't even care? The answer is simply this: as my view of the inhabitants of the Fox/Newsmax/OAN Universe has grown dimmer and dimmer, I've had to lower my standards. Faced with the Make Earth Great Again resistance, I've decided I'll take my stand. I say you're doing fine, Oankali, Oankali, OK.

It is, however, hard to maintain a generally dim view of one's species when your most immediate representatives of it, the ones living with you every day, the ones with whom you choose to Zoom over before-dinner drinks, are so delightful. But then, who gets to have the privilege of taking refuge in this way? Certainly not the people living in abusive relationships. Certainly not the people living in the border cages that defined the Trump administration's immigration policy and seemed drawn directly from the film version of *Children of Men*. Certainly not the refugees, including the climate refugees, who never even made it to those cages. And how much longer will those kinds of refuges exist, as the number of climate refugees increases to the point at which they themselves (more precisely, the conditions that produce them) become a global crisis? Even in a landscape as blasted as that of Butler's Parables, garrisoned refuges are still there, stocked with virtual-reality devices, though we never see into them. Perhaps the people in them, and the people in Atwood's Compounds, felt themselves to be fortunate, safe, and insulated too.

The first pandemic year, 2020, was the year I was tempted to take constant refuge in life with Finn and his parents, even after they moved to a rental house a mile from us, and in the ongoing adventure with Janet and Jamie. It was also the year I postponed writing this book while I wrestled with my sense that Octavia Butler had it basically right, that the combination of high intelligence and hierarchical thinking isn't ultimately sustainable—and shouldn't be. I wrote some other things instead, and that was great, because (as they say) it kept me occupied. And now, starting in early 2021 and stitching and unstitching over the course of two and a half years, I have finally managed to write *this* thing, which may indicate that I haven't quite given up entirely. And I haven't. I don't really mean the title of this epilogue, so please don't just kill me now. As I revised my book 139 times (but who's counting?), Russian troops were committing innumerable war crimes in Ukraine, millions of Europeans and maybe a hundred million Americans have apparently decided to give fascism another chance, and my second grandchild, Evie, has arrived. Darkness and light, once again, "Night on Bald Mountain" and "Ave Maria." And then, as this book went into production, Hamas decided to torture, kidnap, and/or kill over a thousand Israeli civilians, and Israel decided to try to wipe out Hamas, killing over twenty thousand Palestinians in the process, and the Middle East once again became an inferno of escalating atrocities.

So even after we have weathered the pandemic, and whatever the wars in Ukraine and the Middle East will mean (surely enough to offset many human accomplishments in a game of *Blood and Roses*), I will still think that at this point in our collective lives together, the life worth living—the good life—is necessarily a life in which we have to ask ourselves about what would constitute a good death. If we can find ways of postponing that question until after Finn and Evie and their cohort around the world have had a chance to try to salvage things, great. For the sake of those children—really, all of them, gay and straight and bi and trans and queer and ace and cyborg, of all abilities and disabilities—I have to hope we do. We must go on. We can't go on. We'll go on. But fiction will always remind us that another world is possible, and it may indeed be possible that some of those worlds are places none of us—except for the preppers, who will make terrible neighbors—will want to live in. In which case it only makes sense for us to consider all our options, Crakers, Trisolarans, androids, and Oankali included. The optimists among us can continue to hold out hope for a Hainish future—so long as they agree to forgive the Hainish for experimenting with us in the past.

There is another way to end, though—and it behooves me to end this way, because, dear and patient reader, in the end, at the end, I want you to have enjoyed reading this book. Let me imagine, let us imagine, that the Oankali do not show up after all. Let us imagine that the records of our civilizations, the achievements and the atrocities, will not be deliberately expunged from the face of the Earth. Let us imagine that we get to go out on our own terms. If we do get that chance, let me suggest that we take the perspective of a sentient being so alien that I cannot articulate it to the project of the ex-human. In Ted Chiang's 2008 short story "Exhalation," a metallic creature discovers, by means of an audacious experiment on its own brain, that the air pressure differential on which its universe depends is decreasing. These creatures breathe argon, which is piped from air pockets deep underground in their world and stored in aluminum cylinders everywhere, so that each creature can literally refill its air supply each day, like exchanging propane tanks. The narrator is an anatomist; seeking to discover the nature of memory and the basis for its species' form of cognition, it constructs an elaborate apparatus that allows it to examine the gossamer-thin gold leaves, suspended from wires in tiny air capillaries, that constitute the mechanism of its very thoughts: "my consciousness could be said to be encoded in the position of those tiny leaves, but it would be more accurate to say that it was encoded in the ever-shifting pattern of air driving these leaves."[13]

As my students would say, this creature is not very relatable. This is why it comes at the very end of this book: you do not have to divorce yourself from the idea of the human and become ex-human to see the universe as it does, because its universe appears to have no point of contact with our own. I mean that in a physical as well as an intellectual and affective sense: its universe has chromium walls, and the creature's discovery about the changing air pressure in that universe implies that "our universe is a sealed chamber rather than an open well. And air is gradually accumulating within that chamber, until it equals the pressure in the reservoir below" (*E* 50).

The implications of this discovery are staggering, insofar as the equalization of air pressure in this universe will be analogous to heat death in ours: equilibrium will have been achieved, and with it the end of all life. Along the way, because these creatures depend on the interaction of argon with the gold leaves in their brains, the gradual equalization of air pressure will mean that their brains will work less and less efficiently, winding down agonizingly in a super-slow-motion version of HAL's final minutes of consciousness. Understandably, the anatomist's fellow-creatures do not take the news well. After a brief period of denial, there is "widespread panic," followed by the realization that the process will take untold centuries, followed by efforts to resist or reverse what seems to be an inexorable fact of physics. To the narrator, these efforts seem futile, and yet, it writes, "I maintain a slender hope" (*E* 54). Perhaps there is more than one universe, and perhaps the inhabitants of some other universe might someday find a way to breach the chromium walls of this one—not to save it but to explore it or to use its physical properties in some way.

The narrator explains its decision to inscribe its account on the sheets of copper that make up its civilization's stationery: this, it writes, "is why I have written this account. You, I hope, are one of those explorers. You, I hope, found these sheets of copper and deciphered the words engraved on their surfaces. And whether or not your brain is impelled by the air that once impelled mine, through the act of reading my words, the patterns that form your thoughts become an imitation of the patterns that once formed mine. And in that way I live again, through you" (*E* 55).

It is altogether fitting, then, that this creature's account—and mine, imitating its patterns of thought, close with a formal farewell that can stand as a counterpoint to Nietzsche's dismissal of the human intellect and Deckard's sense that even Mozart will vanish:

> Even if a universe's life span is calculable, the variety of life that is generated within it is not. The buildings we have erected, the art and music and verse we have composed, the very lives we've led: none of them could have been predicted, because none of them was inevitable. Our universe might have slid into equilibrium emitting nothing more than a quiet hiss. The fact that it spawned such plenitude is a miracle, one that is matched only by your universe giving rise to you.
>
> Though I am long dead as you read this, explorer, I offer to you a valediction. Contemplate the marvel that is existence, and rejoice that you are able to do so. I feel I have the right to tell you this because, as I am inscribing these words, I am doing the same.

(*E* 56–57)

In that spirit, thank you again, dear and patient reader, whether you be one of my species, one of the Hainish, one of the giant enlightened music-loving but nonhipster insects from Paxil 8, or an argon-breathing metallic creature from a chromium-walled universe. I hope this book will have been worth the time and trouble, for me and for you.

NOTES

PREFACE

1. See Emily VenDerWerff, "How Conservatives Took Over Sci-Fi's Most Prestigious Award," *Vox*, April 26, 2015, https://www.vox.com /2015/4/26/8495415/hugos-sad-puppies-controversy. The origin of the Sad Puppies was immediately followed by the formation of a group calling itself the Rabid Puppies, led by the white supremacist provocateur Vox Day (real name Theodore Robert Beale).

2. I don't mean to suggest that sci-fi is now a multicultural Valhalla. As Jemisin wrote in her 2018 preface to Butler's *Parable of the Sower*, "For every attempt made by marginalized people to express anguish and seek change for historical (and ongoing) harm, there's always pushback. . . . What we have touched has changed: the SFF [science fiction and fantasy] genre has improved slightly. . . . Instead of just Butler and a handful of others, now there are dozens of published black writers—and disabled writers, queer writers, indigenous writers, and more. But what we have changed has changed us in turn; I and other marginalized writers must be constantly braced for internet harassment, death threats, and campaigns to Make Science Fiction Racist Again." N. K. Jemisin, "Three Reads," foreword to Octavia E. Butler, *Parable of the Sower* (New York: Grand Central, 2018), xi. See also Aja Romano, "The Hugo Awards Just Made History, and Defied Alt-Right Extremists in the Process," *Vox*, August 21, 2018, https://www .vox.com/2018/8/21/17763260/n-k-jemisin-hugo-awards-broken-earth -sad-puppies.

3. Elizabeth Kolbert, *The Sixth Extinction: An Unnatural History* (New York: Henry Holt, 2014); Toby Ord, *The Precipice: Existential Risk and the Future of Humanity* (New York: Hachette, 2020), hereafter cited parenthetically as *P*; David Wallace-Wells, *The Uninhabitable Earth: Life After Warming* (New York: Tim Duggan, 2019); Alan Weisman, *The World Without Us* (New York: Thomas Dunne, 2007).

INTRODUCTION: LEARNING TO DIE

1. Sven Birkerts, "Present at the Re-Creation," review of *Oryx and Crake*, *New York Times*, May 18, 2003, https://www.nytimes.com/2003/05/18 /books/present-at-the-re-creation.html.

2. Cixin Liu takes an even more dismissive view of those gatekeepers and their turf: "Literature has always given me the impression of indulging an intense anthropocentric narcissism. . . . Literature needs to get past this narcissism, and the genre that is working hardest to do so is science fiction." Cixin Liu, "Beyond Narcissism: What Science Fiction Can Offer Literature," *Science Fiction Studies* 40, no. 1 (2013): 22. I have taken my cue accordingly. I have a less reductive view of literature than Liu and a less reductive view of science fiction than Birkerts, and I want to wean myself (and you) from anthropocentric narcissism.

3. See Susan Squier, *Babies in Bottles: Twentieth-Century Visions of Reproductive Technology* (New Brunswick, NJ: Rutgers University Press, 1994).

4. Quoted in David Barnett, "Science Fiction: The Genre that Dare Not Speak Its Name," *The Guardian*, January 28, 2009, https://www.the guardian.com/books/booksblog/2009/jan/28/ science-fiction-genre.

5. Matthew Hart suspects, rightly, that "the 'speculative' label is merely a gentrifying term, designed to launder the subcultural stink of the fantastic." Matthew Hart, *Extraterritorial: A Political Geography of Contemporary Fiction* (New York: Columbia University Press, 2020), 110. Hart cites Ursula K. Le Guin's rejoinder: "This arbitrarily restrictive definition seems designed to protect her novels from being relegated to a genre still shunned by hidebound readers, reviewers and prize-awarders. She doesn't want the literary bigots to shove her into the literary ghetto." Ursula K. Le Guin, review of Margaret Atwood, *The*

Year of the Flood, The Guardian, August 29, 2009, https://www.the guardian.com/books/ 2009/aug/29/margaret-atwood-year-of-flood.

6. Margaret Atwood, "Life After Man," interview with Maggie Mcdonald and Eleanor Case, *New Scientist,* May 2, 2003, 40–43. See also Margaret Atwood, "The Road to Ustopia," *The Guardian,* October 14, 2011, https://www.theguardian.com/books/2011/oct/ 14/margaret-atwood-road-to-ustopia. As Atwood explains, "ustopia" is a word "I made up by combining utopia and dystopia."

7. Mary Shelley, *Frankenstein; or, the Modern Prometheus,* ed. Michael Bérubé (New York: Norton, 2021), 5. Hereafter cited parenthetically as *F.*

8. Philip K. Dick, interview with Yves Breaux and Francis Luxereau (1977). Reproduced at *Scraps from the Loft,* 2018, https://scrapsfromtheloft .com/comedy/an-interview-with-philip-k-dick-1977-by-yves-breux -and-francis-luxereau/.

9. Darko Suvin, *Metamorphoses of Science Fiction: On the Poetics and History of a Literary Genre* (New Haven, CT: Yale University Press, 1979).

10. Rob Latham, "American Slipstream: Science Fiction and Literary Respectability," in *The Cambridge Companion to American Science Fiction,* ed. Eric Carl Link and Gerry Canavan (Cambridge: Cambridge University Press, 2015), 99.

11. Link and Canavan, introduction to *Cambridge Companion,* 1. See also Fredric Jameson, who makes of pulp a virtue: "The officially 'non-serious' or pulp character of SF is an indispensable feature in its capacity to relax that tyrannical 'reality principle' which functions as a crippling censorship over high art, and to allow the 'paraliterary' form thereby to inherit the vocation of giving us alternate versions of a world that has elsewhere seemed to resist even *imagined* change." Fredric Jameson, "World-Reduction in Le Guin: The Emergence of Utopian Narrative," *Science Fiction Studies* 2, no. 3 (1975): 223. Isiah Lavender brings this argument to bear on race, writing that "the resources that sf can bring to bear on black experiences are simply greater than realistic modes of writing." Isiah Lavender, *Race in American Science Fiction* (Bloomington: Indiana University Press), 64.

12. This is not to say anything about Alan Weisman's attempt to imagine the world without us; he's just explaining what would and wouldn't survive and why.

13. Gerry Canavan, "Hope, but Not for Us: Ecological Science Fiction and the End of the World in Margaret Atwood's *Oryx and Crake* and *The Year of the Flood*," *LIT: Literature Interpretation Theory* 23, no. 2 (2011): 149.

14. William Faulkner, "Banquet Speech," Nobel Prize in Literature, 1949, December 10, 1950, https://www. nobelprize.org/prizes/literature/1949 /faulkner/speech/.

15. Caspar Weinberger was perhaps the most prominent of those war planners, but he was far from alone. See Richard Halloran, "Weinberger Defends His Plan on a Protracted Nuclear War," *New York Times*, August 10, 1982, https://www.nytimes.com/1982/08/10/world/ weinberger-defends-his-plan-on-a-protracted-nuclear-war.html.

16. See Priscilla Wald, *Contagious: Cultures, Carriers, and the Outbreak Narrative* (Durham, NC: Duke University Press, 2007).

17. Dipesh Chakrabarty, "The Climate of History: Four Theses," *Critical Inquiry* 35, no. 2 (2009): 197–222.

18. John Searle, *The Construction of Social Reality* (New York: Free Press, 1995).

19. Dipesh Chakrabarty, *Provincializing Europe: Postcolonial Thought and Historical Difference* (Princeton, NJ: Princeton University Press, 2000), 26. Hereafter cited parenthetically as *PE*.

20. As the film *The Island President* makes painfully clear, the Maldives will very likely be the first islands to disappear, followed swiftly by many more. *The Island President*, dir. Jon Shenk (Samuel Goldwyn Films, 2011), 1:41.

21. Richard Grusin, introduction to *After Extinction*, ed. Richard Grusin (Minneapolis: University of Minnesota Press, 2018), 2. Gerry Canavan offers a similar reading: "To say 'the Anthropocene' is in some sense to name ourselves and our society as all already dead," and the term should therefore be understood "as a kind of neo-Romantic revival of the melancholic fascination with death, illness and morbidity, ruin, and a vanishing natural world." Gerry Canavan, "Science Fiction and Utopia in the Anthropocene," *American Literature* 93, no. 2 (2021), 261–62. See also Rebecca Evans, who argues that the term "Anthropocene" is science fictional: "The science fictionality of the Anthropocene reminds us that the cognitive estrangements of climate change are as intent on rewriting historical narratives as they are on

addressing possible futures." Rebecca Evans, "Nomenclature, Narrative, and Novum: 'The Anthropocene' and/as Science Fiction," *Science Fiction Studies* 45, no. 3 (2018): 496.

22. See Richard Grusin, *Premediation: Affect and Mediality After 9/11* (New York: Palgrave Macmillan, 2010), in which he develops his theory of how media "premediate" future events.

23. This view has gained some mainstream acceptance, as evidenced by a 2018 editorial in *Scientific American*, "The Term 'Anthropocene' Is Popular—and Problematic," December 1, 2018, https://www.scie ntificamerican.com/ article/the-term-anthropocene-is-popular-and -problematic/.

24. Donna Haraway, *Staying with the Trouble: Making Kin in the Chthulucene* (Durham, NC: Duke University Press, 2016).

25. See Donna Haraway, "Tentacular Thinking: Anthropocene, Capitalocene, Chthulucene," *e-flux* 75 (September 2016), https://www.e-flux .com /journal /75 /67125 /tentacular-thinking-anthropocene -capitalocene-chthulucene/: "Still, if we could only have one word for these SF times, surely it must be the Capitalocene." The note to this sentence gives the credit for the term to Malm. See also Jason Moore, *Capitalism in the Web of Life; Ecology and the Accumulation of Capital* (New York: Verso, 2015); and Jason Moore, *Anthropocene or Capitalocene? Nature, History, and the Crisis of Capitalism* (New York: PM, 2016).

26. See Gregg Mitman, "Reflections on the Plantationocene: A Conversation with Donna Haraway and Anna Tsing," *EdgeEffects*, June 28, 2019, https://edgeeffects.net/haraway-tsing-plantationocene/.

27. See Janae Davis, Alex A. Moulton, Levi Van Sant, and Brian Williams, "Anthropocene, Capitalocene, . . . Plantationocene? A Manifesto for Ecological Justice in an Age of Global Crises," *Geography Compass* 13, no. 5 (May 2019), https://onlinelibrary.wiley. com/doi /10.1111/ gec3.12438.

28. Nicholas Mirzeoff, "It's Not the Anthropocene, It's the White Supremacy Scene: or, The Geological Color Line," in *After Extinction*, ed. Grusin, 123–50.

29. Roy Scranton, *Learning to Die in the Anthropocene: Reflections on the End of a Civilization* (San Francisco: City Lights, 2015), 16. Hereafter cited parenthetically as *LDA*.

30. Rosi Braidotti, *The Posthuman* (Cambridge: Polity, 2013), 135. Hereafter cited parenthetically as *Post*.

31. *Melancholia*, dir. Lars von Trier (2011, Zentropa Entertainments), 2:16.

32. My memory for pre-COVID conversations is not perfect, but I believe I owe this line to David Ferguson, a participant in my seminar on literature and intellectual disability at the School for Criticism and Theory in 2013.

33. Quoted in Caitlin O'Kane, "Senator Lindsey Graham Says He Has an AR-15 to Protect His Home from Gangs," CBS.com, March 29, 2021, https://www.cbsnews.com/news/lindsey-graham-ar-15-protect -home-gangs/. The combination of the pandemic and the public demonstrations against police violence produced a great deal of this doughy-white-boy bravado, epitomized by the St. Louis attorney Mark McCloskey, who with his wife, Patricia, pointed loaded guns at peaceful protestors walking by their house—and thereby became right-wing heroes. In McCloskey's fantasy land, "an angry mob showed up at my doorstep to attack my home & my family," as he put it on Twitter, and "I made it clear . . . I will not back down from the fight." "I made it clear when an angry mob showed up at my doorstep to attack my home & my family: I will not back down from the fight. Last night, I shared my next big move to defend you & our values against the radical mob Help me FIGHT BACK." @mccloskeyusa [Mark McCloskey], Twitter, May 19, 2021, 10:29 AM, https://twitter.com /mccloskeyusa/status/ 1395023765587779587. McCloskey then attempted to parlay his new he-man status into a political career.

34. The locus classicus of this argument is Kwame Anthony Appiah, "Is the Post- in Postmodernism the Post- in Postcolonial?," *Critical Inquiry* 17, no. 2 (1991): 336–57.

35. There are three more prefix options, so far as I have been able to determine. For the *non*human, see Richard Grusin, ed., *The Nonhuman Turn* (Minneapolis: University of Minnesota Press, 2015), based on the conference Grusin organized at the Center for Twenty-First Century Studies at the University of Wisconsin–Milwaukee. The "nonhuman" of that collection, however, doesn't have the connotations I want here; it is more an assemblage of contemporary theoretical schools—new materialism, object-oriented ontology, animal studies,

digital humanities, and information sciences—that decenter the human but not in order for us to shed our skins. There is also the *inhuman*, as in Jean-François Lyotard's 1989 book of that title: *The Inhuman: Reflections on Time*, trans. Geoff Bennington and Rachel Bowlby (Stanford, CA: Stanford University Press, 1991). But that is about the alienation and exploitation of humans in advanced capitalism and retains much of the sense of the *inhumane*. Finally, there is the *ahuman*, as in Patricia MacCormack, *The Ahuman Manifesto: Activism for the End of the Anthropocene* (New York: Bloomsbury, 2020), which argues for a *Children of Men* scenario in which humans stop reproducing and die out, the sooner the better.

36. Adam Kirsch, *The Revolt Against Humanity: Imagining a Future Without Us* (New York: Columbia Global Reports, 2023), 11. Hereafter cited parenthetically as *R*.

37. See Scott F. Gilbert, Jan Sapp, and Alfred I. Tauber, "A Symbiotic View of Life: We Have Never Been Individuals," *Quarterly Review of Biology* 87, no. 4 (2012): 325–41, https://www.journals.uchicago.edu/doi/10.1086/668166.

38. See, for example, Myra Hird, *The Origins of Sociable Life: Evolution After Science Studies* (New York: Palgrave Macmillan, 2009), which opens with a compelling account of how Margulis and Dorion Sagan's book *What Is Sex?* (New York: Simon and Shuster, 1997) literally changed her life—and her understanding of "life."

39. The foundational text of object-oriented ontology is Graham Harman, *Tool-Being: Heidegger and the Metaphysics of Objects* (Chicago: Open Court, 2002); see also Timothy Morton, *The Ecological Thought* (Cambridge, MA: Harvard University Press, 2010), and Timothy Morton, *Humankind: Solidarity with Non-Human People* (New York: Verso, 2017), for an account of the "symbiotic real." As we will see in chapter 2, Morton's position is very close to that of Mike Evans's "Pan-Species Communism" in *The Three-Body Problem*, save for Evans's desire for genocide. For an agenda-setting example of the new materialism, see Jane Bennett, *Vibrant Matter: A Political Ecology of Things* (Durham, NC: Duke University Press, 2009). Carolin Gebauer cites Morton and Haraway in a reading of *Oryx and Crake* as a novel that "raises readers' awareness of the fact that the relationship between the

notions of nature and humanity, or nature and (human) culture, goes beyond a simple binary divide." Carolin Gebauer, "Imagining Posthuman Environments in the Anthropocene: The Function of Space in Post-Apocalyptic Climate Change Fiction," in *Narrating Nonhuman Spaces: Form, Story, and Experience Beyond Anthropocentrism*, ed. Marco Caracciolo, Marlene Karlsson Marcusson, and David Rodriguez (New York: Routledge, 2021), 110.

40. I am not including Jemisin's Broken Earth trilogy here because it is much too far-future and does not entertain or encourage an ex-human perspective, but as I note in chapter 4, I am struck by the fact that the orogenes are simultaneously people with disabilities and people with awesome, potentially terrifying powers, along the lines of people with hyperempathy ("sharers") in Butler's Parables.

41. As I will argue in chapter 3, Hampton Fancher and David Peoples's decision to make Rick Deckard in *Blade Runner* a brooding handsome single man with a romantic interest in an android is especially problematic given the source material. And even more problematic for the gratuitous and unwatchable rape scene.

42. Indeed, the Nigerian information minister Dora Akunyili asked movie houses in the capital city of Abuja not to screen the film. See Julie Bloom, "Nigeria Says 'District 9' is Not Welcome," *New York Times*, September 20, 2009, https://www.nytimes.com/2009/09/21/movies/21arts-NIGERIASAYSD_BRF.html.

43. However, as I was writing this book, FX on Hulu began streaming Butler's *Kindred*, adapted by the Obie Award–winning playwright Branden Jacobs-Jenkins.

44. Kyle Powys White, "Indigenous Science (Fiction) for the Anthropocene: Ancestral Dystopias and Fantasies of Climate Change Crises," *Environment and Planning E: Nature and Space* 1, nos. 1–2 (2018): 226.

45. Kyle Powys White, "Our Ancestors' Dystopia Now: Indigenous Conservation and the Anthropocene," in *Routledge Companion to the Environmental Humanities*, ed. Ursula K. Heise, Jon Christensen, and Michelle Niemann (New York: Routledge, 2017), 208–9.

46. Toby Ord, *The Precipice: Existential Risk and the Future of Humanity* (New York: Hachette, 2020), 17. Hereafter cited parenthetically as *P*.

47. In a thoughtful review that raises similar objections to Ord's homogenizing "on average" and his unsettlingly un-self-conscious use of the

first person plural, Alexa Hazel suggests that despite its flaws, "*The Precipice* may be the *Silent Spring* that the futurists have been waiting for." Hold that thought for chapter 2, in which we will see what happens when Ye Weinjie encounters *Silent Spring*. Alexa Hazel, "In Optimism Lies Urgency: Toby Ord and the Future of Humanity," *Los Angeles Review of Books*, May 9, 2020, https://lareviewofbooks.org/article/in-optimism-lies-urgency-toby-ord-future-humanity/.

48. This is the premise of Kim Stanley Robinson's *The Ministry for the Future* (London: Orbit, 2020), in which the ministry exists precisely to represent the interest of future generations of human beings whose rights are equal to our own.

49. Claire Colebrook, "Lives Worth Living: Extinction, Persons, Disability," in *After Extinction*, ed. Grusin, 161. For Colebrook's larger argument about the prospects of human extinction and the difficulty of justifying our continued existence, see Claire Colebrook, *The Death of the PostHuman: Essays on Extinction* (London: Open Humanities Press, 2014).

50. David Benatar, *Better Never to Have Been: The Harm of Coming Into Existence* (New York: Oxford University Press, 2006).

51. For a useful introduction to the connections tying Oxford philosophers to tech billionaires and their assorted scammers, see Sigal Samuel, "Effective Altruism's Most Controversial Idea," *Vox*, September 6, 2022, https://www.vox.com/future-perfect/23298870/ effective-altruism-longtermism-will-macaskill-future.

52. This is not the place for a full-bore discussion of physician-assisted suicide (an especially fraught subject in disability studies), but it is not uncommon for people experiencing painful terminal illness to want to hasten the inevitable end of their own lives.

53. *Blade Runner*, dir. Ridley Scott (Warner Brothers, 1982), 1:50.

1.THE AUGMENTATION OF THE COMPLEXITY AND INTENSITY OF THE FIELD OF INTELLIGENT LIFE: THE POTENTIAL EX-HUMAN OF *THE LEFT HAND OF DARKNESS*

1. They are Stephanie Brown at Ohio State–Newark, Jeff Clymer at the University of Kentucky, and Jane Elliott at King's College London.

2. For historiographic metafiction as the dominant mode of literary post-modernism, see Linda Hutcheon, *A Poetics of Postmodernism: History, Theory, Fiction* (New York: Routledge, 1988); for postmodern literature and ontological uncertainty (as opposed to the merely epistemological uncertainty of modernist literature), see Brian McHale, *Postmodernist Fiction* (New York: Routledge, 1987). The bit about characters dissolving into neutrinos is something I made up, but takes as its inspiration the inexplicable fate of Tyrone Slothrop in Thomas Pynchon's *Gravity's Rainbow* (New York: Vintage, 1973), who somehow becomes a crossroads. What made my students' abreactions especially curious, I thought, was that there was a lively critical conversation throughout the 1990s on the complex relations between science fiction and post-modernism, as evidenced by the journal *Science Fiction Studies*, whose special issue on the subject was published in 1991.

3. Lewis Call, "Postmodern Anarchism in the Novels of Ursula K. Le Guin," *SubStance* 36, no. 2 (2007): 87–105.

4. Becky Chambers, "How *The Left Hand of Darkness* Changed Everything," *Literary Hub*, September 10, 2018, https://lithub.com/how-the-left-hand-of-darkness-changed-everything/. Interestingly, this isn't quite true; there was a period when the novel fell out of favor and Le Guin all but repudiated it. Its reputation has recovered, and it is back in the canon, but it has been a surprisingly rocky ride.

5. Charlie Jane Anders, "*The Left Hand of Darkness* at Fifty," *Paris Review*, March 12, 2019, https://www.theparisreview.org/blog/2019/03/12/the-left-hand-of-darkness-at-fifty/.

6. Ursula K. Le Guin, *The Left Hand of Darkness* (New York: Ace, 1969), 89. Hereafter cited parenthetically as *LHD*.

7. An aside: when I first taught the novel in 1991, I used two pedestrian examples to illustrate the ubiquitous gendering of childcare in our own (North American) society, noting that none of my undergraduate students had yet become parents. One was the fact that when I took my toddling firstborn to a home improvement store in 1987, I found that there were no shopping carts with child seats, the kind to which he and I had become accustomed at supermarkets. The other was from the supermarkets themselves, where I found upon my first diaper-buying errand that the diaper aisle was also the feminine-hygiene-products aisle. The implicit message was *here are paper products for those*

of you who are menstruating, next to products for those of you who have given birth. Somehow, over the course of the 1990s, things were rearranged. The home improvement stores not only acquired shopping carts with child seats but also installed changing tables in the men's bathrooms; the supermarkets moved the feminine hygiene products to health and beauty aisles and rearranged the diaper aisle so that it juxtaposed Pampers and Depends. The new implicit message was *remember that we enter this world with no control over our excretory functions and may exit it the same way. It is the Circle of Life.* I have no idea how the degendering of such commercial spaces took place.

8. However, as Barbara Bengels points out, Genly acknowledges that "I thought of him as my landlady, because he had fat buttocks that wagged as he walked, and a soft fat face, and a prying, spying, ignoble, kindly nature" (*LHD* 48). Bengels, focusing on the physical description, rightly notes that Genly's "equation of effeminacy and fleshiness is not very different from his displeasure with the female form itself." Barbara Bengels, "Sex and the Single Man: *The Left Hand of Darkness*," *Science Fiction: A Review of Speculative Literature* 9, no. 1 (1987): 17.

9. Pamela J. Annas goes further, adding to the pronoun problem the fact that Le Guin's male narrator skews the novel's presentation of androgyny: "Feminist criticism of this novel has focused on the use of the generic 'he' and on the choice of a man, Genly Ai, as the main character and interpreter of Gethen. Gethen would have looked different to us if Genly Ai had been a woman, but instead we see this androgynous society through the eyes of a biological and culturally conditioned male. What Le Guin has done is to embody in Genly Ai the main problem feminists have had with the concept of androgyny: that it has usually been looked at and defined from a male perspective." Pamela J. Annas, "New Worlds, New Words: Androgyny in Feminist Science Fiction," *Science Fiction Studies* 5, no. 2 (1978): 151. More emphatically, Joanna Russ, working the same side of the sci-fi street as Le Guin throughout the 1970s, dismissed the novel as "a world of men." Joanna Russ, "The Image of Women in Science Fiction," in *Images of Women in Fiction: Feminist Perspectives*, ed. Susan Koppelman Cornillon (Bowling Green, OH: Bowling Green Popular Press, 1972), 90.

10. And yet how much trouble would it have been for Ong Tot Oppong to write "anyone can turn their hand to anything" instead of "anyone

can turn his hand to anything"? Similarly, "when you meet a Gethenian you cannot and must not do what a bisexual naturally does, which
is to cast him in the role of Man or Woman" could easily have been
"when you meet Gethenians you cannot and must not do what a bisexual naturally does, which is to cast them in the role of Man or Woman."

11. Jewell Parker Rhodes's canny critique of the novel's pronouns is now
a standard go-to argument: "If as an artist [Le Guin] can invent a new
futuristic world with new religions and new cultural groupings, then,
can't she invent new words to depict accurately her vision of the andro-
gyne? Perhaps this argument is extreme: but Le Guin's fictional world
is called *Gethen*, Gethen's religions are called *Haddara* and *Yomesh*, and
the planet's cultural groups are named *Karhiders* and *Orgota*; given
these nouns are alien to English, would it not be equally simple to refer
to the Gethenians in such a way as to reflect better their ambisexual
being? . . . Pronoun distinctions between Ai and the Gethenians would
make more immediate the xenophobia which must be overcome." Jewell Parker Rhodes, "Ursula K. Le Guin's *The Left Hand of Darkness*:
Androgyny and the Feminist Utopia," in *Women and Utopia: Critical
Interpretations*, ed. Marleen Barr and Nicholas D. Smith (Lanham,
MD: University Press of America, 1983), 115–16. Indeed, Rhodes's critique goes deeper, taking issue with Le Guin's idea of androgyny in
toto for its gender essentialism: "androgyny as a possible utopian device
aimed at exploding our culture's sexual restraints is a deception. The
myth inherently reinforces and encourages the stereotyping feminists
would so dearly love to deny" (109).

12. In the 1976 essay "Is Gender Necessary?," Le Guin dug in hard on her
use of "he": "I call Gethenians 'he' because I utterly refuse to mangle
English by inventing a pronoun for 'he/she.' 'He' is the generic pronoun, damn it, in English. (I envy the Japanese, who, I am told, do
have a he/she pronoun.) But I do not consider this really very important." Ursula K. Le Guin, "Is Gender Necessary? Redux," in *The Language of the Night: Essays on Fantasy and Science Fiction*, rev. ed. (New
York: HarperCollins, 1992), 169–70. Hereafter cited parenthetically as
"IGN." In her 1988 notes on the essay, published side by side with the
original text and titled "Redux," Le Guin wrote that "I now consider
it very important" ("IGN" 170)—and made an argument that would

resonate strongly three decades later: "This 'utter refusal' of 1968 restated in 1976 collapsed, utterly, within a couple of years more. I still dislike invented pronouns, but now dislike them less than the so-called generic pronoun he/him/his, which does in fact exclude women from discourse; and which was an invention of male grammarians, for until the sixteenth century the English generic singular was they/them/their, as it still is in English and American colloquial speech. It should be restored to the written language, and let the pedants and pundits squeak and gibber in the streets" ("IGN" 169–70). The issue was brought to the forefront by trans activists in the 2010s, and there was, and still is, much squeaking and gibbering among the pedants and pundits—and, even more lamentably, among elected representatives throughout much of the United States.

13. Barbara Bengels notes the curious fact that "he mentions the 3–4% of perverts . . . none of whom he seems to have sought out for companionship or sexual relief in his two years of virtual isolation on Gethen." Bengels, "Sex and the Single Man," 17.

14. In her reading of "Is Gender Necessary?," Sarah Lefanu notes more generally (and accurately), "As is so often the case with Le Guin, she responds to criticism with self-criticism." Sarah Lefanu, *Feminism and Science Fiction* (Bloomington: Indiana University Press, 1989), 137. Indeed, in "Redux" Le Guin bears this out by being self-critical about her initial self-criticism: she asks us to "strike 'his'" from "his children," to "place 'him' in quotation marks, please" for "see him as a man," and "Read: . . . as I did" for "to see Estraven as I saw him" ("IGN" 170–71). The original passage is eloquent testimony to how the pronouns consistently undermine Le Guin's project even as she issues a mea culpa for casting Estraven in traditionally male-protagonist roles.

15. Not long thereafter, in his audience with the king, Ai will remark that the truculent monarch "stood there sullen as an old she-otter in a cage" (35). This gendered otter, however, is clearly tinged with Genly's misogyny.

16. Arthur C. Clarke, *2001: A Space Odyssey* (New York: Roc, 1968), 243–44. Hereafter cited parenthetically as *2001*.

17. As Patricia Frazer Lamb and Diana L. Veith point out (drawing on Leslie Fiedler's *Love and Death in the American Novel*), Genly's and

Estraven's harrowing journey effectively codes Estraven as male and invites us to read the adventure as homosocial/homoerotic, and since they are presented as men throughout the novel, "Estraven's and Genly's barrier is that theirs is a socially and psychologically homosexual love that, as such, cannot be fulfilled. Thus, not only do they turn aside from one another at the time of Estraven's kemmer, but a few pages later Estraven dies." Patricia Frazer Lamb and Diana L. Veith, "Again, *The Left Hand of Darkness*: Androgyny or Homophobia?," in *Erotic Universe: Sexuality and Fantastic Literature*, ed. Donald Palumbo (New York: Greenwood, 1986), 227. Lamb and Veith are right about this but oddly mistaken to claim that it is Genly who refuses kemmering with Estraven (223–24); Estraven quite clearly tells Genly, at the climactic moment at which the latter sees the former as the manwoman they are, that "he was in kemmer and had been trying to avoid me, insofar as one of us could avoid the other. 'I must not touch you,' he said, with extreme constraint; saying that he looked away" (*LHD* 249).

18. In his audience with King Argaven, Ai explains, "The principle it works on, the constant of simultaneity, is analogous in some ways to gravity" (*LHD* 37). Unfortunately, that's not how gravity works, but this is a problem that bedevils all of science fiction: how to imagine communication across vast distances. Le Guin later corrected the error in *The Dispossessed*, which explains (among other things) Shevek's invention of the ansible. I'll return to *The Dispossessed* at the end of this chapter.

19. Victor mentions the destruction of "the empires of Mexico and Peru" in his warning to Walton to always "preserve a calm and peaceful mind" (*F* 40), and the creature himself learns, via Volney's *Ruins of Empires*, of "the discovery of the American hemisphere" and weeps "over the hapless fate of its original inhabitants" (*F* 98).

20. Jean-François Lyotard, *The Postmodern Condition: A Report on Knowledge* [1979], trans. Geoff Bennington and Brian Massumi (Minneapolis: University of Minnesota Press, 1984), 81–82. I doubt whether many readers will want me to rehearse the details of that debate at this late date; for my part, I wrote extensively about it—and offered my own attempt to address the impasse—in Michael Bérubé, *What's Liberal About the Liberal Arts? Classroom Politics and "Bias" in Higher Education* (New York: Norton, 2006), chap. 6, "Postmodernism," 206–72.

21. See, e.g., reader-response accounts of the novel by John Pennington, "Exorcising Gender: Resisting Readers in Ursula K. Le Guin's *Left Hand of Darkness*," *Extrapolation* 41, no. 4 (2000): 351–58; and Christine Cornell, "The Interpretative Journey in Ursula K. Le Guin's *The Left Hand of Darkness*," *Extrapolation* 42, no. 4 (2001): 315–27. As Cornell writes, "The narrative of *Left Hand of Darkness* is crafted in such a way that the reader of the novel is restrained so that he or she must retrace Genly Ai's . . . intellectual and emotional development while following his physical journey" (317). (Though Cornell insists that she uses the word *restrained* "advisedly" [317], I would prefer to say "encouraged." Texts can't force readers to do anything, after all; that was one of the central insights of reader-response criticism.) Some years earlier, Craig and Diana Barrow had argued that the readers who are retracing Genly's missteps are implicitly male: "herein lies the key both to her own feminism and the feminist misunderstanding of her contribution to the cause. . . . Le Guin is arguing for sexual equality but with male fans and science-fiction writers." Craig Barrow and Diana Barrow, "*The Left Hand of Darkness*: Feminism for Men," *Mosaic* 20, no. 1 (1987): 84. Sarah Lefanu, however, is a bit more specific and more skeptical, suggesting that the novel "speaks to liberal rather than misogynistic male readers, to readers who feel at ease with the kind of feminism that seeks to remove conflict and difference." Lefanu, *Feminism and Science Fiction*, 140.

22. That inscrutability carries with it an unfortunate whiff of Orientalism, underscored by the fact that Karhiders cannot pronounce the letter "l," so that Estraven consistently refers to Genly Ai as "Genry." Genly, for his part, is Black; some readers miss this detail, because Le Guin has cannily placed a Black character in a landscape where his Blackness does not signify as it would on Earth. Indeed, even Isiah Lavender's discussion of race in the novel says nothing about Genly's Blackness. Instead, Lavender claims (correctly) that Gethenians are "a dark-skinned race" and that (mistakenly) "the roots of racial tension between the two dominant nations of Gethen—Karhide and Orgoreyn—are clearly on display as they struggle over the possession of a strip of land known as the 'Sinoth Valley.'" Isiah Lavender, *Race in American Science Fiction* (Bloomington: Indiana University Press),

159–60. There is no evidence in the novel that the tension between Karhide and Orgoreyn is racial in nature. For a compelling critique of the apparent insignificance of Genly's Blackness, see Jamil Khader, "Race Matters: People of Color, Ideology, and the Politics of Erasure and Reversal in Ursula Le Guin's *The Left Hand of Darkness* and Mary Doria Russell's *The Sparrow*," *Journal of the Fantastic in the Arts* 16, no. 2 (2005): 110–27. Because of "the framing of the novel within the trappings of liberal multiculturalism," Khader writes, "Blackness is evacuated, especially the African-American experience, from its cultural memory and its foundational narratives. Instead, the Black subject is reframed within the Eurocentric narrative of imperialism as an agent of Empire and as an equal partner to European imperialists" (114). This isn't quite right: the Ekumen is not an empire, and there is no reason to read Genly as specifically African American (rather than African), so it is a bit of an overreach for Khader to complain that Genly "definitely lacks the slave's ultimate realization of the evils of slavery" (116) because he does not connect his experience in Pulefen Farm to the experiences of slaves escaping from plantations. That said, Khader is right that Le Guin presents Genly's Blackness as if it does not have any connotations for Blackness as we know it; on Gethen it is meaningless, totally subsumed by sex/gender difference, and for that matter, as Joan Vinge notes, the Ekumen seems to have "no visible racial prejudice," so Genly's Blackness does not signify anywhere. Joan Vinge, "Introduction to *The Left Hand of Darkness*," *New York Review of Science Fiction* 43 (March 1992): 15.

23. The association of *The Left Hand of Darkness* with anthropology is common, since both Ong Tot Oppong and Genly Ai are engaged in an anthropological exercise, and this association was remarked as early as Fredric Jameson's 1975 *Science Fiction Studies* article, which cast the novel as a mash-up of genres including "the travel narrative (with anthropological data)." Fredric Jameson, "World-Reduction in Le Guin: The Emergence of Utopian Narrative," *Science Fiction Studies* 2, no. 3 (1975): 221. Mona Fayad writes that "Ai's refusal to see the Gethenians as androgynous is symptomatic of the kinds of cultural assumptions that Master Narratives project onto their interpretation of other cultures. Ai's contact with the Gethenians, despite his claims regarding

the benevolence of the Ekumen, brings with it a cultural imperialism which insists on its own superiority, a superiority based on the sameness of its patriarchal vision." Mona Fayad, "Aliens, Androgynes, and Anthropology: Le Guin's Critique of Representation in *The Left Hand of Darkness*," *Mosaic* 30, no. 3 (1997): 59–73.

24. Vine Deloria, *Custer Died for Your Sins: An Indian Manifesto* (New York: Macmillan, 1969), 79, 81. For a long-range assessment of Deloria's impact on the field, see Thomas Biolsi and Larry J. Zimmerman, *Indians and Anthropologists: Vine Deloria, Jr., and the Critique of Anthropology* (Tucson: University of Arizona Press, 1997).

25. Apparently Le Guin was so aware of anthropological thinking that she was like the fish that does not know it is wet. Joan Vinge reports that "I once had an opportunity to talk with Ursula Le Guin at an awards banquet. I told her that my anthropologist friends and I had been impressed by her use of anthropology in creating *The Left Hand of Darkness*, with its fully realized cultures, which are so human and at the same time so alien. She looked somewhat surprised, and said that she had not intentionally approached the novel that way. She must have learned her approach from her parents 'by osmosis,' she said. She had grown up with that particular way of seeing, taking for granted what most people have to learn like a second language (if they ever learn it at all)." Vinge, "Introduction," 14.

26. This reexamination of the field continues today, as, for example, in Margaret M. Bruchac's 2018 study of five early-twentieth-century American anthropologists (including even the determinedly antiracist Franz Boas) and their relations with their Native informants. Margaret M. Bruchac, *Savage Kin: Indigenous Informants and American Anthropologists* (Tucson: University of Arizona Press, 2018).

27. Trinh Minh-Ha, *Woman, Native, Other: Writing Postcoloniality and Feminism* (Bloomington: Indiana University Press), 59. The ableism entailed in calling native informants "handicapped" has not aged well, but the critique holds up. See also Fayed, "Aliens, Androgynes, and Anthropology," who claims that the novel offers "critiques of anthropological discourse that are similar to Trinh Minh-ha's attempts to problematize the colonialist beginnings and imperialistic undertones of anthropology as a science" (61). Fayad does not, however, pursue this

perceptive line of thought so far as to see Estraven as a vexed native informant shackled by shifgrethor.

28. Gayatri Spivak, *A Critique of Postcolonial Reason: Toward a History of the Vanishing Present* (Cambridge, MA: Harvard University Press, 1999), ix, 6.

29. For Genly's journey from misogyny, see also Barbara Brown, "*The Left Hand of Darkness*: Androgyny, Future, Present, and Past," *Extrapolation* 21, no. 3 (1980): 227–35. But Rhodes points out that at the very end of the novel, "despite Genly's growth, he cannot help but remark about the now dead Estraven's son: '(he had a girl's quick delicacy in his looks and movements, but no girl could keep so grim a silence as he did)' (*LHD*, p. 299)." Rhodes, "Androgyny and the Feminist Utopia," 119.

30. Ursula K. Le Guin, *The Dispossessed* (New York: Harper and Row, 1974), 279. Hereafter cited parenthetically as *D*. In 2022, the writer Jeff VanderMeer offered a reading of *LHD* as a novel about climate change as well: Jeff VanderMeer, "Landscape, Change, and the Long Road Ahead," *Orion*, 2022, https://orionmagazine.org/article/left-hand-of-darkness-book-review/.

31. In the following chapter, I will note that when we learn about Trisolaris in Cixin Liu's *The Three-Body Problem*, we hear it described in very similar terms—a planet where there is nothing to live for but bare life itself. However, Trisolaris's totalitarian government and resource rationing have nothing to do with the rapaciousness of the Trisolarans themselves and everything to do with their planet's unstable orbital path around three stars.

2. DESPERATE MEASURES: JUSTIFIABLE DESPAIR IN *THE THREE-BODY PROBLEM* AND *ORYX AND CRAKE*

1. I am aware that since the Chinese use *last name, first name*, I should say "Liu Cixin," but I am going by the way his name appears on the covers of the English translations of his work.

2. Alexandra Alter, "How Chinese Sci-Fi Conquered America," *New York Times Magazine*, December 3, 2019, https://www.nytimes.com

/2019/12/03/magazine/ken-liu-three-body-problem-chinese-science
-fiction.html.

3. Curiously, however, as Hans-Georg Erney points out, the original
serial publication of *Three-Body* in *Science Fiction World* opened with
the scenes set during the Cultural Revolution. Only in book form were
these scenes considered politically risky. Hans-Georg Erney, "Ecological Science Fiction with Chinese Characteristics: *The Three-Body
Problem*," *MOSF Journal of Science Fiction* 5, no. 1 (2021): 82.

4. Cixin Liu, *The Three-Body Problem* (New York: Tor, 2014), 19. Hereafter cited parenthetically as *TBP*.

5. In my fall 2022 class, however, a very talented Chinese-American student suggested to me—privately, so as not to upset Chinese students
in the class—that the authoritarian world of Trisolaris is basically an
allegory of contemporary China. Writing in the *MOSF Journal of Science Fiction*, Hans-Georg Erney concurs: "Some of the sections set on
the alien planet Trisolaris come closest to a critique of contemporary
China." Erney, "Ecological Science Fiction," 87. My student pointed
out, moreover, that on the final page of the novel, the stone tablet
marking the site of Red Coast Base had been placed by the Chinese
Academy of Sciences on March 21, 1989—less than a month before the
death of Hu Yaobang and the beginning of the Tiananmen Square
protests. No Chinese reader, she insisted, could read that tablet without thinking of the massacre of June 4, 1989.

6. Jiayang Fan, "Liu Cixin's War of the Worlds," *New Yorker*, June 17, 2019,
https://www.newyorker.com/magazine/2019/06/24/liu-cixins-war-of
-the-worlds. In 2021, the United States officially accused China of
genocide and crimes against humanity with regard to the Uighurs.

7. See, e.g., Ezra Glinter, "Review: China's Most Popular Science Fiction Writer, Cixin Liu, Brings His Spectacular Trilogy to an End,"
Los Angeles Times, September 22, 2016, https://www.latimes.com/books
/la-ca-jc-cixin-liu-20160914-snap-story.html. Googling "Cixin Liu
weak women characters" yields rafts of fan commentary that finds the
trilogy lamentably full of misogynist characters and narrative strategies, such as the "fridging" of Luo Ji's wife, Zhuang Yan, herself a
male-fantasy figure, in *The Dark Forest* ("fridging" means that she is

taken away from him and disappears from the novel so that he can be motivated to work seriously); for a vivid, pulling-no-punches example of fan commentary, see Thea James and Ana Grilo, "Joint Review: *The Dark Forest* by Cixin Liu," *The Book Smugglers*, December 11, 2015, https://www.thebooksmugglers. com/2015/12/joint-review-the-dark-forest-by-cixin-liu.html. (Grilo gives the book a 1 out of 10.)

8. There is a somewhat similar figure in Colson Whitehead's zombie novel *Zone One*: the minor character of Abel, "one of those apocalypse-as-moral-hygiene people, with a college-sophomore socialist slant. The dead came to scrub the Earth of capitalism and the vast bourgeois superstructure, with its doilies, helicopter parenting, and streaming video, return us to nature and wholesome communal living." Colson Whitehead, *Zone One* (New York: Doubleday, 2011), 153. The protagonist, called Mark Spitz by his human cohort (ironically, for his inability to swim; we never learn his real name), reflects that "the divine-retribution folks" greet the zombie plague on the grounds that "the human race deserved the plague, we brought it on ourselves for poisoning the planet, for the Death of God, the calculated brutalities of the global economic system, for driving primordial species to extinction" (153). Abel is not quite in the class of Crake and Dr. Peters, however, because he does not release a virus to wipe us out; he and his fellow travelers simply interpret the plague as our just deserts. Granted, he does manage to bring about the deaths of most of the humans in his immediate vicinity by opening the gates to the "skels" (zombies), but this produces merely local mayhem. Crake and Peters have global ambitions, and Crake almost realizes his.

9. Weisman's book was written eons ago, in 2007. We are just over eight billion now, but who's counting? Alan Weisman, *The World Without Us* (New York: Thomas Dunne, 2007), 310.

10. I am trying to adopt Liu's dry, deadpan-dispassionate tone here, but in all seriousness, this phenomenon is real. As Adam Kirsch writes, "Even if the revolt against humanity remains only a worldview or value system, it has the potential to turbocharge the central ideological struggle in American and European politics today. Much analysis has been devoted to the clash between liberalism, the creed of the educated classes who have held the levers of power in the West since the

Cold War, and populism, which appeals to those left behind by this regime—the religious, rural, working-class, nationalistic, and socially conservative. This division has made Western politics in the era of Brexit and Donald Trump more volatile than at any time since World War II. The revolt against humanity maps all too neatly onto this division" (*R* 93). As we will see in the epilogue, I am inclined to read Butler's Lilith's Brood trilogy through this lens as well.

11. The most simplistic version of this scenario has to be Roland Emmerich's 1996 film *Independence Day*, though I have to admit I enjoyed the film's mainstreaming of the Roswell/Area 51 conspiracy theory (i.e., that aliens crash-landed in Roswell, New Mexico, in 1947 and the U.S. government has been hiding their bodies in a secret military installation in Nevada), as well as the fact that the grizzled Jewish father, Julius Levinson (Judd Hirsch), is aware of the presence of alien bodies in Area 51 but the president of the United States (Bill Pullman) is not. By contrast, in *Arrival*, when the world's powers begin to worry that the alien heptapods are hostile, they immediately revert to petty, parochial intraspecies disputes and territorialisms. *Independence Day*, dir. Roland Emmerich (Twentieth Century Fox, 1996), 2:25; *Arrival*, dir. Denis Villeneuve (Paramount, 2016), 1:56.

12. Alan Moore and Dave Gibbons. *Watchmen* (New York: Warner Books, 1987); "The Architects of Fear," *The Outer Limits*, written by Meyer Dolinsky, dir. Byron Haskin (WABC, New York), September 30, 1963. See also President Ronald Reagan's address to the United Nations in 1987: "In our obsession with antagonisms of the moment, we often forget how much unites all the members of humanity. Perhaps we need some outside, universal threat to make us recognize this common bond. I occasionally think how quickly our differences worldwide would vanish if we were facing an alien threat from outside this world." Ronald Reagan, Address to the 42nd Session of the United Nations General Assembly in New York, New York, September 21, 1987, https://www.reaganlibrary.gov/archives/speech/address-42d-session-united-nations-general-assembly-new-york-new-york.

13. *Mars Attacks!*, dir. Tim Burton (Warner Brothers, 1996), 1:50.

14. Michael Bérubé, *Life as Jamie Knows It: An Exceptional Child Grows Up* (Boston: Beacon, 2016), 196.

15. In one of my classes, a group of students suggested that the timeframe for the Trisolaran invasion—450 years hence—maps interestingly (in a relatively optimistic scenario) onto the timeframe for climate change: that is, it presents humankind with a doomsday that seems to many people too far off to require drastic action now.

16. Thomas Moran pursues a similar line of argument, writing that the novel offers "a mode with which to apprehend extinction not as a threat to be avoided but as the inevitable destiny of terrestrial life" and that as the novel "pushes the rationalist hard science fiction form to its allegorical limit . . . the text begins to become interesting, calling not for the ethical salvation of humanity but for the radical annihilation of existing forms of political and ethical commitment." Thomas Moran, "The Perverse Utopianism of Willed Human Extinction: Writing Extinction in Liu Cixin's *The Three-Body Problem*," in *Ethical Futures and Global Science Fiction*, ed. Zachary Kendal, Aisling Smith, Giulia Champion, and Andrew Milner (New York: Palgrave Macmillan, 2020), 133–34.

17. We eventually manage a truce with the Trisolarans, and we survive centuries longer—until another intelligent species discovers us and decides to neutralize us as a potential threat by reducing our solar system from three dimensions to two. Some of us escape in time to avoid the fatal flattening, and thanks to the laws of relativity and some timely help from a Trisolaran representative, two of us manage to make it all the way to the death of the universe—and perhaps to the new universe to be born.

18. *12 Monkeys*, dir. Terry Gilliam (Universal, 1995), 2:10; *Contagion*, dir. Stephen Soderberg (Warner Brothers, 2011), 1:46.

19. Margaret Atwood, *Oryx and Crake* (New York: Anchor, 2003), 53. Hereafter cited parenthetically as *OC*.

20. Heather J. Hicks writes that "after the loss of his father, Crake is sociopathically detached from the world around him, his only emotion expressed in screams while sleeping." Heather J. Hicks, *The Post-Apocalyptic Novel in the Twenty-First Century: Modernity Beyond Salvage* (New York: Palgrave Macmillan, 2016), 39. That screaming seems to me a fairly important exception, however, even (or especially) if Crake is telling the truth about being unaware of it. Ariel Kroon offers

a more nuanced reading of Crake by way of affect theory and is almost as sympathetic to Crake's motivations as I am: "Atwood challenges readers to empathize with Crake's twin drives to eugenics and genocide, as the dominant culture around him is engaged in the active persecution of humans and non-humans alike." Ariel Kroon, "Reasonably Insane: Affect and Crake in Margaret Atwood's *Oryx and Crake*," *Canadian Literature* 226 (2015): 19.

21. As Earl G. Ingersoll noted in one of the first essays on the novel: "the gesture toward Shakespeare's tragedy is provocative because Hamlet's revenge plot leaves the stage at the end of Act V looking a bit post-apocalyptic, too." Earl G. Ingersoll, "Survival in Margaret Atwood's Novel *Oryx and Crake*," *Extrapolation* 45, no. 2 (2004): 169.

22. Kroon writes, "Crake's father's assumption that others would be motivated by horror to move against HelthWyzer resulted in his betrayal and murder by his confidants. Crake thus recognizes that faith in knowledge to motivate others to act morally is a false hope and deliberately avoids it." Kroon, "Reasonably Insane," 29. Deploying trauma theory, Katherine V. Snyder offers a perceptive reading of Jimmy in order to capture the novel's "portrayal of familial and domestic relations as prologue and analogue for the near-future obliteration of the human race" but strangely does not extend the analysis to Crake. Katherine V. Snyder, "'Time to Go': The Post-Apocalyptic and the Post-Traumatic in Margaret Atwood's *Oryx and Crake*," *Studies in the Novel* 43, no. 4 (2011): 486.

23. One critical exception is that of Gerry Canavan, who discusses this scene for precisely the right reason: "In the face of man's mania for self-destruction, which now threatens not only the future of *Homo sapiens* but all life on the planet as a whole, Crake's virulent misanthropy unexpectedly becomes transformed into something like a virtue, the truest form of love. (If this is not genocide as humanitarianism, exactly, then it is at the very least genocide as environmental policy: global death, in the name of preserving life.) This bizarre, murderous love directs itself not only towards preventing the predictable suffering of humans in the face of inevitable catastrophic collapse but towards all other life forms on the planet as well; when Crake witnesses a television report on peasant revolts in the Third World, his reaction is to want to kill

the police state suppressing the riots—not because they are harming guerillas ('there are always dead peasants') but because in the process they are massively defoliating the forest (179)." Gerry Canavan, "Hope, but Not for Us: Ecological Science Fiction and the End of the World in Margaret Atwood's *Oryx and Crake* and *The Year of the Flood*," *LIT: Literature Interpretation Theory* 23, no. 2 (2011): 150–51.

24. Atwood's characterization of the news in the pleeblands bears mention. "There were the usual political assassinations out there in the pleebs, the usual strange accidents, the unexplained disappearances. Or there were sex scandals: sex scandals always got the newscasters excited. For a while it was sports coaches and little boys; then there was a wave of adolescent girls found locked in garages" (*OC* 254). One of those girls is Oryx. But it was my singular misfortune to be teaching this novel in November 2011 just as the Jerry Sandusky scandal swept through Penn State, and a few of my students remarked, altogether appropriately, on the horror of the reference to sports coaches and little boys—precisely what our scandal, which persisted for decades, was all about.

25. There is an ominous preview of this at the end of *Oryx and Crake*, when Jimmy stumbles upon what initially appears reason for hope—a footprint in the sand, straight out of *Robinson Crusoe*—but turns out to be a pair of men and a woman, whom, we learn in *The Year of the Flood*, the men have been raping and brutalizing on a daily basis (and who turns out to be Jimmy's former girlfriend, Amanda Payne).

26. In an ingenious reading, Slawomir Koziol casts the Crakers as works of art and Crake as an avant-garde transgenic artist—while marking the connections between the Italian avant-garde and fascism. For Koziol, Crake "reduces the status of humans to that currently ascribed to animals in most scientific laboratories"—just as transhumanists are accused of doing today. Slawomir Koziol, "Crake's Aesthetic: Genetically Modified Humans as a Form of Art in Margaret Atwood's *Oryx and Crake*," *Critique: Studies in Contemporary Fiction* 59, no. 4 (2018): 500. Jihun Yoo pairs Crake with Butler's Oankali but muddies his otherwise savvy reading of (what I am calling) the ex-human in these texts by insisting that Crake and the Oankali are engaged in *transhumanist* projects, which they most certainly are not. Jihun Yoo, "Transhumanist

Impulse, Utopian Vision, and Reversing Dystopia in Margaret Atwood's *Oryx and Crake* and Octavia E. Butler's *Dawn*," *Modern Language Review* 114, no. 4 (2019): 662–81.

27. The novel deliberately invites this reading, most obviously when Jimmy cries out, "Crake! . . . Why am I on this earth? How come I'm alone? Where's my Bride of Frankenstein?" (*OC* 169).

28. The novel deliberately, emphatically invites this reading as well, and many readers have accepted the invitation. We are told explicitly that the Watson-Crick Institute at which Crake studies "was known to the students there as Asperger's U. because of the high percentage of brilliant weirdos that strolled and hopped and lurched through its corridors. Demi-autistic, generally speaking; single-track tunnel-vision minds, a marked degree of social ineptitude—these were not your sharp dressers—and luckily for everyone there, a high tolerance for mildly deviant public behavior" (*OC* 193–94). In his *New Republic* review of the novel, Richard Posner kicked off the reading of Crake as a figure of disability horror: "Crake is a perfectly credible twenty-first-century intellectual psychopath, with his faintly autistic, ascetic hyper-rationalism and his techie-bureaucratic talk." Richard Posner, "The End Is Near," *New Republic*, September 22, 2003, 31–32. J. Brooks Bouson concurs: "Pointing to the Asperger's-like traits of her character, Atwood provides a contemporary twist on the well-worn stereotype of the mad—and impersonal-amoral—scientist, creating in the process a puzzling, and troubling, character, one whose game-like approach to life ultimately leads to his gruesome destruction of humanity." J. Brooks Bouson, "'It's Game Over Forever': Atwood's Satiric Vision of a Bioengineered Posthuman Future in *Oryx and Crake*," *Journal of Commonwealth Literature* 39, no. 3 (2004): 145. Oddly, although Bouson cites Atwood's claim that "from a certain perspective, Crake is the most altruistic person around" (149; citing Brian Bethune, "Atwood Apocalyptic," *Maclean's* 116, no. 17 [April 28, 2003]: 48), he insists that even Crake's murders of his parents must be understood as "behaviour that points to the emotional void at the heart of Atwood's impersonal and amoral scientist character" (146). Chung-Hao Ku adds, after citing Bouson, "this pathological reading, though explaining (if not exonerating) Crake's destruction of humankind, still fails to take

into account such exterior forces as capitalism and technocracy." Chung-Hao Ku, "Of Monster and Man: Transgenics and Transgression in Margaret Atwood's *Oryx and Crake*," *Concentric: Literary and Cultural Studies* 32, no. 1 (2006): 120. The most severe indictment I have seen is that of Sara Schotland, who sees Crake as "the ultimate villain" whose representation by Atwood "does a disservice" to people with Asperger's. Sara Schotland, "Atwood's Crake: The Aspergic Mad Scientist," *Lincoln Humanities Journal* 7 (2019): 122. Stephen Dunning's mostly sympathetic reading of Crake, arguing that he "clearly acts with therapeutic intent," nevertheless manages to characterize the Watson-Crick students as "pampered, socially retarded [!], corporate student associates who lead painfully impoverished lives, and appear incapable of any intimacy lying outside the narrow definitions of their work." Stephen Dunning, "Margaret Atwood's *Oryx and Crake*: The Terror of the Therapeutic," *Canadian Literature* 186 (2005): 89–90.

29. Hannes Bergthaller, "Housebreaking the Human Animal: Humanism and the Problem of Sustainability in Margaret Atwood's *Oryx and Crake* and *The Year of the Flood*," *English Studies* 91, no. 7 (2010): 731, 737.

30. Bergthaller, "Housebreaking the Human Animal," 735, 741. Jane Glover proposes a similarly ambivalent reading of Crake, claiming that he "displays two particularly human characteristics in his own life's work: the instrumentalism which has played such a major role in the destruction of nature, and the human creativity to imagine a more utopian world." Jane Glover, "Human/Nature: Ecological Philosophy in Margaret Atwood's *Oryx and Crake*," *English Studies in Africa* 52, no. 2 (2009): 59.

31. The phrase "intellectually honourable" goes back to Jimmy's mother Sharon (*OC* 69), from when she first meets Crake, a few months before her escape from the Compound. "'Your friend is intellectually honourable,' Jimmy's mother would say. 'He doesn't lie to himself.' Then she'd gaze at Jimmy with that blue-eyed, wounded-by-him look he knew so well. If only *he* could be like that—intellectually honourable. Another baffling item on the cryptic report card his mother toted around in some mental pocket, the report card on which he was always

just barely passing. *Jimmy would do better at intellectual honourableness if only he would try harder.* Plus, if he had any fucking clues about what the fuck it meant" (*OC* 69–70). What it means, certainly, is that from a very young age—from his first entry into the novel—Crake understands the world as Jimmy's mother does.

32. The legendary Reddit post from a player of *Civilization II*, going by the handle u/Lycerius, seems apposite here:

> I've been playing the same game of Civ II for 10 years. Though long outdated, I grew fascinated with this particular game because by the time Civ III was released, I was already well into the distant future. I then thought that it might be interesting to see just how far into the future I could get and see what the ramifications would be. Naturally I play other games and have a life, but I often return to this game when I'm not doing anything and carry on. The results are as follows.
>
> • The world is a hellish nightmare of suffering and devastation.
>
> • There are 3 remaining super nations in the year 3991 A.D., each competing for the scant resources left on the planet after dozens of nuclear wars have rendered vast swaths of the world uninhabitable wastelands.
>
> • The ice caps have melted over 20 times (somehow) due primarily to the many nuclear wars. As a result, every inch of land in the world that isn't a mountain is inundated swamp land, useless to farming. Most of which is irradiated anyway.

There's more in this vein, but you get the idea. The post dates from 2012 and has generated 3,600 comments (comments are now closed), offering the advice the poster asked for. One popular suggestion was that the player needed to change his form of government: "Change to fundamentalism, I remember this was bad for research but you don't need it now anyway, but the people will stop hating you and you'll have more coin." "Fundamentalism is what you need. Fanatics are as cheap as anything." This may indeed be where we are headed.

33. Canavan, "Hope, but Not for Us," 144.

34. See also Ingersoll: "If traditional human qualities have to be sacrificed in order to survive, it may not be worth surviving." Ingersoll, "Survival," 167. Sara Schotland, whom I cited above for her argument that Atwood's portrayal of Crake does harm to people with Asperger's, extends her disability critique even to the Crakers, arguing that "Crake's absence of empathy is shown not only by his lack of feeling for human subjects but by the abnormal nature of the substitute androids that he designs to populate the postplague world. . . . The Crakers represent an extreme caricature of the intellectually disabled." Schotland, "Atwood's Crake," 128–29.

35. This vision of the fate of the performing arts was especially hard to read—and easy to contemplate—in the first phases of the COVID-19 pandemic, with theaters and performing venues shuttered around the globe.

36. In Ariel Kroon's affect theory reading, "the main characters' lack of emotional response to obvious suffering and the derision of moral values as useless (or active hindrances) to their hyper-capitalist system work to present an overarching dystopic mood." Kroon, "Reasonably Insane," 25. In what follows, I extend this analysis to the narrative itself.

37. Philip K. Dick, *Do Androids Dream of Electric Sheep?* (New York: Del Rey, 1968), 4. Hereafter cited parenthetically as *A*.

38. One important index of the worth of this society is its purely instrumental treatment of animals, such as the headless creatures that produce "Chickienobs" and the pigoons that are harvested for organ transplants—though the pigoons manage to create a place for themselves in the post-pandemic world. For an analysis of the novel from an animal studies perspective, see Stephanie Lance, "The Cost of Production: Animal Welfare and the Post-Industrial Slaughterhouse in Margaret Atwood's *Oryx and Crake*," *MOSF Journal of Science Fiction* 4, no. 1 (2020): 60–74. I will return to the question of human-animal relations in my discussion of *Do Androids Dream of Electric Sheep?* in chapter 3.

39. There are at least two clever against-the-grain feminist readings of the MaddAddam trilogy that foreground the role of women: Heather J. Hicks reads *Oryx and Crake* as a feminist reworking of the Book of Revelation and *Robinson Crusoe*: "As Snowman confronts 'zero hour'

in the final scene of the novel, Atwood resets the clock and opens the door for a new era to begin. In the wake of the long histories of apocalypse, gender, colonization, and science the novel has excavated, she invites us to imagine this new Crusoe setting out with his gun to defend the new Friday(s)." Hicks, *The Post-Apocalyptic Novel*, 53. And Calina Ciobanu writes that the end of *The Year of the Flood* "suggests that imagining a fundamentally different kind of future for humanity will require destabilizing the dominant biopolitical order by injecting into it a female ethics of incommensurability. . . . The only guarantee at the end of the Anthropocene is contingency. Hope, however, for better or worse, remains bound up in the figure of the woman." Calina Ciobanu, "Rewriting the Human at the End of the Anthropocene in Margaret Atwood's *MaddAddam* Trilogy," *Minnesota Review* 83 (2014): 157, 160–61.

3. INHERIT THE WASTELAND: OR, HOW I LEARNED TO STOP WORRYING AND CEDE THE PLANET TO THE SMART MACHINES

1. Ord may be right about the dangers of AI, but it was difficult to contemplate this in the middle of a pandemic, even as many of us were looking past the pandemic to the growing threats associated with climate change. But after the release of ChatGPT in 2023, suddenly the media focus shifted to the existential risk posed by AI. Nevertheless, "existential risk" theory has come under withering critique for its inattention to global inequities and its suspect use of statistics. See Joshua Schuster and Derek Woods, *Calamity Theory: Three Critiques of Existential Risk* (Minneapolis: University of Minnesota Press, 2021). No doubt Ord and his fellow transhumanists are more concerned with AI than with other existential risks precisely because they are basing their hopes for the future on marrying a smart, well-connected machine someday.

2. *The Matrix*, dir. Lana Wachowski and Lilly Wachowksi [as the Wachowski Brothers] (Warner Brothers, 1999), 2:16.

3. Dolly Jorgensen, "Resurrecting Species Through Robotics: Animal Extinction and Deextinction in *Do Androids Dream of Electric Sheep?*,"

in *Literary Animal Studies and the Climate Crisis*, ed. Sune Borkfelt and Matthias Stephan (New York: Palgrave Macmillan, 2022), 230. For more on Dick and the Anthropocene, see Ursula Heise, "Philip K. Dick's Futuristic Ecologies," in *Philip K. Dick: Essays of the Here and Now*, ed. David Sandner (Jefferson, NC: McFarland, 2020), 14–31.

4. As James Reich points out, "the Germanic Voigt-Kampff is an ironic compound derived from an antiquated usage for 'farm steward/land-owner' or manager, and 'struggle/fight'. Voigt also puns 'Vogt' in the sense of 'overseer/bailiff'. It's a classic Dick joke which refers to the jurisdiction and trials of the novel's shepherd and bounty hunter Rick Deckard. . . . Deckard is also a pun on the Germanic 'Dekker', a name common among farmers, indicating one who makes thatched roofing or enclosures. Deckard's electric sheep is kept on the roof of his apartment building. Deckard is also a pun on Descartes, after René Descartes—the two men share initials—whose cogito is undermined by the novel, and *Blade Runner*." James Reich, "Voigt-Kampff: Germanicity and Empathy in *Do Androids Dream of Electric Sheep?*," *Outsider Academy*, June 25, 2017, https://www.jamesreichbooks.com/voigt-kampff-germanicity-and-empathy-in-do-androids-dream-of-electric-sheep/.

5. Pauline Kael asked this sensible question in her review of the film in the *New Yorker*: "Why is Deckard engaged in this urgent hunt? The replicants are due to expire anyway. All the moviemakers' thinking must have gone into the sets." Pauline Kael, "Baby, the Rain Must Fall," *New Yorker*, July 12, 1982, https://www.newyorker.com/magazine/1982/07/12/baby-the-rain-must-fall. Kael's snark about the sets is misaimed, however, since this question is even more pertinent to the novel, in which the androids will expire *and* the human species will die a slow, agonizing death.

6. His name is Baty in the book, but if I am citing the film, I use Batty, since that is his listing in the credits and on the Internet Movie Database. And for whatever reason Fancher and Peoples added the extra *t*—to suggest that Roy is kind of batty, perhaps?—there is no way to hear that extra *t* in the film.

7. For a close reading of the duet Luft is singing with Papageno in her role as Pamina and its relevance to the novel's treatment of empathy,

see Patrick A. McCarthy, "Do Androids Dream of Magic Flutes?," *Paradoxa: Studies in World Literary Genres* 5, nos. 13–14 (1999): 44–52. Dick's evocatively titled novel has inspired some of the best-titled academic essays I have ever come across (see also Cole and Seegert, below).

8. It is entirely possible that this is Dick's reply to Kierkegaard's remarks in *Either/Or: A Fragment of Life*: "With his *Don Giovanni* Mozart enters that small, immortal band of men whose names, whose works, time will not forget, for they are remembered in eternity." Søren Kierkegaard, *Either/Or: A Fragment of Life*, ed. Victor Eremita, trans. Alastair Hannaty (New York: Penguin, 1992), 62. The passage is cited by Alan Weisman in the context of the Voyager missions' golden records, which, Weisman suggests, hold out the chance that music, the most ephemeral of human accomplishments, might indeed survive until the heat death of the universe. Alan Weisman, *The World Without Us* (New York: Thomas Dunne, 2007), 323. Hold that thought for the epilogue and my reservations about being conquered by the Oankali of Lilith's Brood.

9. In 1995, Simon A. Cole was able to claim, correctly, that "most critics have ignored" the theme of animals in the novel, largely because the theme is almost completely absent from the film. Simon A. Cole, "Do Androids Pulverize Tiger Bones to Use as Aphrodisiacs?," *Social Text* 42 (1995): 176. Cole's essay is a fascinating meditation on what he calls the novel's "animal-human-android love triangle" (176) in the context of our ongoing mass species extinction events and stands up exceptionally well three decades later. Cole also notes that "there is . . . an air of denial surrounding the outpouring of concern for animal welfare in blade-runner society. It is not clear that humans, faced with the choice between extinction or self-imposed exile, are in any position to pity other creatures" (183). Since 1995, however, and no doubt because of the increased interest in animal studies in the humanities, this aspect of the novel has drawn considerably more attention. See, e.g., Ursula Heise, "From Extinction to Electronics: Dead Frogs, Live Dinosaurs, and Electric Sheep," in *Zoontologies: The Question of the Animal*, ed. Cary Wolfe (Minneapolis: University of Minnesota Press, 2003), 59–81, making the now-canonical argument that Deckard's acceptance of the artificiality of the toad he found marks an empathic breakthrough

("his insight actually amounts to an acknowledgment that the lives and needs of his species, organic humans, are not the only ones that count" [76]); Sherryl Vint, "Speciesism and Species Being in 'Do Androids Dream of Electric Sheep?,'" *Mosaic* 40, no. 1 (2007): 111–26; Angus Taylor, "Electric Sheep and the New Argument from Nature," in *Animal Subjects: An Ethical Reader in a Posthuman World*, ed. Jodey Castricano (Waterloo, ON: Wilfrid Laurier University Press, 2008), 177–93; Art Seegert, "Ewe, Robot," in *Philip K. Dick and Philosophy: Do Androids Have Kindred Spirits?*, ed. D. E. Wittkower (Chicago: Open Court, 2011), 39–49; Casey R. Riffel, "Animals at the End of the World: Notes Toward a Transspecies Eschatology," in *Making Animal Meaning*, ed. Linda Kalof and Georgina M. Montgomery (Lansing: Michigan State University Press, 2011), 159–72; Megan E. Cannella, "Do Androids Dream of Derrida's Cat? The Unregulated Emotion of Animals in Philip K. Dick's *Do Androids Dream of Electric Sheep?*," in *Seeing Animals After Derrida*, ed. Sarah Bezan and James Tink (Lanham, MD: Lexington, 2018), 145–62.

10. Dick wisely left it to his readers to discern the shoddiness of the empathy criterion, and they have not failed him. Donald Palumbo, for example, points to "this society's willful self-deception . . . to allow its members to claim as exclusively theirs those very qualities, empathy and intelligence, that the historical fact of WWT demonstrates humanity does not possess in sufficient abundance." Donald Palumbo, "Faith and Bad Faith in *Do Androids Dream of Electric Sheep?*," *Journal of Popular Culture* 46, no. 6 (2013): 1280. As for Mercerism, which is exposed as a fraud by Buster Friendly, N. Katherine Hayles notes that "Dick's treatment of Mercerism remains completely ambiguous. The text refuses an either/or choice and implies that Mercerism is both political hucksterism and a genuinely meaningful experience." As a devout agnostic, I might extend that observation to religions in general. N. Katherine Hayles, *How We Became Posthuman: Virtual Bodies in Cybernetics, Literature, and Informatics* (Chicago: University of Chicago Press, 1999), 175. Sherryl Vint adds that "it is essential that Mercerism is founded on empathy *with animals* as it is precisely the human/animal boundary that provides the grounds upon which to deny empathy and continue exploitation" (i.e., with regard to the androids).

Vint, "Speciesism," 118; emphasis in original. Similarly, Riffel argues that "humans have invested entire legal, political, and economic institutions to policing (and thereby reinforcing) the anxious border between human and android, using animals as the criterion while simultaneously relegating those animals to a hyperbolic commodity fetishism." Riffel, "Animals at the End of the World," 162.

11. Palumbo, "Faith and Bad Faith," 1283.

12. In my fall 2021 class, a young Black woman, unprompted by me, asked whether this aspect of the book amounted to a critique of aggressive-to-lethal policing. "I would say so," I replied, adding that I have never understood (to take one example among many) why I need police officers to protect me from people selling loose cigarettes. Later in the week, after doing some Googling, I referred her and the rest of the class to Noah Berlatsky's extraordinary essay on the subject, published in 2017, which concludes, "*Blade Runner* presents a run-down but beautiful future, filled with tragic emotion and powerful moral decisions. *Do Androids Dream of Electric Sheep?* seems truer to our blander, bleaker present, in which a clockwork bureaucracy blandly declares that certain lives are worthless, that only a chosen few people are worthy of protection, and that equality under the law would somehow hold the nation back. The central insight of Black Lives Matter is that the state is programmed for petty hatred and genocidal violence, and that bystanders' apathy or resignation constantly gets in the way of lasting change. Book-Deckard, the smaller-than-life policeman as mass-murderer, still seems grubbily prescient, half a century after Dick first sent him off to kill." Noah Berlatsky, "*Blade Runner*'s Source Material Says More About Modern Politics Than the Movie Does," *The Verge*, October 5, 2017, https://www.theverge.com/2017/10/5/16428544/blade-runner-philip-k-dick-do-androids-dream-of-electric-sheep-analysis-adaptation.

13. Sci-fi fans will know I am alluding to Ray Bradbury's *Martian Chronicles*; this note is for everybody else. I just want to add that the inclusion of Los Angeles's renowned Bradbury Building in *Blade Runner* is a nice touch, a kind of tip of the hat. Additionally, *Three Stigmata* can be considered a very early climate change novel, another example of Jorgensen's "Anticipatory Anthropocene," insofar as temperatures on

Earth have risen to the point at which the planet is barely habitable. Philip K. Dick, *Martian Time-Slip* (New York: Ballantine, 1964); Philip K. Dick, *The Three Stigmata of Palmer Eldritch* (New York: Doubleday, 1964); Philip K. Dick, *Ubik* (New York: Doubleday, 1969); Philip K. Dick, *We Can Build You* (New York: DAW, 1972).

14. Michael Bérubé, "Disability and Narrative," *PMLA* 120, no. 2 (2005): 568–76.

15. Disability studies came even later than animal studies to the novel, tending to eschew science fiction in general (except for the work of Sami Schalk, about which more in chapter 4). Ryan Morrison makes the somewhat reductive argument that although the human/android boundary is porous, "the novel relies on harmful representations of neurodivergence to make its point"—and that those harmful representations are the androids themselves, who are "recognizably neurodivergent." Ryan Morrison, "Ethical Depictions of Neurodivergence in SF About AI," *Configurations* 27, no. 3 (2019): 396, 389. Adam Pottle, however, sees *Androids*—especially the character of Isidore—as "a novel that criticizes eugenics as a posthuman endeavour that emphasizes reason as the sole human characteristic while eliminating human diversity and empathy for others." Adam Pottle, "Segregating the Chickenheads: Philip Dick's *Do Androids Dream of Electric Sheep?* and the Post/humanism of the American Eugenics Movement," *Disability Studies Quarterly* 33, no. 3 (2013): https://dsq-sds.org/index.php/dsq /article/view/3229/3262. Though Pottle stops short of interrogating the novel's treatment of empathy, his reading of Dick as a fierce critic of eugenics is sound in itself and applicable as well, a fortiori, to *Martian Time-Slip.*

16. Although Rosen certainly has a point about police killing humans, his claim that his innocent niece is human is of course a lie—and Eldon's and Rachael's pretense that she did not know she was an android is another lie, since (as we learn later) Rachael has made a habit of having sex with bounty hunters in order to prevent them from doing their jobs. In other words, Deckard's position is extremely bad morally, and the Rosens' is . . . also bad.

17. As one of my students pointed out in his final exam, because humans have come to rely on Penfield mood organs to control their emotions,

"the primary difference between humans and androids feels very minor. . . . Plus, while renegade androids have certainly committed a series of crimes to get to Earth, the past crimes of humanity outweigh anything the androids have done. The reason why the planet is a nuclear wasteland at all is because of humanity." That's a very good final exam answer, and I can assure you it was not written by ChatGPT.

18. Sherryl Vint likens Pris instead to a callous adult, writing that she is "mirroring the technique of scientists who were (and often still are) able to perform painful experiments on living creatures without any concern." Vint, "Speciesism," 113.

19. Cannella, "Derrida's Cat," 148.

20. Indeed, for Cannella, Rachael's desire for revenge is a mark of her humanity: "Rick rejecting Rachael in favor of an animal capable of empathetic affect enables Rachael to transcend her programming. In this moment of confrontation, Rachael engages in a completely humanistic, emotional display of revenge." Cannella, "Derrida's Cat," 157.

21. Quoted in *Sacrificial Sheep: The Novel vs. the Film*, dir. Charles de Lauzirika (Warner Home Video, 2007), 0:15. In that short documentary, Dick also explains that his sense of the narrative arc of the novel is that Deckard is gradually dehumanized as a result of his pursuit of the androids; the film takes another tack altogether, dropping emphatic hints (including a brief, enigmatic dream sequence involving a unicorn, which only came to light in the director's cut) that Deckard himself is an android. Obviously, my argument in this chapter makes sense only if we accept Dick's insistence that the Rick Deckard in his novel is human. In his short monograph on *Blade Runner*, Scott Bukatman suggests that "Dick protests a bit too much" about the callousness of androids and that "his text is inconsistent, shifting scene by scene." Quite so. Scott Bukatman, *Blade Runner* (London: BFI, 2012), 80.

22. In *Literary Bioethics: Animality, Disability, and the Human* (New York: New York University Press, 2020), Maren Tova Linett reads the cloning program in *Never Let Me Go* by way of Michael Pollan's *The Omnivore's Dilemma* (New York: Penguin, 2007), which is not only brilliant but deeply unsettling for anyone (like me) otherwise sympathetic to Pollan's argument for eating humanely raised animals.

23. The sequel released twenty-five years later, *Blade Runner 2049*, offers another fascinating possibility—that the androids could find a way to reproduce sexually. Despite the presence of Jared Leto, the film is (in my opinion) a remarkably good sequel, faithful to the spirit and the letter of both the original film and its literary source. *Blade Runner 2049*, dir. Denis Villeneuve (Warner Brothers, 2017), 2:43.

24. The ending, in which Alquist sends off the robots, crying "Go, Adam. Go, Eve—be a wife to Primus. Be a husband to Helena, Primus," strongly suggests that Alquist has decided that the robots will find some way to reproduce themselves. Karl Čapek, *R.U.R. (Rossum's Universal Robots)* [1920], trans. Claudia Novak, intro. Ivan Klíma (New York: Penguin, 2004), 84. The robots, like the replicants of *Androids*, are keenly aware of their limited life spans (twenty years, an eon compared to the replicants) and demand of their creators that they turn over Rossum's formula for designing sentient life. Rossum's formula has been lost (more specifically, his papers have been deliberately burned), so Alquist had determined that he should dissect either Helena or Primus to try to see how they function. Hence, his reversal, his decision to let them go, implies that he has faith that some kind of *Blade Runner 2049* scenario awaits them—and their progeny.

25. Ray Bradbury, "A Sound of Thunder," in *R Is for Rocket* (New York: Doubleday, 1962), 79–93.

26. Similarly, why do the far-future five-dimensional humans in *Interstellar* (dir. Christopher Nolan [Paramount 2014], 2:49) give us twelve options rather than directing us to the one exoplanet where we can save the species? Many people noted that the film relies on a chicken-and-egg device; as David Crow wrote in "Interstellar Ending Explained," "there is a time travel paradox in this, like so much with science fiction, which ultimately suggests that humanity only survived because Cooper was sent by future beings into this black hole to communicate with Murph, thereby necessitating Cooper having already made the journey before '*they*' first summoned him with gravitational anomalies, but . . . does your head hurt yet?" David Crow, "Interstellar Ending Explained," *Den of Geek*, August 7, 2016, https://www.denofgeek .com/ movies/explaining-the-interstellar-ending/. But the twelve-possible-exoplanets idea seems to me the strangest of all the many

things in *Interstellar* that make no sense. Similarly, as James Hibberd put it in *Entertainment Weekly*, "Ultimately, if aliens/future humans wanted to save us, couldn't they have simply given the professor the secret equation?" James Hibberd, "15 Maddening 'Interstellar' Plot Holes," *Entertainment Weekly*, November 8, 2014, https://ew.com/article/2014/11/08/interstellar-plot-holes/.

27. Octavia E. Butler, *Kindred* [1979] (Boston: Beacon, 2003), 112.

28. *Kindred* is sometimes considered at outlier in Butler's oeuvre, an exception to her life's work in science fiction, but Isiah Lavender argues that it belongs to more than one genre: "very few sf stories can be remotely classified as belonging to both the neo-slave narratives and the meta-slavery tales. *Kindred* is the only novel that comes to mind." Isiah Lavender, *Race in American Science Fiction* (Bloomington: Indiana University Press), 63.

29. Michael Bérubé, "Paranoia in a Vacuum: *2001* and the National Security State," in *Public Access: Literary Theory and American Cultural Politics* (New York: Verso, 1994), 181–202.

30. *2001: A Space Odyssey*, dir. Stanley Kubrick (MGM, 1968), 2:19.

31. More recently, in fall 2022, one of my students, a U.S. Army veteran, argued that Heywood Floyd and Mission Control are right to keep Bowman and Poole in the dark. Arguing from experience, he told me and the rest of the class that he executed any number of counterintelligence missions in which he was told what to do but not why. My response was that NASA is and always was a civilian operation, to which the protocols of military intelligence should not apply, and that the decision to apply those protocols leads directly to HAL's breakdown. But he had a point.

32. Attention must be paid to Clarke's characterization of the state of information technology in 2001:

> Floyd sometimes wondered if the Newspad, and the fantastic technology behind it, was the last word in man's quest for perfect communications. Here he was, far out in space, speeding away from Earth at thousands of miles per hour, yet in a few milliseconds he could see the headlines of any newspaper he pleased. (That very word "newspaper," of course, was an anachronistic

hangover into the age of electronics.) The text was updated automatically on every hour; even if one read only the English versions, one could spend an entire lifetime doing nothing but
absorbing the everchanging flow of information from the news
satellites.

It was hard to imagine how the system could be improved or
made more convenient. But sooner or later, Floyd guessed, it would
pass away, to be replaced by something as unimaginable as the
Newspad itself would have been to Caxton or Gutenberg.

There was another thought which a scanning of those tiny electronic headlines often invoked. The more wonderful the means of
communication, the more trivial, tawdry, or depressing its contents
seemed to be. Accidents, crimes, natural and man-made disasters,
threats of conflict, gloomy editorials—these still seemed to be the
main concerns of the millions of words being sprayed into the ether.
(*2001* 64)

33. Ray Kurzweil, *The Singularity Is Near: When Humans Transcend Biol-
    ogy* (New York: Viking, 2005).
34. Robert Savage, "Paleoanthropology of the Future: The Prehistory of
    Posthumanity in Arthur C. Clarke's *2001: A Space Odyssey*," *Extrapo-
    lation* 51, no. 1 (2010), 109–10.

4. BETTER CHILDREN: OCTAVIA BUTLER AND GENETIC DESTINY

1. See Rebecca Onion, "Why So Many Readers Are Turning to Octavia
   Butler's Apocalypse Fiction Right Now," *Slate*, September 19, 2020,
   https://slate.com/culture/2020/09/octavia-butler-parable-of-the
   -sower-talents-pandemic.html. And as Alexis Lothian notes, "black
   feminist organizers at the Allied Media Conference, which brings
   together activists working for media justice, use Octavia Butler's work
   as a gathering point from which to focus the speculative, world-
   changing energies of radical activists." Alexis Lothian, "Feminist and
   Queer Science Fiction in America," in *The Cambridge Companion to
   American Science Fiction*, ed. Eric Carl Link and Gerry Canavan (Cambridge: Cambridge University Press, 2015), 80.

2. Octavia Butler, *Parable of the Sower* (New York: Grand Central, 1993), 12; hereafter cited parenthetically as *PS*. As Olamina's journal will explain at the outset of *Talents*, "it also boosted the performance of ordinary, healthy young people. They read faster, retained more, made more rapid, accurate connections, calculations, and conclusions. As a result, Paracetco became as popular as coffee among students, and, if they meant to compete in any of the highly paid professions, it was as necessary as a knowledge of computers." Octavia Butler, *Parable of the Talents* (New York: Grand Central, 1998), 13; hereafter cited parenthetically as *PT*. Basically, Paracetco is an extra-strength version of Adderall (albeit a version whose side effects can be passed down to one's offspring), which therefore locates one of the most "speculative" aspects of the fiction of *Parables* in a reasonably recognizable form of the here and now.

3. Katrina's death toll in 2005 is estimated at anywhere from 1,200 to over 1,800; the U.S. National Hurricane Center puts the death toll at 1,833. In this as in some other respects, the only problem with Butler's dystopia is that it's not quite as bad as the world we live in. Richard D. Knabb, Jamie R. Rhome, and Daniel P. Brown, "Tropical Cyclone Report—Hurricane Katrina," National Hurricane Center, 2005, https://www.nhc.noaa.gov/data/tcr/ AL122005_Katrina.pdf.

4. One minor but striking detail is that dogs have already become feral. "I've read books about them being intelligent, loyal pets, but that's all in the past. Dogs now are wild animals who will eat a baby if they can" (*PS* 209). What takes centuries to happen in Russell Hoban's remarkable *Riddley Walker* (London: Jonathan Cape, 1980), in which humans in a neo–Stone Age postnuclear hellscape have to fortify their villages against bands of roving dogs, takes only a couple of decades in the *Parables* books. I think this seems somewhat less likely, given what we know of the development of human-canine interdependence over ten or twelve thousand years, than the election of a white nationalist president who promises to make America great again.

5. The parallel to Donald Trump is not exact, of course, since Trump is not an evangelical Christian (however much he is beloved and worshipped by that constituency), and "Jarret supporters have been known, now and then, to form mobs and burn people at the stake for being witches" (*PT* 19). As of this writing, witch burnings have not yet been

revived as a feature of life in the United States; the Christian right is preoccupied with campaigns against gay, lesbian, and (especially) trans Americans. But there is time.

6. In a 1999 interview that is reprinted as a "Reading Group Guide" in the most recent edition of *Talents*, published by Grand Central, Butler explains that the Destiny has to involve exoplanets rather than terraforming Mars: "a world that offers breathable air, potable water—or water that can easily be made potable—and arable land is much more desirable than a dead world like the moon or Mars. Where water must be mined like gold; where air must be caged in vast community-wide bubbles and carefully maintained; where normal temperature extremes range, literally, between freezing and boiling; where even small mistakes may be fatal; chances of survival are less." Thus, because "a human settlement on an extrasolar world would not be able to depend on resupply from Earth," "the more our new world can do for us the more likely we are to be able to survive on it"—though Butler acknowledges that "on the other hand, the more our new world can do for us, the more it might be able to do to us" (*PT* 413). Thus, even though we learn in 2032 that "on the planet Mars, living, multi-cellular organisms have been discovered" (*PT* 81), Olamina takes no inspiration from the discovery and never considers Mars a viable option for Earthseed. The immensity of the task, Olamina believes, requires the kind of commitment only a religion can provide: "The truth is, preparing for interstellar travel and then sending out ships filled with colonists is bound to be a job so long, thankless, expensive, and difficult that I suspect that only a religion could do it. A lot of people will find ways to make money from it. That might get things started. But it will take something as essentially human *and as essentially irrational* as religion to keep them focused and keep it going—for generations if it takes generations" (*PT* 357; my emphasis). Earthseed is therefore the delivery vehicle for the Alpha Centauri mission, something Olamina cooks up in order to snooker—the novel repeatedly uses the word "seduce"—people into leaving Earth.

7. Canavan, "'There's Nothing New / Under The Sun, / But There Are New Suns': Recovering Octavia E. Butler's Lost Parables," *Los Angeles Review of Books*, June 9, 2014, https://lareviewofbooks.org/article

/theres-nothing-new-sun-new-suns-recovering-octavia-e-butlers
-lost-parables/.

8. Sami Schalk, *Bodyminds Reimagined: (Dis)ability, Race, and Gender in Black Women's Speculative Fiction* (Durham, NC: Duke University Press, 2018), 90–91. For a more general account of how Butler's critics tend to misapprehend the role of disability in her work, see Therí A. Pickens, "Octavia Butler and the Aesthetics of the Novel," *Hypatia* 30, no. 1 (2015): 167–80.

9. Because this might sound confusing to readers unfamiliar with disability studies, I will point out simply that (a) some disabilities do not have disease etiologies, and not all diseases are necessarily disabling, and that (b) in disability studies, "disability" is commonly distinguished from "impairment," whereby "disability" refers to the social organization of impairment. In the classic example, a wheelchair user might have a mobility impairment but is not *disabled* in the "social model" of disability unless s/he has no access ramps, curb cuts, or widened doors. The "social model" has come under pressure with regard to intellectual and psychosocial disabilities, but the distinction will suffice for an understanding of why the stigma associated with hyperempathy corresponds to a disability-studies understanding of the condition.

10. Doug Stark, "'A More Realistic View': Reimagining Sympoietic Practice in Octavia Butler's *Parables*," *Extrapolation* 61, nos. 1–2 (2020): 160.

11. Olamina's hyperempathy is thus rather more like the power of Rogue in the X-Men, who has the ability to absorb the memories, feelings, strength, and life force of anyone she touches. She considers her mutant superpower to be a curse.

12. Before that happens, there is one doomed attempt at rebellion and escape, led by a man named David Turner, whose name evokes Nat Turner and David Walker. He is thwarted, tortured into insanity, and finally hanged.

13. Gerry Canavan, *Octavia Butler* (Urbana: University of Illinois Press, 2016), 174; hereafter cited parenthetically as *OB*. In Butler's archives, Canavan discovered to his surprise what else was skipped over in this fast-forward: "lost stories and cut scenes set during Olamina's missing decades reveal her as a steely and callous power-broker when she needs

to be, even ordering a local politician's assassination for daring to defy her. (One version even has Olamina slave-collaring people who try to leave her Earthseed villages: 'Boy,' she said, 'the dogs eat what's left of people who try to break into our Communities. We burn what's left of people who try to break out.') For anyone who has read the published versions of the novels, this is absolutely startling; Butler's personal reflections on Olamina reveal her as a much, much darker character than the one we get to know in the books, a character Butler never really trusted and only grew to like despite herself over time." Canavan, "Nothing New."

14. In that December 30, 2035, journey that closes the book proper, Olamina notes that "I've flown to Newark, Delaware; Clarion, Pennsylvania; and up to Syracuse, New York. Next, I go to Toledo, Ohio; Ann Arbor, Michigan; Madison, Wisconsin; and Iowa City, Iowa" (*PT* 389). That is her first book tour. I just want to suggest that Joel and Irma Elford made a serious mistake booking Olamina into Clarion University rather than Penn State, with more than ten times the number of students and a larger airport.

15. Adam Serwer, *The Cruelty Is the Point: The Past, Present, and Future of Trump's America* (New York: One World, 2021).

16. Isiah Lavender, *Race in American Science Fiction* (Bloomington: Indiana University Press), 24.

17. Asha Vere, for her part, dislikes her mother intensely, largely because Olamina had the chance to leave Acorn with Bankhole and live in a nearby gated village. Had Olamina taken that chance, she would not have endured Camp Christian, Bankhole would not have been gassed to death, and Asha herself would not have wound up in a Christian America foster home with a father who molested her. "If only my mother had agreed to go with my father to live peacefully, normally in Halstead, it wouldn't have happened. Or at least, it wouldn't have happened to us" (*PT* 182). Perversely, she blames Olamina for all the abuse she suffers at the hands of Christian America and identifies strongly with Marc. Thus, although Butler ultimately decided not to portray Olamina as a steely and callous power broker, she did decide to frame her narrative by way of the account of a hostile daughter who

believes that her mother's first duty was to her immediate family even if it would mean abandoning the Acorn community she founded and ultimately proved unable to save.

18. One of my students suggested that when Marc leaves Acorn, despite the fact that Olamina has saved him from a life of slavery and torture by collar, he tips off Christian America as to the presence of "heathen" and is therefore responsible for all the atrocities that ensue. It is an entirely plausible scenario.

19. Canavan, "Nothing New." More recently, Ji Hyun Lee has proposed a reading of the unfinished project of the Parables by way of trauma theory: noting that Butler produced 186 drafts amounting to roughly 1,500 pages of false starts, he writes, "With her repeated attempts to write the third novel, Butler appeared to be suffering from 'archive fever,' wherein the elements of traumatic futurity, including repetition and the death drive, were enacted on the level of her writing, in the very act of her writing." Ji Hyun Lee, "Trauma, Technology, and the Trickster: Reading Octavia E. Butler's Unfinished Trilogy," in *The Bloomsbury Handbook to Octavia E. Butler*, ed. Gregory J. Hampton and Kendra R. Parker (London: Bloomsbury, 2019), 214.

20. Ji Hyun Lee comes to the same conclusion, though hers involves an avoidance of traumatic repetition and doesn't necessarily involve fanfic (though it might!): "although Butler's unfruitful, abandoned writing of *Trickster* may seem like a product of archive fever and repeat a death drive problem, it is actually an important form of resistance that constitutes a mode of survival. . . . By not finishing *Trickster*, Butler offers the possibility of an alternative, an adaptive mode of survival that hints at hope, at life." Lee, "Trauma, Technology, and the Trickster," 217.

21. Stephanie Burt, "Octavia Butler Wanted to Write a 'Yes' Book," *The New Republic*, May 27, 2021, https://newrepublic.com/article/162251 /octavia-butler-kindred-fledgling-review-yes-book.

22. A representative example is afforded by Patricia Melzer, who writes that "because of the aliens' third sex/gender and the number of members necessary to form a reproductive unit, the Oankali 'queer' the process of reproduction and challenge the gendered relations of power within a heterosexual context." Patricia Meltzer, *Alien Constructions:*

Science Fiction and Feminist Thought (Austin: University of Texas Press, 2006), 318–19. Melzer makes this (quite defensible) claim even while acknowledging that the sex involved is literally rape. The first major statement from the pro-Oankali/hybridity party was that of the formidable Donna Haraway, *Simians, Cyborgs, and Women: The Reinvention of Nature* (New York: Routledge, 1991), 226–30, which also advanced a reading of Lilith as cyborg heroine.

23. Sherryl Vint, *Bodies of Tomorrow: Technology, Subjectivity, Science Fiction* (Toronto: University of Toronto Press, 2007), 65.

24. Octavia Butler, *Lilith's Brood* (New York: Grand Central, 1989), 189; hereafter cited parenthetically as *LB*.

25. In what follows, I do not mean to suggest that Canavan's is the only anti-Oankali argument worth engaging at length, but it is the most relentless and unforgiving and therefore (for my own argument) the most unavoidable. But see also Isiah Lavender, who writes that "the Oankali starship is a slave ship where the aliens enact a breeding program on a captive humanity." Lavender, *Race in American Science Fiction*, 70. This almost makes the Oankali ship sound like the massive interstellar ship *Matilda* in Rivers Solomon's debut novel *An Unkindness of Ghosts* (New York: Akashic Books, 2017), which is modeled on the antebellum South (the *Matilda* is a rhyming echo of the *Clotilda*, the last slave ship to reach the United States). For more Oankali-skeptical critics, see note 27, below.

26. At which point one wonders what would convince Canavan once and for all that the humans did it. Perhaps a documentary clip of Charlton Heston breaking down on a beach in front of a remnant of the Statue of Liberty and damning the human "maniacs" who "blew it up"?

27. Other notable dissents construing the Oankali as imperialists/enslavers include those of Rachel Pollack, whose review of *Dawn* called attention to rape and slavery in ways that I am echoing here: "Dawn (Xenogenesis I)," *Foundation* 44 (1988): 68–71; Frances Bonner, "Difference and Desire, Slavery and Seduction: Octavia Butler's Xenogenesis," *Foundation* 48 (1990): 50–62; Michelle Erica Green, "'There Goes the Neighborhood': Octavia Butler's Demand for Diversity in Utopias," in *Utopian and Science Fiction by Women: Worlds of Difference*, ed. Jane L. Donawerth and Carol A. Kolmerten (Syracuse, NY:

Syracuse University Press, 1994), 166–89 ("the human resistance to the Oankali parallels the resistance of a slave to rape by a master who will later claim her child as his property," 188); Amanda Boulter, "Polymorphous Futures: Octavia E. Butler's Xenogenesis Trilogy," in *American Bodies: Cultural Histories of the Physique*, ed. Tim Armstrong (New York: New York University Press, 1996), 170–85; and Rebecca J. Holden, "The High Costs of Cyborg Survival," *Foundation* 72 (1998): 49–56, taking issue specifically with Haraway.

28. United Nations Office on Genocide Prevention and the Responsibility to Protect, https://www.un.org/en/genocideprevention/about -responsibility-to-protect.shtml.

29. Michael Bérubé, *The Left at War* (New York University Press, 2009), esp. chap. 3, "Iraq: The Hard Road to Debacle," 116–52.

30. I am decidedly in the minority here; most critics, whatever their position on Butler's alleged essentialism, agree that the question of whether the Human Contradiction is baked in is important and unavoidable. See, e.g., Hoda M. Zaki, "Utopia, Dystopia, and Ideology in the Science Fiction of Octavia Butler," *Science Fiction Studies* 17, no. 2 (1990): 239–51, taking the hard line that Butler's biological determinism "represents an essentially retrogressive view of politics" (242); more ambivalent critics of Butler's uses of biology include Cathy Peppers, "Dialogic Origins and Alien Identities in Butler's *Xenogenesis*," *Science Fiction Studies* 22, no. 1 (1995): 47–62; Jim Miller, "Post-Apocalyptic Hoping: Octavia Butler's Dystopian/Utopian Vision," *Science Fiction Studies* 25, no. 2 (1998): 336–60; Nancy Jesser, "Blood, Genes, and Gender in Octavia Butler's *Kindred* and *Dawn*," *Extrapolation* 43, no. 1 (2002): 36–61; Jessie Stickgold-Sarah, "'Your Children Will Know Us, You Never Will': The Pessimistic Utopia of Octavia Butler's *Xenogenesis* Trilogy," *Extrapolation* 51, no. 3 (2010): 414–30; and J. Adam Johns, "Becoming Medusa: Octavia Butler's *Lilith's Brood* and Sociobiology," *Science Fiction Studies* 37, no. 3 (2010): 382–400 (reading Butler as a follower of the sociobiologist E. O. Wilson). More recently (and perhaps most ambivalently), Lisa Dowdall has argued that the trilogy "offers a radical vision of human biology and evolution": "By contrasting the genetic determinism and colonial enterprise of the alien Oankali with the human resisters' insistence on biological and reproductive

independence, Butler enacts a politics of ambivalence that situates reproduction within the rapidly evolving bioeconomic machinery of late capitalism. At the same time, Butler constructs human evolution as an ongoing dialectical process within living systems of interspecies becoming." Lisa Dowdall, "Treasured Strangers: Race, Biopolitics, and Human in Octavia E. Butler's *Xenogenesis* Trilogy," *Science Fiction Studies* 44, no. 3 (2017): 506. There has also been lively critical debate over gender essentialism in Butler's work, beginning with Dorothy Allison's complaint about Butler's maternal heroines in "The Future of Female: Octavia Butler's Mother Lode," in *Reading Feminist, Reading Black*, ed. Henry Louis Gates Jr. (New York: Meridian, 1990), 471–78, but that argument is tangential to the question of whether we are all hardwired into the Human Contradiction. For her part, Butler did say that it is an open question: when Larry McCaffery suggested to her that "one of the underlying concepts in *Dawn* [is] that we are biologically programmed for self-destruction," Butler replied, "It's less a matter of being programmed for self-destruction than it is that self-destruction occurs because we're not willing to go beyond that principle of who's got the biggest or the best or the most. We can; in fact we do, individually. And if we know we are like that, we ought to be able to go beyond it." Larry McCaffery and Jim McMenamin, "Interview with Octavia Butler" [1988], in *Conversations with Octavia Butler*, ed. Consuela Francis (Jackson: University Press of Mississippi, 2010), 10.

31. China Miéville writes of "Weird Fiction's obsession with the tentacle, a limb-type absent from European folklore and the Gothic, and one which, after early proto-Weird variations by Victor Hugo, Jules Verne, and H. G. Wells, viralled suddenly in Haute Weird Fiction until it is now, in the post-Weird debris of fantastic horror, the default monstrous limb-type." China Miéville, "Weird Fiction," in *The Routledge Companion to Science Fiction*, ed. Mark Bould, Andrew M. Butler, Adam Roberts, and Sherryl Vint (New York: Routledge, 2009), 512.

32. In 2019 I began asking students to write their final paper for the class in the form of fanfic; my reward was that in 2022, when I taught *Dawn*

for the second time, two students independently wrote brilliant mash-ups of *Dawn* and *Frankenstein* in which the creature does not immolate himself after the close of the novel but rather freezes in the Arctic and is revived centuries later by the Oankali. This works out extremely well all around; the Oankali are the first sentient beings the creature has met who are not repelled by his appearance, and the Oankali are relieved and impressed at how gentle and accommodating the creature is, especially when compared to those volatile and disgust-filled humans.

33. Inexplicably, Elizabeth Billinger claims that "it is possible for the humans in the novel to accept the Oankali's control in this way because they trust the Oankali's reading of human genetic flaws, flaws which will lead to the ineluctable self-destruction of humanity if left to its own devices." Elizabeth Billinger, "After Earth: How Far Away Does the Far Future Have to Be? Estrangement and Cognition in Clarke and Butler," in *Earth Is but a Star: Excursions Through Science Fiction to the Far Future*, ed. Damien Broderick (Crawley: University of West Australia Press, 2001), 103. Naomi Jacobs offers a more accurate assessment of the scenario: "extremely long-lived and healthy, brilliantly intelligent, capable of mind-melding and many other superhuman feats, the Oankali represent a state of being that matches point by point many utopian fantasies of a better human future, an improved human type. And yet, because to merge with the Oankali would bring the disappearance of the human type and the diffusion of the humanist subject, such metamorphosis is regarded with horror by the human beings to whom it is offered." Naomi Jacobs, "Posthuman Bodies and Agency in Octavia Butler's *Xenogenesis*," in *Dark Horizons: Science Fiction and the Dystopian Imagination*, ed. Raffaella Baccolini and Tom Moylan (New York: Routledge, 2003), 100.

34. *Passengers*, dir, Morten Tyldum (Columbia, 2016), 1:56. See Matt Miller, "This One Small Change Could Have Made *Passengers* a Good Movie," *Esquire*, April 21, 2017, https://www.esquire.com/entertainment/movies/news/a54678/passengers-good-movie-fix-video/.

35. "Learn and run" is "an echo of many slave narratives," as Stickgold-Sarah, "Your Children Will Know Us," 421–22, points out.

36. Amanda Boulter, "Polymorphous Futures," 178, makes this connection as well. "However," she adds, "unlike Malintzin, Lilith is not despised by her children." I agree that this is a significant "however." Gregory J. Hampton, by contrast, likens Lilith to the compromised figure of Ariel in Aimé Césaire's *Une Tempête (A Tempest)*. Gregory J. Hampton, "Octavia E. Butler's Discourse on Colonialism and Identity: Dis/eased Identity in "Bloodchild," *Dawn*, and *Survivor*," in *The Bloomsbury Handbook to Octavia E. Butler*, 140.

37. The Oankali do have some very strange gaps in their understanding of humans. As Nancy Jesser observes, "It is striking that in the Oankali's 250-year study of human behavior and human culture, they never came across a reference to 'faggot' and have to ask Lilith what it means." Jesser, "Blood, Genes, and Gender," 46–47. It is all the more striking when one recognizes, as has Amanda Boulter, "Polymorphous Futures," 175, that "among the humans, deviation from the heterosexual norm is synonymous with the non-human."

38. Jacobs, "Posthuman Bodies and Agency," 99.

39. George Estreich (personal correspondence) suggests to me that Colson Whitehead's "American Phoenix" in *Zone One*, the rebranding of the United States launched by the provisional government in Buffalo, is a hat-tip to Butler. Despite the ubiquity of the phoenix as a symbol of rebirth (in apocalypses and otherwise), I suspect that he is right.

40. See, e.g., Milo W. Obourn, *Disabled Futures: A Framework for Radical Inclusion* (Philadelphia: Temple University Press, 2020), 114–15; and Claire P. Curtis, "Utopian Possibilities: Disability, Norms, and Eugenics in Octavia Butler's *Xenogenesis*," *Journal of Literary and Cultural Disability Studies* 9, no. 1 (2015): 27–28. Obourn's larger argument in chapter 4, "Speculative Disabled Futures: Octavia Butler's *Xenogenesis* Trilogy," is a fascinating and nuanced discussion of ableism in both human and Oankali society, though it relies too heavily on a complete conflation of disability and disease.

41. As Aparitaja Nanja puts it, Akin "understands that the Oankali choice of genetic healing does not merely alleviate suffering for humans but comes at a huge cost. It recalls the consequences of colonialism as a solution to alleged native problems." Aparitaja Nanja, "Power, Politics,

and Domestic Desire in Octavia Butler's *Lilith's Brood*," *Callaloo* 36, no. 3 (2013): 782.

42. Cathy Peppers sees Butler's use of Margulis as part of the trilogy's critique of eugenics and sociobiology. Peppers, "Dialogic Origins," 53–55.

43. Still, there is a sense in which the Oankali decision speaks well of Oankali political culture. Whereas Hoda Zaki claims that the Oankali "group mind . . . represents a notion of community which we would do well to approach with caution, as it resonates all too closely with certain ideologies inimical to individual freedom—e.g., fascism," Naomi Jacobs counters, sensibly, that what actually happens here is that "an individual has powerfully moved the collective to acknowledge an alternative view and to assist a dissenting group to achieve its wishes. A truly fascist consensus would brutally repress dissent to achieve a fully unified collective; but although the Oankali link their minds for purposes of decision making, the individual mind is never unaware of itself in this complex relation, nor must any individual give up an independent view once the decision has been reached." Hoda M. Zaki, "Utopia, Dystopia, and Ideology," 243; Naomi Jacobs, "Posthuman Bodies and Agency," 105. On the other hand, as Nolan Belk observes, "no humans are allowed to participate in the Oankali decision about the Mars colony." Nolan Belk, "The Certainty of the Flesh: Octavia Butler's Use of the Erotic in the *Xenogenesis* Trilogy," *Utopian Studies* 19, no. 3 (2009): 379. Clearly Oankali participatory democracy has its limits.

44. As Amanda Boulter observes, "Lilith's response to her pregnancy echoes the ambivalent feelings of those women slaves whose pregnancies were the result of forced matings or rape, and whose children represented an increase in the white man's property." Boulter, "Polymorphous Futures," 177.

45. Obourn offers an appropriately ambivalent reading of the Oankali-human state of affairs at the end of *Imago*: "What in one reading looks like a willingness to accept difference, otherness, fluidity, and change reveals in another a potentially genocidal drive to rid the world/universe of those with mental illness or cognitive or physical impairments." Obourn, *Disabled Futures*, 118.

46. For a postcolonialist reading of Jodahs in terms of Homi Bhabha's theory of colonial mimicry, see Aparajita Nanda, "Teaching the 'Other' of Colonialism: The Mimic (Wo)Men of *Xenogenesis*," in *The Bloomsbury Handbook to Octavia E. Butler*, 117–32.

47. Citing Jeffrey A. Tucker, "'The Human Contradiction': Identity and/as Essence in Octavia Butler's Xenogenesis Trilogy," *Yearbook of English Studies* 37, no. 2 (2007): 174.

48. Claire Curtis agrees, noting quite sensibly that "there are repeated instances, throughout the trilogy, of the resisters failing to learn any lesson after the near total destruction of life as we know it." Curtis, "Utopian Possibilities," 28.

49. J. Adam Johns is sure that "they will almost certainly all die," but that conclusion (however plausible) has no textual support in the novel. Johns, "Becoming Medusa," 392. By contrast, Sherryl Vint argues that this is precisely why we cannot read Butler as a biological essentialist: "We never get to discover the fate of the Mars colony: perhaps it self-destructs as the Oankali predict, but hope that it will succeed remains." Thus, "the Oankali may be genetic essentialists, but Butler's readers are encouraged not to be." Vint, *Bodies of Tomorrow*, 77, 67. This seems to me exactly right.

50. William M. Miller Jr., *A Canticle for Liebowitz* (Philadelphia: J. B. Lippincott, 1959).

EPILOGUE: JUST KILL ME NOW

1. Allie Brosh, *Hyperbole and a Half: Unfortunate Situations, Flawed Coping Mechanisms, Mayhem, and Other Things That Happened* (New York: Gallery, 2013); Viktor Frankl, *Man's Search for Meaning*, part 1, trans. Ilse Lasch (Boston: Beacon, 1959); Jeff Sharlet, *This Brilliant Darkness: A Book of Strangers* (New York: Norton, 2020).

2. But Rachel would like to add this qualifier: "We were all eventually okay from the 2021 Omicron strain, but fuck all the antivaxxers who took up all the monoclonal antibody treatments, for which I qualified but was put at the back of the line, since I was up to date on vaccines. I was seven months pregnant and have never been more miserable (it caused a sinus infection so bad that it messed up my teeth and I needed

to have a double root canal—and since I was pregnant, had severe restrictions on the type of novocaine and pain management I could use—so I am alive and well, but still SO MAD about the anti vaxxers who got that treatment ahead of me, and just need to state it every so often for the official record." Rachel Harris, personal correspondence. Rachel would also like to endorse my characterization of antivaxxers more generally.

3. It is remarkable how effective baby laughter is. Witnessing Finn crack up, a friend of the family asked, "What *is* it about baby laughter, anyway?" To which I replied, "It's pure." She thought for a moment and then said, "That's true—there is fake baby crying but there is no fake baby laughter." Or, I added, derisive or sarcastic baby laughter.

4. Lee Edelman, *No Future: Queer Theory and the Death Drive* (Durham, NC: Duke University Press, 2004), 2. Hereafter cited parenthetically as *NF*.

5. Jim Holt, "The Power of Catastrophic Thinking," review of Toby Ord, *The Precipice, New York Review of Books*, February 25, 2021, 28, https://www.nybooks.com/articles/2021/02/25/ power-catastrophic-thinking -toby-ord-precipice/.

6. Intriguingly, Obourn reads Lilith's Brood as a response to the ideology of reproductive futurism: "Butler's speculation is about survival into a future that does not rely on the logic of white reproductive futurity." Milo W. Obourn, *Disabled Futures: A Framework for Radical Inclusion* (Philadelphia: Temple University Press, 2020), 128. I think this is just about right and needs only a slight ex-human twist.

7. This was part of a larger question posed to me by Nick: when do we start allowing him to make mistakes? Obviously we're not going to let him find out for himself what it is like to fall off a bed or a chair, but what things are OK for him to learn by himself? It is a question all parents ask, even among the Oankali.

8. It is safe to say that I am not the only person thinking these thoughts. As Adam Kirsch notes in *The Revolt Against Humanity*, most humans of childbearing age now have a pretty bleak view of their prospects: "In 2018, the *New York Times* polled people who had or expected to have fewer children than they wanted and asked them why; 33 percent mentioned their fear of climate change. A study of 600 people of

childbearing age published in the journal *Climatic Change* in 2020 found that 92 percent believed that the future would be worse than the present, while less than 1 percent said it would be better." Adam Kirsch, *The Revolt Against Humanity: Imagining a Future Without Us* (New York: Columbia Global Reports, 2023), 50. World Bank, *Turn Down the Heat: Why a 4°C Warmer World Must Be Avoided, a Report for the World Bank by the Potsdam Institute for Climate Impact Research and Climate Analytics* (Washington, DC: World Bank, November 2012); IPCC [Intergovernmental Panel on Climate Change], *Climate Change 2014: Synthesis Report. Contribution of Working Groups I, II and III to the Fifth Assessment Report of the Intergovernmental Panel on Climate Change*, ed. R. K. Pachauri and L. A. Meyer (Geneva: IPCC, 2014); *Climate Change 2021: The Physical Science Basis. Contribution of Working Group I to the Sixth Assessment Report of the Intergovernmental Panel on Climate Change*, ed. V. Masson-Delmotte, P. Zhai, A. Pirani, et al. (Cambridge: Cambridge University Press, 2021).

9. Elizabeth Kolbert, "The Case for Catastrophe," *National Geographic*, Earth Day 50th Anniversary Special Issue, April 2020, 14–21; Emma Marris, "The Case for Renewal," *National Geographic*, April 2020, 18–28.

10. Marris's essay acknowledges the challenges—most of them, anyway—but ends hopefully with a vision of her daughter living in a solar-powered city in a building constructed of "drawdown blocks" consisting of "carbon captured from the atmosphere" and boarding a zero-emissions train. "She's invited to a party to celebrate the 100th Earth Day—a party, not a protest. There are no reluctant politicians left to convince" (28). Much as I would like to see Finn and his parents live in that world, I suspect that Marris has fallen prey to climate-change-denialist denial. Those politicians will infest our globe forever, some of them bought by oil companies, some of them religious fundamentalists, some of them simply criminally incompetent and unspeakably stupid.

11. Theodore McCombs and Gemma Webster, "Akin's Choice: Octavia Butler's 'Adulthood Rites' as a Coming-of-Age Story," *Fiction Unbound*, November 18, 2016, https://www.fictionunbound.com/blog/2016/11/17/adulthood-rites.

12. I cop to being one of those jerks myself—or even worse, a know-some-of-it-all—but I find this to be a convenient ideological fiction for right-wingers and centrists determined to ignore that the Democratic base consists mostly of people of color, however much the Democratic elite is dominated by neoliberal technocrats.

13. Ted Chiang, "Exhalation," in *Exhalation* (New York: Knopf, 2019), 47. Hereafter cited parenthetically as *E*.

INDEX

internet, 97; Jimmy (Snowman), 84–85, 86, 89, 90, 91, 92, 94–101, 102, 239n22, 240n25, 241n27, 242–43n31, 244–45n39; and Last Man character, 83, 84; and MaddAddam trilogy, 84, 86, 87, 89, 103, 151, 244n39; moral fulcrum of, 86–87, 101–2; Oryx, 84, 87, 102, 240n24; and pandemics, 84; and racism, 88; RejoovenEsence Compound in, 84; and *Robinson Crusoe* (Defoe), 240n25, 244–45n39; and sexual violence, 87, 88, 91, 95, 151, 240n24, 240n25; and Shakepeare's *Hamlet*, 85–86, 239n21; Sharon in, 98, 99–102, 242–43n31, 243n31; threat of violence in, 87, 103; and treatment of animals, 101–2, 123–24, 244n36; and Victor Frankenstein, 88; and viral apocalypse, 4, 7, 86, 90; and viruses, 4, 7, 83–86, 89; and war, 57, 95
"Our Ancestors' Dystopia Now" (Whyte), 21–22

Paltrow, Gwenyth, 83
pandemics, 199–203, 204, 206–8, 212–13, 222n33, 236n8. *see* viruses
Parable of the Sower (Butler): Alicia Catalina Godinez Leal, 153–54; and Alpha Centauri, 157, 163; and American space program, 153–55; and arson, 150; and conditions on Earth, 154, 156, 157; and crewed space travel, 155–57; and disability, 161–62, 165; and disparity between rich and poor, 150; drugs in, 147–48, 150, 161; and dystopian society, 148–52, 255n3; Earthseed, 152–53, 154, 163; and extraterrestrial life, 154; and fate of humans, 152–54; father in, 149, 150, 155, 157, 161; government in, 149, 150–51, 153–55; hurricane in, 151, 255n3; and hyperempathy condition, 147, 159–63, 165; Lauren Olamina, 147–54, 155, 157, 158, 159–64; and Mars, 153, 155, 157; and money, 149, 150, 154; and moon, 154, 155; mother in, 147–48, 161; Olamina's group, 163; pain and suffering in, 159–60, 162; President Christopher Morpeth Donner, 154–55, 156; and rape, 150; and science fiction, 155; Taylor Franklin Bankhole in, 149, 163; and torture, 162; and virtual reality, 149; and voting, 154
Parable of the Talents (Butler): Acorn (Earthseed colony), 163, 164, 258–59n17, 259n18; Alpha Centauri, 148, 151, 166, 167, 168; Asha Vere (Larkin), 151, 164, 167, 258n17; Christian America sect in, 160, 163, 164–65, 167, 258n17; and conditions on Earth, 167, 168; and Destiny, 157, 158, 163, 164, 167;

208–10, 212; virtual reality land in, 210–11; and Caspar Weinberger, 220n15; and white nationalist/Christian fascism, 166–67, 203, 207, 208, 213. *See also* NASA; Native Americans; pandemics
universalism, 10, 16
utopia, 23, 40–41, 177, 196, 242n30, 263n33

Verne, Jules, 2, 262n31
Vint, Sherryl, 171, 248–49n10, 251n18, 266n49
viruses: and agency, 109; and AIDS virus, 6, 83; and antivaxxers, 202, 209, 266n2, 267n2; and COVID-19, 6, 74, 83, 199, 202–3, 208, 244n35, 266–67n2; and Crake, 236n8; explanations for, 82–83; films about, 82, 83; and pandemics, 74, 82–83, 105, 125, 184, 199–203, 208; spreading of, 130, 236n8; vaccines for, 202; and viral apocalypse, 6–7, 71, 83,

109. *See also Oryx and Crake* (Atwood)
Voyager missions, 139–40, 247n8

Walker, Riddley (Hoban), 197
Wandering Earth, The (film), 59
Watchmen (Moore), 74
Waterworld (film), 14
Watson, Ian, 176
We Can Build You (Dick), 118
Weird Tales, 3
Wells, H. G., 2, 262n31
Wharton, Edith, 3
Whitman, Walt, 3
Whyte, Kyle Powys, 21–22, 26
Woman, Native, Other (Minh-Ha), 52
World War II, 6, 237n10
World Without Us, The (Weisman), 71, 199, 201, 236n9

Yeats, William Butler, 13

Zone One (Whitehead), 7, 236n8, 264n39

Printed and bound by CPI Group (UK) Ltd, Croydon, CR0 4YY

22/04/2024

14487213-0001